CENTRAL COAST

from San Francisco to Santa Barbara

Artwork by

Sebastian Titus

Written by

Richard Paul Hinkle

Reviews by

William H. Gibbs, III

A Vintage Image Book

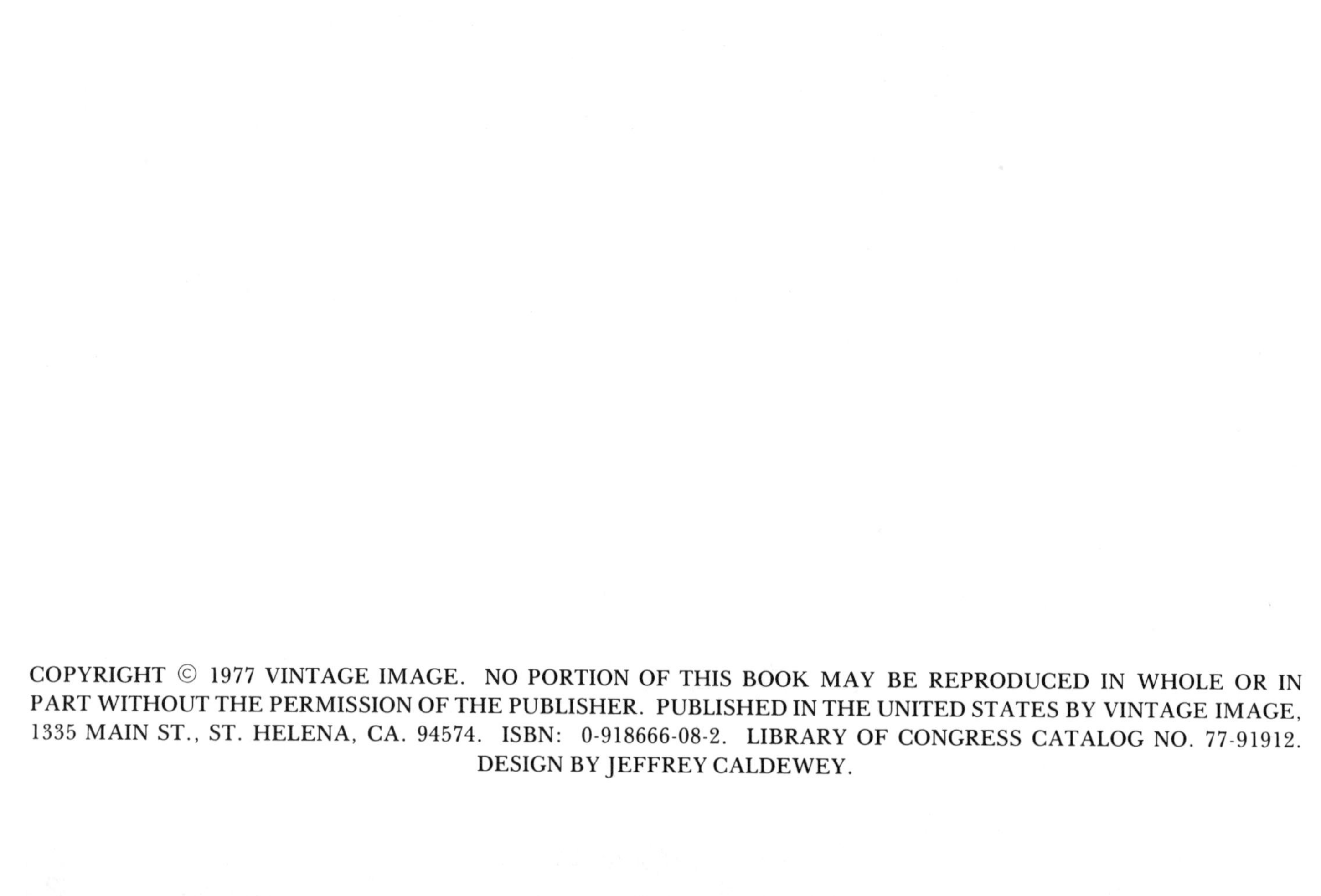

 PUBLISHED IN THE UNITED STATES BY VINTAGE IMAGE, 1335 MAIN ST., ST. HELENA, CA. 94574. ISBN: 0-918666-08-2. LIBRARY OF CONGRESS CATALOG NO. 77-91912.
DESIGN BY JEFFREY CALDEWEY.

Table of Contents

Contra Costa County
Alameda County
San Mateo County
Santa Cruz County
Santa Clara County
San Benito County
Monterey County
San Luis Obispo County
Santa Barbara County
DEL NORTE
SISKIYOU
MODOC
HUMBOLDT
TRINITY
SHASTA
LASSEN
TEHAMA
PLUMAS
MENDOCINO
BUTTE
GLENN
SIERRA
LAKE
YUBA
NEVADA
COLUSA
SUTTER
PLACER
YOLO
EL DORADO
SONOMA
NAPA
SOLANO
AMADOR
ALPINE
MONO
SACRAMENTO
TUOLUMNE
MARIN
SAN JOAQUIN
CALAVERAS
CONTRA COSTA
ALAMEDA
MARIPOSA
MADERA
SANTA CLARA
STANISLAUS
MERCED
FRESNO
INYO
SAN MATEO
TULARE
SAN BENITO
MONTEREY
KINGS
SAN LUIS OBISPO
KERN
SAN BERNARDINO
SANTA BARBARA
VENTURA
LOS ANGELES
RIVERSIDE
ORANGE
SAN DIEGO
IMPERIAL

Foreword

The Central Coast encompasses a widely divergent area, in winegrowing history, in viticultural microclimates, and in manner of winemaking. Such a mix not only makes its exploration intriguing, but renders simple characterizations null.

We have used the term Central Coast as a means of general description. It is more a convenient handle than it is a pinpoint definition. The area we are covering spans roughly the middle of California's north/south grape growing belt, and nearly all of it is directly under the coastal influence. We have subdivided the Central Coast into five broad regions, i.e., The Opposite Coast (Contra Costa - Alameda Counties), The Near Coast (San Mateo - Santa Cruz Counties), Santa Clara County, Monterey - San Benito Counties, and San Luis Obispo - Santa Barbara Counties. Specific regional appellations - to the point of individual vineyard appellations - have become increasingly more important to industry and consumer alike. Strict geographic parameters to appellations such as Salinas Valley, Santa Cruz Mountains, Livermore Valley, Hecker Pass, Cienega Valley, Pinnacles, Paso Robles, Templeton, Santa Maria Valley and Santa Ynez Valley are evolving.

Historical Perspective

The presence of a wine industry in California is the direct result of our Spanish heritage and the indirect result of at least a half dozen other European cultures. That the industry is as vital today as it is, is remarkable when one considers the forces brought to bear against it, whether by design or by natural causes.

Think about it. When the missions were secularized in 1833, the culture of the vine that was integral to mission life was nearly discarded. When James Marshall discovered gold in John Sutter's millwright, great numbers of young men ceased hoeing weeds and began picking at the earth for flecks of yellow metal. Yet, as we shall see, the rush to the Mother Lode later yielded sufficient impetus to the winegrowing industry to put it on its feet for good in California.

Phylloxera vastarix posed the greatest threat to the fledgling industry in the 1890's, an even greater danger than Prohibition. The tiny, yellowish root louse, which had fed upon the vines of America's Northeast for thousands of years--causing the native vines to tighten their bark so as to withstand the aphid invader--was introduced to Europe in the early 1860's, wreaking widespread damage. The pest was later brought to California, having been identified here in 1873, with similar results.

Phylloxera nearly did in grape growers in California and, if it hadn't been for the pioneering efforts of a few growers to discover resistant rootstocks, led by University of California researchers E.W. Hilgard, Frederic Bioletti, and Arthur Hayne, Prohibition might easily have finished off the industry.

Instead, Prohibitionists found a revitalized industry opposing them, one that had withstood phylloxera, disastrously low prices during depressions, and wars and was willing to take on this new enemy in toe-to-toe combat. Into the mid-twenties, as it happened, grape prices soared to heights not scaled again until the early years of the present decade. When commercial wineries were put out of business, hundreds of home wineries took each of their places, creating a tremendous demand for grapes from those growers who had kept faith in the vine and not turned their soils to other crops.

Sociologically, it was only a matter of time until Repeal came, but you couldn't have proved it by Senator Morris Sheppard, author of the Eighteenth (Prohibition) Amendment. He was quoted as saying, in his best Texas hyperbole, "There is as much chance of repealing the Eighteenth Amendment as there is for a hummingbird to fly to the planet Mars with the Washington Monument tied to its tail."

There is no record of the flight, but on December 5, 1933, the "Noble Experiment" came to an end and commercial winemaking became legal once again. It had never lost its respectability. In 1920, when the Volstead Act officially went into effect, California had 700 bonded wineries; by 1933 only 160 remained. Business hurriedly picked up again during the following year.

Horatio F. Stoll, author, publisher, and proponent of the wine industry through much of the first half of this century, offered a colorful glimpse (in a 1941 radio broadcast) of the introduction of the vine into Alta (Upper) California: "The history of our wine industry goes back to April, 1769, when Don Gaspar de Portola and Father Serra came into California, bringing with them civilization and Christianity. They found the wild grape vines growing along the creeks and rivers and felt at once that this new land was the natural home of the vine. Undoubtably, in the following spring they planted the grape, the fig, and the olive in the garden of the first mission established at San Diego.''

The El Camino Real (U.S. 101 for the most), alternately translated as ''The Royal Way'' or ''The King's Highway,'' is the mission trail in California, extending from San Diego to Sonoma. It is the central aspect of that trail that we are concerned with in this volume; in mission terms, from Mission Santa Barbara to Mission San Francisco de Asis (Dolores).

Wine was a vital segment of mission life. It was necessary to fulfill the sacraments and to add spice to what must have been common fare at the padres' table. A sign of hospitality to travelers and a comfort to the ill, wine was also essential to the mission economy.

We derive our love of wine in California, however, not only from the representatives of Spain, but also from those French, German, Italian, Swiss, Portuguese and even Irish immigrants who followed. As noted above, the Gold Rush was initially a drain on California agriculture, but its aftermath was a blessing of the greatest magnitude. The simplicity of it all is so apparent to us now, with a century and a quarter's perspective: there was insufficient gold to sustain the multitudes of miners who hailed from all over the European continent (not to mention the American). When the economic truth of the matter became apparent, the discouraged Forty-Niners picked up their hoes once again and tilled a different sort of gold from the fertile valleys of an adopted land.

Winegrowing, as a commercial enterprise in northern California, dates from the end of the Gold Rush.

By 1880 grapes, wheat, and barley were the major agricultural products of California. In fact, grapes ranked seventh among all manufactures of the state. The making of wine emerged as an industry separate from the growing of grapes as early as 1860 and by the 1870's San Francisco had become the center for the manufacture of cooperage, glassware, and wine related machinery. By 1873 nearly a million gallons of wine were being exported--sold out of state--annually. Though the first transcontinental railroad had begun to open up new markets for California wines in the seventies, the industry would also face its most trying depression then.

Perhaps the singular most exciting phenomenon in the California wine industry of today, particularly in the regions covered in this volume, is the proliferation of what can best be termed ''cottage industry'' wineries. In the suburbs of the Bay Area, the mountains of Santa Cruz, the hills of the southern Santa Clara Valley, and along the broad expanse stretching from Monterey to Santa Barbara, bonded wineries with strong community orientations are springing up like mushrooms after a December rain. For the owners of many, it will work into a vocation, but several seek only a satisfying avocation or retirement plan. It is this fresh, personable movement that gives vitality to an increasingly more dynamic winegrowing industry

The whole of the East Bay was once called *Contra Costa*, the "opposite coast," for it lies directly across the bay from the San Francisco Peninsula. What is now Contra Costa County runs east from Richmond nearly to Stockton. A large part of the county's identity derives from the hulking presence of Mount Diablo ("devil's mountain") and the vast array of pastel petroleum tanks dotting the northernmost hillsides from Martinez to Antioch.

The latter area was once populated mostly by grape vines and fruit trees, both of which were initially set out be Francisco Maria Castro, grantee of Rancho San Pablo in 1823. As in most parts of California, many of the early ranchers laid out small vineyards and made a little wine. Wheat, however, was the county's main cash crop in the early days.

Perhaps the most successful pre-phylloxera winegrowing estate in the county was John Theophil Strentzel's Alhambra Ranch, three miles south of Martinez. Born in Poland in 1813, son of a prominent physician, he attended medical school at the University of Budapest. After the Russian conquest of Poland, Strentzel left for America, settling first in east Texas. After marrying Louisiana Irwin, Strentzel moved west in 1849, settling first on the Tuolumne River, then the Merced, and then in Benicia (then the state capital), where he was told of the beneficial climate and agricultural possibilities across the Carquinez Strait.

In 1853 Strentzel purchased a small tract from the Ygnacio Martinez family and, three years later, set out the first "foreigns" (European grapes) in the county. In 1861 Strentzel won awards at the State Fair for his "red wine, two years old and over" and his 1860 vintages of red and white generics. He urged others to plant foreign varieties in place of Missions (the coarse variety brought to California by the padres) and had at least 150 acres in vines by the 1870's. In 1880 his daughter, Louise Wanda, married the honored naturalist, John Muir.

A group of scholastics, The Christian Brothers, began their winemaking activities at their original Novitiate in Martinez in 1882, making table and altar wines there until 1931.

The biggest winemaking operation in the county came to Richmond as a consequence of the 1906 San Francisco earthquake. When the quake and fire burned them out of the city, the California Wine Association moved across the Bay to erect what would be the world's largest winery. Called Winehaven, the twelve million gallon winery and distillery also included its own company town. Prohibition, however, shut down the operation after only eight years of use. Winehaven was dismantled in 1937 and, four years later, sold, only to be condemned by the U.S. Navy for its own use as a storage depot for the war.

However limited in size, Contra Costa's grape industry was always widely diversified. As late as 1940 there were at least ten wineries in the county, 119 farms grew table grapes, 55 had raisin grapes, and another 519 farmed juice (wine) grapes. But, as Prohibition had caused many farmers to turn to orchards, the late forties brought homes by the tract-full to the western part of the county. Grape acreage dwindled rapidly until, by the mid-seventies, barely a thousand acres of wine grapes remained, mostly in the eastern expanses of delta lands.

Alameda County is white wine country. The warm clime and gravelly soils are well suited to white wine varieties. A 1965 vineyard survey showed that all but two of the ten most planted varieties were for white wines. Semillon led the list with 498 acres (it still did a decade later, though down to 338 acres), with Zinfandel second (217 acres), and Sauvignon Blanc third. Grey Riesling, largely due to the Wente plantings, now holds the second slot (282 acres in 1975), followed by Chardonnay, Zinfandel, Chenin Blanc, Sauvignon Blanc, and French Colombard.

In the early years of the county vine culture stayed close to the Mission San Jose. The county's first large scale winegrower was Elias L. Beard, who acquired 30,000 acres of secularized mission lands in 1849. The property included the old mission vineyard, so Beard, with his son, John L. Beard, and stepson, Henry Ellsworth, set about to revive the neglected vines. Elias was making over 20,000 gallons of wine per year by 1851 and was elected vice president of the California Agricultural Society in the year of its organization, 1854.

In 1856 a Frenchman, Clement Colombet, received the first award ever given by the California Agricultural Society for California wine at the Society's Fair in San Jose. Born in Nice, Colombet had worked as a tanner in Santa Cruz and San Jose before opening a general store in Mission San Jose in 1851. By 1853 he was making wine. In the year of his award he purchased the 9500 acre Agua Caliente Rancho from Fulgencio Higuera. Colombet planted 60,000 vines, built a winery, and erected a resort hotel around the warm springs. The earthquake of 1868 destroyed the Warm Springs Hotel and put Colombet out of business.

The following year the property was purchased by railroad builder, governor, later senator and university founder Leland Stanford. Under the able direction of Stanford's brother Josiah, vineyard plantings were extended, orchards were planted, and a brick winery built (finished in 1870) that is still in use by Weibel.

At the 1887 Viticultural Exhibition in San Francisco, 455 vintages of California wine were displayed. Over a hundred came from Alameda County wineries, including 24 from Linda Vista, 21 from Cresta Blanca, and 14 from Mont Rouge. Over 150 people grew grapes in the county at that time.

J.C. Palmer imported some 10,000 cuttings from France and Spain in 1862 and began laying out a vast planting southwest of Mission San Jose, in the Washington Township. Named Palmdale, rows of palm trees and acres of prunes and olives accompanied the vineyards. Located on what is now the site of the Holy Family Novitiate and Ohlone Junior College, the property was broken up in the early 1880's. Two highly significant wine operations took up where Palmer left off.

That which retained the Palmdale name was headed by Juan Gallegos, who had made a fortune in coffee in Costa Rica. By the late 1880's Gallegos had over a thousand acres in vineyards and had dug hillside tunnels and erected a distillery and a million dol-

Chardonnay grape cluster

lar, three story, brick winery. Gallegos made clarets, which he exported to South and Central America, and maintained a large experimental vineyard. Said to have owned 5000 acres at one time, Gallegos lost it all rather swiftly: A boatload of wine was lost, a superintendent and $85,000 became missing at the same time, and phylloxera did in the vineyards to the vine. The winery, which had been sold to San Francisco wine dealer Henry Lachman in 1901, was so severly damaged by the quake of '06 that it had to be razed.

The legend of Charles Clark McIver's Linda Vista Vineyards and Winery survives in a colorful, almost flamboyant public relations brochure, published in 1894 by the H.S. Crocker Company of San Francisco. In it, McIver (presumably) lauded the soil his grapes were planted in--"rich with calcareous washings from the adjacent mountains"-- and the area's climate: "semi-tropical, and yet fanned by the cooling and moist breezes from the San Francisco Bay, which prevents the baking and caking effect on the soil so frequently met with in the interior....dew forming on the grapes during the night has ample time to evaporate before the morning sun shines on the fruit to blister and do it harm."

A destructive fire in 1884 nearly destroyed the town of Mission San Jose, but the quick thinking of Mr. Joseph Sunderer, who suggested using the claret under the old adobe to put out the fire, saved the new church and other buildings. Sunderer was later made fire chief. Local vineyards succumbed to the combined ravages of phylloxera and wild animals, though some operations continued until the spread of suburbia put them out of business.

Today, Fred Weibel's Champagne Vineyards is the sole link with the Mission San Jose area's winegrowing past. Even so, one must wonder how long the Weibels will fend off the spread of "little boxes" before they move even more of their operations to the open spaces of Mendocino County.

Pleasanton is, today, but a short drive north of Mission San Jose on Interstate 680. Curiously, the town's name is actually misspelled, for it was named after General Alfred Pleasonton in 1867. Only two wineries of any significance have ever existed near Pleasanton, and both are still in business.

John Crellin set out the 223 acre Ruby Hill Vineyard in 1883, four miles east and slightly south of town. Four years later he erected a three story, brick, 125,000 gallon winery, later enlarged to 300,000 gallons. Over a thousand olive trees were planted to divide the vineyard sections.

In 1921 Ernest Ferrario purchased the winery from Crellin's brother, C.L. Crellin. It was during Ferrario's tenure that the winery became known as Ruby Hill, for the reddish soil of the slope behind the winery. Largely a bulk winery (Ferrario's personal preference was a Barbera/Zinfandel blend), it became a storage facility in the sixties when Ferrario retired. The brothers Rosingana now operate the property as Stony Ridge Winery.

The Garatti Winery was built in downtown Pleasanton in 1902 by Frank Garatti, a native of Lombardy. Most of the wines were bulked to other wineries, though some were sold under the family's name. Garatti died in 1948, after which his son-in-law, F.W. "Bill" Brenner, took over until his own death in 1960. The facility was operated as Loretto Winery for a short time until it was purchased by New Yorker Anthony Scotto and rechristened Villa Armando.

Further east, a town and valley bear the name of Robert Livermore, an English sailor who married heiress Josefa Higuera and purchased the Rancho Las Positas in 1838 with Jose Noriega. Noriega raised Arabian horses and Livermore became a grandee, building the first wooden house in the valley, planting olives, pears, wheat, and vines, and running cattle and sheep.

Though the valley might justifiably be called Wente/Concannon Valley today, their families were merely two amongst a flock of early winegrowers in the Livermore area. Olivina, for example, was established in 1881 by Julius Paul Smith, a student of European winegrowing who had been born in Wisconsin. A vital man, he founded the Pacific Borax Company, better known by its famous "Twenty Mule Team." It was the means of Smith's wealth and retirement to Olivina. He planted a large vineyard and built a 300,000 gallon winery.

To a ranch near Olivina, in 1882, came the man who had been the first valedictorian of the first graduating class of the new University of California (1868). He had gone on to newspaper work, first with the *San Francisco Chronicle*, later with the *Alta California*. Assigned by the State Vinicultural Society as a delegate to the Paris Exposition of 1878, he returned to California to author a series of thirty-four articles advising California winegrowers on how to build a prosperous industry. Charles A. Wetmore did all that and more.

In 1882, however, he came to Livermore, planted a vineyard with cuttings from Ch. Margaux and Ch. d'Yquem (on resistant rootstock), and founded the winery named for the sheer, white, limestone cliff that dominated the head of the valley: Cresta Blanca. Aged in the winery's caves, Wetmore's "Souvenir" wines became widely known, winning many laurels. Yet Wetmore was more interested in promoting the industry than he was in making wine, so in 1892, at the age of forty-five, he retired from business to pursue his avocation, leaving the winery to his brother, Clarence, and son, Louis.

Eighteen eighty-three was the year of the Wentes and the Concannons. In that year, with Louis Busch and Herman Oterson, Carl Heinrich Wente purchased the Bernard ranch, which had already been planted to Zinfandel, Charbono, Colombard, and Mataro. At the same time, James Concannon was putting the wandering life behind him and settling just up the road, toward town, from Wente. The families continue to be the closest of friends and neighbors.

Prohibition and the rapid expansion of suburbia drastically curtailed winegrowing in Alameda County. Housing developments with names like Vintage Hills and Heritage Valley swallowed former sheep, orchard, and vine lands whole. In Indian times elk roamed the tawny hills and horses were the primary means of transportation

While San Francisco has never been a threat to any other county as far as grape growing, it has since the Gold Rush days been the center of trade for much of California's winegrowing industry. So great has been its historical influence--both in and of itself and as the hub of California's great grape growing regions to north, east, and south--that the delegate from Uruguay, in the debate in the United Nations committee appointed to select a permanent site for the U.N., strongly advocated San Francisco. When pressed for a reason in a public meeting that followed, the delegate replied: "In San Francisco we find wines, good California wines, and where you find wines you find also civilization and culture."

Though many of the larger wineries now have their corporate offices in San Francisco, it was during the last two decades of the nineteenth century (and until the 1906 Earthquake in this century) that San Francisco was truly in its glory as America's wine center. For it was then that the important wineries had their wine "vaults" (cellars) in the city. Wines were brought to San Francisco in bulk, usually in horse-drawn wagons loaded to near the bursting point with puncheons and barrels. They were then bottled in the vaults and sold by one of the many wine merchants.

Pre-eminent among the early San Francisco wine dealers was the firm of Kohler & Frohling. While Kohler was one of the most dynamic men of his time, Frohling remains relatively obscure. Kohler had begun as a grower in Los Angeles with Frohling. In 1856 he became the first San Francisco dealer to specialize in California wines, the firm's official title then being: "Kohler, Chas. & Co., Los Angeles wine, 102 Merchant" (Street).

By 1858 the firm had moved to Montgomery Street and the name changed to "Kohler & Frohling, dealers and producers of California wines and brandies."

During their early days Kohler used his talents as a violinist, professionally, to support the store. Later, when the firm was solid, it purchased property in Glen Ellen, called Tokay Vineyard (part of which was later acquired by Jack London).

By 1860 the firm had an agency in New York City (Perkins, Sterns & Co.), the only New York wine house to deal solely in California wines. Later it had representatives in China, Japan, Siberia, and Peru, an odd collection of connoisseurs.

When Charles Kohler died in 1887, the firm passed to his two sons, Hans and Charles, Jr., and his son-in-law, Herman Bohrman. They built a large new cellar at Second and Folsom in San Francisco and bought a large brick winery in Windsor. In 1894 the firm merged with several others to form the California Wine Association. However, due to overexpansion, Kohler's heirs had lost their stock in C.W.A. by 1896.

Two north coast families of today have antecendents who were dealers in the city as well as growers in the country. J. Gundlach & Co. had their offices and cellars on the southeast corner of Market and Second Street and a branch office in New York. The Rhinefarm their vineyards and winery, was and is located in Vineburg, at the foot of the Sonoma Valley. Charles Carpy, whose grandson of the same name is part owner of Freemark Abbey, came from Bordeaux in the late sixties and by 1887 owned his own company. By 1891 he had purchased a million and a half gallon winery in San Jose and three years later he acquired the three and a half million gallon Greystone Cellars in St. Helena.

Like its neighbor to the north, *San Mateo County* has never loomed as a threat to other winegrowing areas. Its highest grape acreage might have been 800 acres. What little future the area might have had viticulturally died when the whole of the San Francisco Peninsula was engulfed--over a long period of time--by homes.

Leaving aside the Bay on the one side and the Pacific Ocean on the other, the two primary bodies of water in the county are the San Andreas Lake and the Crystal Springs Reservoir, water supplies for the peninsula and part of a State Fish and Game Refuge. The valley of the lakes was formed by earthquakes along the San Andreas Fault, responsible for the 1906 monster, and it was near the lower lake (Crystal Springs) that the Hungarian nobleman, Haraszthy, planted thirty acres of his 640 acre ranch to grapes in 1854. But the cooling fogs from the Pacific retarded ripening too much, so the Count moved north to Sonoma and his liason with General Vallejo.

Dr. Robert O. Tripp, a versatile fellow, was another early grower. Dentist, deputy sheriff, county supervisor, and general store owner, Tripp had come to Woodside in 1849 in failing health. He passed on in 1909 at the age of 94.

Due to the housing shortage in San Francisco, caused by the Gold Rush, Woodside had become a roaring lumber camp, then known variously as Squealer Gulch or Whiskey Hill. Tripp, a member of the Dell Temperance Union, planted a five and a half acre vineyard and built a small winery on King's Mountain Road, just a half mile from today's Woodside Vineyards. He sold his wines to the lumberjacks and pulled their teeth at the store. His winery is now a residence and the store an historical museum.

The county's greatest contributions to the wine industry came between the seventies and a few years before World War I. Its greatest single contributor was Emmett H. Rixford.

In 1883 Rixford planted five acres in central Woodside to Cabernet Sauvignon, Merlot, and Petit-Verdot, so as to match the *cepage* (blend) of Chateau Margaux. The vineyard site was on a hill that featured a sharp slope on one side and a gentle one on the other, what the Spanish call a *cuesta*. Thus, Rixford's Cabernets acquired their reputation under the La Questa Vineyard label.

Rixford was not one to hide the secrets of winemaking, publishing in the same year of his first plantings a small volume entitled "The Wine Press and The Cellar: A Manual for the Winemaker and the Cellar-Man." In it, besides offering sound advice on cellar management and a survey of wines being made in the state, he made a wry statement on the depression of '76: "In 1876 the Mission grape sold in California for from $7.50 to $10 per ton, and foreign varieties for from $14 to $18 per ton, and consequently many vineyardists in districts remote from the market turned their hogs

Vineyards high in the Santa Cruz Mountains

into the vineyard to gather the fruit.'' Two years later, he noted, Missions were up to $12 to $14 and by the opening years of the eighties to around $20. By then the foreigns were commanding $22 to $35 per ton and as high as $40.

There were others, but those that didn't feel the pinch of phylloxera were convinced by Prohibition and the spread of tract homes. Only five acres of grapes exist today in the county. With the removal of Nepenthe Cellars to Santa Cruz County, only Woodside and Sherrill remain to represent San Mateo County to the California winegrowing fraternity.

The mountains immediately north of *Santa Cruz* have long been considered a home of premium wine grapes. In 1892 professor E.W. Hilgard declared it ''the county for growing grapes for high-grade wines'' and Frona Eunice Wait (three years earlier) referred to it as the ''future Chablis district.'' The latter comment was in obvious reference to the county's oceanic climate, which well serves varieties as Pinot Noir and Chardonnay--the grapes of French Chablis--but causes the maturity of late varieties, especially Cabernet Sauvignon, to be questionable. Yet there are warmer pockets and fine Cabernets have been grown and vinified in the region.

Santa Cruz was well-known as wine country in the decades before Prohibition. Some reporters claim as many as 39 wineries and a high of nearly 4000 acres, at various times. Historically, the county has been known for small holdings and diversified farming. Grapes were raised alongside grain, buckwheat, corn, potatoes, beans, and sugar beets. Deer fences were a requirement, as the redwood-forested hillsides were abundant with black-tailed deer, bears, and an occasional cougar.

There were 1210 Mission vines in the county according to an 1835 report and Lyman J. Burrell was reported to have planted *viniferas* near the summit (called Highland or Lexington) in 1856. But the earliest commercial planting was made by John Wait Jarvis and his brother George in 1858. In that year they began setting out 300 acres in the Vine Hill district, seven miles northeast of Santa Cruz (east of the present Highway 17).

In 1879 John Jarvis purchased another plot in Vine Hill and named it Union Vineyard, for the ''union of the hills...and my love for the Union represented by the stars and stripes.'' Jarvis' patriotism extended to a giant redwood tree, 234 feet high and 27 feet in circumference, which he named ''General Grant.'' At Union Vineyard Jarvis had sixty-three acres of Zinfandel, White Riesling, Chauche Gris (Grey Riesling), Chauche Noir, Verdel, Baluzat, and others. He reportedly harvested 22 tons from one acre of Verdel one year, which yielded an income of $825 (or $37.50 per ton).

He built a winery on the property and made some 42,600 gallons there in 1888, but most of the wine went to another winery that Jarvis was a partner in: the Santa Cruz Mountain Wine Company.

The Santa Cruz Mountain Wine Company was incorporated in 1887 with John Jarvis as president and school teacher W.H. Galbraith, a native Vermonter, as secretary. The most famous winery in the county, it boasted of three caves dug out of the soft sandstone of the Branciforte cliffs along the Branciforte Creek. The three caves totalled 380 feet in length, the largest being 24 feet wide and 18 feet high. The winery had cooperage for 200,000 gallons of wine and eventually owned over 200 acres of vineyards.

The Ben Lomand Wine Company was established in 1886 by Englishman J.F. Coope, ultimately achieving an annual production of 100,000 gallons. Two-thirds of the winery's vineyard holdings were in Grey Riesling, with the remainder in Cabernet Sauvignon and Chauche Noir. Coope garnered first awards for his Cabernet and Riesling at the 1894 San Francisco Exposition and an honorable mention for the Riesling at the Paris Exposition of 1900. The company succumbed to an invasion of phylloxera and a fire in 1917.

There were nearly two dozen small wineries operating in Santa Cruz County prior to Prohibition, sporting names like Bergazzi, Krilanovich, Locatelli, Campagnoni, and Wildhagen. The cycle is turning again, as a number of small, cottage industry wineries have opened in the last few years.

Though many of the county's vine tracts have been replaced by Christmas tree farms, there are signs that a mild rebirth may not be far away, despite the county's alleged prejudice (in zoning) against new vineyards. Where only three or four wineries existed in the county five years ago, there are no less than thirteen today. It remains to be seen how long this new revival will be sustained.

SANTA CLARA COUNTY

Though the countv no longer has the grape acreage it once had, *Santa Clara* remains a sort of spiritual center of the bay and central coast region. Suburbia has already done in the northern part of the valley, from Fremont to Mountain View and on down to a continually expanding San Jose, and is now quietly working away at the southern part of the valley. Industries, especially aviation and electronics, have also played a role in moving agriculture out of a county that was once a veritable "fruit basket."

San Jose, the state's oldest municipality, and its environs were described as the "Garden City of the State" by early settlers, who appreciated its rich soils and equable climate. Grain was a primary crop until the 1880's, when fruit culture began to assert its dominance.

"Santa Clara county never became as known for winegrowing as Napa or Sonoma," asserts Edmund Mirassou, "because the agriculture of those counties was more restricted by the soils. In the Santa Clara Valley, however, the land was fertile enough for a wide variety of crops." When Pierce's Disease claimed 20,000 acres of grapes and Prohibition loomed, for example, farmers simply turned to strawberries, fruit and nut orchards, and other crops.

"Around 1900," says Mirassou, "the advent of turbine pumps and deep water wells made Monterey attractive to farmers. Finally, by the forties and fifties, the land became too attractive to other interests, industry and 'subdivisionitis.' Monterey had its public relations for being the country's 'lettuce bowl,' but the wineries in Santa Clara got no publicity."

When houses came, grapevines had to go. There had never been a strong identity push for Santa Clara grapes. Curiously enough, the wineries stayed. They merely shifted their agricultural efforts south: Almaden went to San Benito and Monterey; Paul Masson and Mirassou went to Monterey. A wholly new winery, Turgeon & Lohr, has its winery in downtown San Jose and its vineyards in Monterey. In 1976 alone, Paul Masson and Almaden sold twelve million cases between them and the entire county accounted for sixteen million cases, amounting to $750 million in sales.

Experimenters and nurserymen preceeded most of the professional grape growers, especially in San Jose. Among the earliest was Louis Pellier, brother of the Mirassou family's first generation, Pierre Pellier. Louis had come to California seeking gold, working in the mine fields for about a year. In 1850, the year of California's statehood, he came to San Jose and purchased a tract of land fronting on the west side of San Pedro Street, near St. James Street. There he established Pellier's Gardens and was soon joined by Pierre, who brought cuttings of French varieties with him. The pair also began farming the western slopes of Mt. Hamilton, in the Evergreen District.

French nurseryman Antoine Delmas had 14,000 Mission grapes planted in his French Gardens in 1852 and 1853. Circa 1853 Delmas imported 10,000 cuttings of 80 varieties from France. It was later claimed that he had imported Zinfandel at that time under the name Black St. Peter's. He said that he had sent cuttings to General Mariano Vallejo in Sonoma and that he had later grafted the J.P. Pierce vineyard (known as a Zinfandel vineyard) to Black St. Peter's. Historian Charles Sullivan, who has researched the topic, offers the wry comment: "All of a sudden there was no Black St. Peter's in Santa Clara County, and lots of Zinfandel!"

One of the most assertive of the early winemakers in San Jose was General Henry Morris Naglee, a staunch proponent of light-bodied brandies. Naglee had come to California as an Army officer in 1847. The next year he purchased 140 acres in San Jose, from 11th Street east to Coyote Creek and south from Santa Clara Street to William Street. There he set out fruit trees and vines.

In 1849 he resigned his commission and opened the state's first commercial bank, Naglee & Sinton, on Kearny Street in San Francisco, taking advantage of the sudden prosperity from the gold fields. He returned to the Union Army for the Civil War, then retired as a Major General to San Jose. In four trips to France Naglee is credited with having introduced some 150 grape varieties to California viticulture. His own vineyards were set out to Folle Blanche, Chardonnay, Charbono, and White Riesling.

At the 1876 American Centennial Exposition in Philadelphia his brandy was voted "the finest American brandy." He won numerous California State Fair awards and won a gold medal in the 1882 Bordeaux Exposition. Naglee stopped making wine in 1888 and died two years later.

Most of the Evergreen story, however, belongs to the Mirassou clan. From the arrival of the Pellier boys to the current generation of five they have been the moving force there, first as grape growers, later as winemakers.

Still, there were others in Evergreen. The most prominent was William Wehner, a noted architect and artist who planted the 175 acre Highland Vineyard in 1889. An early advocate for the now common Rupestris St. George rootstock (to resist phylloxera), Wehner built two wineries in the Evergreen district. One, called Evergreen, was later purchased by Bisceglia, sold to Anthony Cribari, and finally leased to the ever-present Mirassous.

Los Gatos, south and west of San Jose, is not all Almaden and Paul Masson, but they do provide the key figures. Thee and Lefranc named their winery Almaden for the New Almaden mine south of San Jose, not far from the winery. It was named for the original Almaden mine in Spain, which had yielded cinnabar for rouge in Nero's time. The word itself means "quicksilver" (mercury).

Lone Hill Vineyards had a lengthy history. Vineyards were first planted on the site, off of today's Blossom Hill Road, in 1864 by New Yorker David M. Harwood. He had purchased the property from Almaden's Etienne Thee and Charles Lefranc. In 1888 the vineyard and winery came into the hands of C. Freyschlag.

After Prohibition the business was revived by the sons of Herman Mirassou, who purchased it in 1936 and put up a new winery a decade later at the close of World War II. Four Mirassou brothers were active in the venture: Arthur, Rodolphe, Ambroise, and Clovis. The winery survived until the mid 1960's. The area now seems one continuous housing tract and Lone Hill is no longer a hill by any description.

The Cupertino-Mountain View area was widely planted before phylloxera almost completely shut it down in the late nineties. Montebello Road, above the Stevens Creek Reservoir, was particularly noted as a grape growing area.

The man most responsible for the town of Cupertino was John T. Doyle. In the late seventies Doyle, a retired attorney, purchased half of a vineyard that had been planted off of Stevens Creek Road in 1860. Doyle began making wines right off, crushing his first vintage in 1880. Typical of his candor, he declared it a poor one. By 1886 he had completed the main winery, called Las Palmas for the palm trees which lined the entrance to the vineyard.

Doyle was a quality oriented man. He had given two acres to the University of California for experimental purposes and was highly scientific in his approach to winegrowing. An idealist who refused to bow to purely commercial interests, he was often at odds with Charles Wetmore. He constructed an irrigation system for his vineyards that is still used. An avid promoter of the industry, he was known for his Barbera and Charbono wines.

The cottages Doyle built for his workers became the core of Cupertino, which had earlier been called Westside. The winery was damaged by the 1906 earthquake and Doyle died the following year.

A character by any definition was J.B.J. Portal, who owned the Burgundy Vineyard on Stevens Creek

Cabernet Sauvignon Cluster

Road. A Frenchman, Portal had arrived in California in 1869 and gone into the real estate business. In 1872 he bought a nursery vineyard in San Jose and four years later began making the red wine that he became known for, using Black Pinot and Ploussard. Considered a bit of a rogue (he later deserted his wife, leaving behind vineyard and winery), Portal spoke sensibly in public when, in 1887, he addressed the Grape Growers' and Wine Makers' Association in San Francisco: "We should consider ourselves California winegrowers, and not simply of one district, and not try to run down one another's business...In putting up your wines let the label be a guarantee of quality."

It was an Alsatian German, Pierre Cline, who opened up the Montebello Road area to vineyards. He had opened a restaurant in the Occidental Hotel in San Francisco and wanted to serve his own wine there. So he bought property high on Montebello Road and planted a vineyard to the Medoc blend: Merlot, Cabernet Sauvignon, and Cabernet Franc. Cline won many awards for his Mira Valle wines in the 1890's, including a gold medal at the 1900 Paris Exposition. Considered by some to have been California's greatest pre-Prohibition winemaker, Cline retired in 1910. Now only Ridge Vineyards remains on the hill.

Millefleurs Winery, on Stevens Creek Road, was owned by Charles A. Bladwin, who called the property Beaulieu. The winery (finished in 1895) had an underground cellar and the family's elaborate house was a copy of the French Petite Trianon. Baldwin also had the first swimming pool in the area. Phylloxera did great damage during the first five years of the new century and the earthquake did some two million dollars damage. The property was sold in 1920 and is now the central part of De Anza College. The winery is the school's bookstore and the house is to be a museum.

There is still a good deal of agriculture in the southern stretch of the Santa Clara Valley, from Morgan Hill to Gilroy, but even here the invasion of housing development continues. San Martin and Pedrizzetti are looking to other areas for grapes like the larger wineries to the north. The only wineries that still grow most of their own grapes are those smaller operations in the Hecker Pass district.

In an effort to preserve an insight into winemaking as it was in the last century, a group called Friends of the Winemaker is attempting to reconstruct the old Malaguerra Winery as an historical museum. The winery, or what's left of it, is located at the end of Burnett Road, between Morgan Hill and Coyote. The stone and wood winery was operated by Joseph Malaguerra, but no one is certain as to his exact dates.

Once one of the largest wineries in the county, Madrone Winery was founded after Prohibition by Benjamin Cribari and his three sons, Fiore, Anthony, and Angelo. By 1936 they had cellars in New York City--on the seventh floor of a downtown building--which had a set of casks that each had a carving of one of the California missions on it. Cribari also had a much smaller winery in Paradise Valley, southwest of Morgan Hill.

In 1944 Cribari sold Madrone, his New York winery, and the San Benito label so as to open a three million gallon winery in Fresno (which eventually merged with Guild). Lucky Lager purchased the Madrone Winery, then a four million gallon facility, and marketed the wines first as Grape Gold, then under the Madrone Vineyard label.

In 1950, when the Korean War began, Madrone was merged with Almaden in what turned out to be a short-lived affair. From 1953 to 1959 the building was leased by Walter S. Richert to produce his well known sherries. One or two of the winery buildings still stand, just north of Cochran Road.

In 1932 the Bruno Filice family, which had settled in the valley as grape growers in the 1890's, purchased the San Martin Winery. San Martin had been founded as a cooperative sometime between 1892 and 1908 and had been idle during Prohibition. When Bruno Filice died, the winery went to his four sons and one son-in-law: Michael, John, Peter, and Frank Filice and Pasquale Lico. They later sold the winery to Southdown, who in turn sold recently to Somerset (Norton Simon).

The Hecker Pass area has been thickly populated with small wineries since William Blackstone Rankin opened up the Gilroy area for the California Wine Association in 1905, building the half million gallon Las Animas Winery. A year later, Rankin generously opened the doors of the winery to refugees of the 1906 earthquake.

The area around Hecker Pass Road, which connects Gilroy with Watsonville, was originally called the Bodfish District. The road was called Bodfish Mill Road and Bodfish Creek still meanders along a parallel route. The road wasn't extended over the pass to Watsonville until 1928, the work of long time county supervisor Henry Hecker.

One of the early wineries in the district was Bonesio Winery. Pietro Bonesio originally began making wine in the Rucker district, north of town, then purchased the 600 acre Solis Rancho, at the corner of Watsonville Road and Day Road, in 1921. His sons, Louis and Victor, took over the operation after Prohibition, bottling their best wines under the Uvas label. (The Spanish called the area ''Uvas'' or Grape Valley.) The winery is now run by the Chargin family as Kirigin Cellars.

Hecker Pass has always been a Little Italy. After Prohibition there were at least twenty wineries in the area, owned by people with names like Chappelli, Perelli, Giachino, Roffinella, Bertero, Scagliotti, Massiglia, Masini, Cheisa, and Pappani.

A man who knows the area as well as anyone is John Roffinella, a grape broker on Watsonville Road. The sign advertising his business is a simple one: ''Choice grapes: Wholesale, Retail.'' Roffinella, with his father Filippo, began selling grapes to home winemakers and wineries in 1920. He remembers well the early days of Prohibition, when the instant demand by home winemakers, once it became clear that it was legal to make wine at home, caused grape prices to skyrocket: ''Grapes went from ten dollars a ton to a hundred twenty dollars a ton, just like that!''

There are no longer twenty wineries in the Hecker Pass district, but there are eight who continue the tradition of producing sound, hearty, country wines that are sold with a minimum of fanfare and prices to match.

It has been over a decade and a half since Paul Masson, Mirassou, and Wente Brothers first recognized the coming limitations of agriculture in the Santa Clara and Livermore valleys. The next logical move was south--to *Monterey County,* land of lettuce, artichokes, and Steinbeck.

Climatological studies conducted by University of California viticulturists A.J. Winkler and Maynard A. Amerine in the late thirties (published in 1944) had already concluded that Monterey could be compared favorably with California's northern coastal winegrowing regions. Ranging from a low Region I, near Monterey Bay, to a low Region III at King City, the county's weather was deemed cool, but warm enough to ripen the fruit of vines. The biggest problem, that of water, had already been solved by dams, deep wells, and the underground Salinas River. All that remained was to install the vast network of overhead sprinkler systems that would provide those vines with a "controlled rainfall."

The county's early history was far more concerned with political firsts than grape culture. The city of Monterey was California's first capital, without dispute, for it was the first capital under both Spanish and American rule. In 1842, Monterey was the site of an aborted American takeover when Commodore Thomas Catesby Jones, commander of the U.S. Pacific Squadron, took possession of Monterey under the mistaken impression that the U.S. and Mexico were at war. Two days later he lowered the American flag and sent his apologies to General Micheltorena at Santa Barbara.

Three and a half years later war *was* declared and on the 7th of July, 1846, the first American flag was "again" raised over Monterey, this time by Captain William Mervine, under orders from Commodore John D. Sloat. Mervine read Sloat's carefully worded proclamation and formally took possession of California for the United States. No shots were fired.

Actually, in the earliest days of Monterey County's Spanish period there was at least one secular viticulturist, perhaps the first in California. He was Governor Pedro Fages, who planted orchards and vines at Monterey, at his own expense, as early as 1783.

In 1915 the Sunset Magazine Homeseekers' Bureau ventured to predict that "within a comparatively few years viticulture will be followed extensively." Four years later, Francis William "Will" Silvear planted his first vines in the hills above Soledad, just below the jagged rock formations, The Pinnacles.

Will planted Muscats and Thompson Seedless then and rented the vineyards out during Prohibition. At Repeal, struck with the thought of making sparkling wine, Silvear planted Pinot Noir, Chardonnay, and Pinot Blanc on resistant stocks. From the 1940's until Silvear's death in 1955 Ollie Goulet, at Almaden, made sparkling wines from Silvear's grapes. The ranch is now the site of Chalone Vineyard.

Silvear was practically all of the county's viticulture until the sixties. Mirassou was the first to make a significant vineyard planting, in 1961, followed by Wente and Paul Masson in 1962. Since then Monterey County quickly emerged as a winegrowing region. Virtually all of the new plantings went in on their own roots, for two reasons: the county has no history of phylloxera and the soils are relatively light, therefore not conducive to the growth and spread of the aphid (phylloxera).

What the tally shows, in the end, is that more than 33,000 acres of grapes are now growing in Monterey County, nearly all of them bearing for the 1977 crush. Viticulturally, this represents nearly two-thirds of all the vinelands in the central coast! Such rapid and expansive growth would have been a total disaster if the quality weren't there. Happily, after a false start, it is there.

When some of the first wines began coming out of Monterey County we were exposed to what was called, by detractors, the "Monterey Stench." There seemed to be a lettuce-like quality to some of the young wines, especially Cabernet Sauvignons. Some said it was caused by unclean tanks and others claimed that it was some soil residue from the row crops that had preceeded the vines.

Neither was true, as the same characteristics showed up in wines made in new or stainless steel tanks and from grapes grown in non-lettuce soils. The answer came in a more basic form: ripeness. This requires some explanation.

Monterey's climate is cool and the growing season long. Where most other regions in California have completed harvesting by the middle of October, the Monterey vintage continues until at least Thanksgiving, often well into December. The result of this long season is the development of intense flavors, color, sugar, and fruit acids *if the grapes are picked at complete ripeness*. What was learned there was that good numbers are not always sufficient. Grapes that were picked at sugar and acid levels that would have been satisfactory in other regions yielded wines that were immature and possessed a repugnant vegetative quality. Yet, when the same grapes were left on the vine until their acid level dropped noticeably, without any significant decrease in sugar, the resulting wines had all the nose, flavor, and character that one might expect from sound, fully ripe grapes. In short, there was a vast difference between fruit that was "statistically" ripe and that which was actually ripe.

That this vegetative quality was especially strong in Cabernet Sauvignon was due to the fact that the variety shares a common acid component with bell peppers (only one methyl group is different betwen the two molecules). If Cabernet grapes are picked ripe, the wines possess just a hint of that bell pepperishness. But when the fruit is unripe, that characteristic is so magnified as to be distasteful.

Botrytis cinerea, the noble mold (under the right conditions), is a regular occurance in Monterey County, due to warm summer days tempered by the evening's cool, moist, coastal air mass. Beneficial to varieties like White Riesling, Semillon, and Sauvignon Blanc, it poses a threat to Chardonnay and Chenin Blanc, requiring sprayed retardants.

Summer winds can be destructive in Monterey, so many vineyards sport snow fences or "wind rows" of trees, usually eucalyptus. Birds, like starlings and linnets, may also be a problem.

San Benito County was created from the northeastern

Riesling grape cluster botrytis cinerea

part of Monterey County in 1874. Aside from vines planted at the Mission San Juan Bautista in 1853, the first man to take up winegrowing seriously was a French baker by the name of Theophilus Vache.

The Cienega (''grass valley'') district lies ten miles southwest of Hollister. It was by devious route--via New Orleans, Santa Fe, Mexico, France, and Peru--that Vache first came to the Cienega. Eighteen fifty found Vache in Hollister with a small dairy and some sheep. In 1854, the year the Light Brigade made their infamous charge, he moved south to the Cienega district, having acquired a 320 acre tract. In the sandy foothills he planted his first five acres of grapes. In 1861 he sent to France for cuttings of Black Pinot, Trousseau, and Grey Riesling, which he laid out at a thousand vines per acre, each vine bearing twenty-five pounds of fruit at maturity.

Vache retailed his wines at his own wine depot in Hollister. The vineyard was his pride, but Vache also grew dates, figs, mulberries, plums, peaches, pears, apples, apricots, and other fruits. In 1883 Vache's nephews--Adolphe, Emile, and Theopile II--founded the E. Vache Winery in Redlands, which later developed into today's Brookside Winery. In the same year, Vache sold his Cienega property to William Palmtag.

Palmtag had been born in Germany in 1847. Of a large family, ten of his brothers preceded him to California. Palmtag arrived in 1864 and set upon a series of occupations--miner, grocery clerk, farmer, and truck driver--that eventually led him, in 1872, to Hollister and a wholesale liquor business. Eleven years later Palmtag bought Vache's vineyard and immediately began expanding the operation.

Palmtag was also a bit of a civic leader. A progressive, he was elected mayor and county supervisor, he was a street builder, and he founded and was president of two banks. In 1901 his winery was incorporated as the San Benito Vineyards Corporation with a half million in capitalization, primarily from Palmtag and a couple of eastern investors: John Dickinson and C.M. Lewis. By the end of the decade first Lewis, and then Palmtag, had retired from the venture.

During Prohibition Dickinson traded the winery for the Hotel Washington in San Francisco. Thereafter the winery went through several hands before coming into the ownership of Edwin Valliant Sr. in 1935. He operated the facility as Valliant Winery and Vineyards, winning a silver medal for his Cabernet at the 1941 State Fair. The winery was purchased by W.A. Taylor & Co. (a subsidiary of Hiram Walker) in 1943. Taylor leased the facility to Almaden until 1963, when Almaden finally purchased it.

Viticulturally, Bob Thompson has called San Benito ''a veritable fiefdom'' of Almaden. How true. By the end of 1976 Almaden boasted 4368 of the county's 4575 acres of vinelands--over ninety-five percent. Before purchasing the Cienega properties in 1963, Almaden had acquired the Paicines Orchards from Mrs. George Sykes (in 1956). Most of Almaden's vines are planted there, a vast planting covering nearly 3900 acres, and the winery, with an over 7.5 million gallon capacity, handles white wines and brandies.

What was one of the first viticultural areas in California is now enjoying rebirth as the Golden State's newest. The southern movement into Monterey County in the sixties continued on into San Luis Obispo and Santa Barbara in the early seventies. A decade ago the two counties could claim 443 acres of wine grapes between them, and that had increased to just 675 acres by the end of 1970. But by 1971 the race was on. In that year alone Santa Barbara leaped from 164 acres to 1050 acres. San Luis Obispo, a more established grape growing area in its own small way, grew more slowly, but by 1976 the two counties had over 10,000 acres of vines and a dozen wineries converting juice into the nectar of forgotten deities.

Pierre Hypolite Dallidet is considered to have been the first secular winegrower in *San Luis Obispo County*. He planted 15 acres circa 1860 near what is now Pacific Street in San Luis Obispo and began making wine in 1863. Dallidet had the only distillery in the county prior to World War I.

The most continuous vinicultural saga in the county is that of the Yorks. Andrew York, a native of Indiana, came to California by ox team. After mining, farming, and travelling a great deal, he purchased the Grandstaff ranch, on what is now York Mountain, in 1882. Jacob Grandstaff, a Texan, had been deeded the land seven years earlier by President Grant.

With his sons--Walter, Thomas, and Silas--York built a small stone winery to handle surplus grapes. Called Ascension Winery (York Mountain is in the Ascension district, south of Paso Robles, near Templeton), it was enlarged ten years later with bricks made from clay found on the property. Shortly thereafter, possibly after the turn of the century, additional land was purchased and Zinfandel planted for early maturing, so as to miss fall and winter frosts.

When Andrew York died in 1913, Walter and Silas, who had purchased the operation in 1911, were running things and had changed the name to York Brothers Winery. It was the largest in the county. When the brothers retired in 1944, Walter's son Wilfrid continued operating the winery until 1970.

James Anderson started in the Santa Clara Valley, then went to Hollister, and thence to Bakersfield, where he raised alfalfa. In Washington State he guided a party of settlers out of Indian troubles, then returned to California in 1876, where he purchased a grain ranch from Andrew York. In 1879 he moved for the last time, buying 163 acres from a Mr. Dunn in the Ascension district. He planted an orchard, 20 acres of grapes, and built a 16,000 barrel winery on Anderson Creek.

One historical account of the county notes that many unknowing buyers were sold "orchard land" on the ocean side of the Santa Lucias, having been told that the climate there had been changed after the 1906 earthquake and was then suitable. Commented the writer: "Those orchards as far as wood was concerned were howling successes, but alas for the fruit!"

The county's most famous viticulturist of this century was pianist and Polish patriot Ignace Paderewski. In 1913 Paderewski, who had once been prime minister of Poland, purchased 2000 acres of upland north and west of Paso Robles, adjacent to today's Hoffman

Mountain Ranch. Paderewski had, on the advice of his friend, violinist Sir Henry Heyman, gone to the mineral baths at Paso Robles to calm his arthritis. Heyman also advised him, after he had purchased the ranch, to plant almonds: "You can't imagine anything better to go with port," he is said to have told Paderewski.

Thin Shells, Princesses, and Jordans were planted, amounting to the largest planting of almonds in California. The ranch also had grain, cattle, and poultry. The famed pianist was a gentleman farmer, you see, and he also had farms in England, Switzerland, and Poland. When grape prices soared at the beginning of Prohibition, Paderewski decided to plant Swiss grape varieties at Paso Robles. Fortunately, Horatio Stoll, a friend of Heyman's, persuaded Frederic Bioletti to journey south and advise Paderewski. The pianist took Bioletti's advice, planted Petite Sirah, Zinfandel, and a few others, and got premium prices for them. A friend in San Miguel made some wine from Paderewski's grapes, as did York Mountain Winery. One of the former's wines, a Zinfandel, won a prize at the State Fair after Prohibition.

There was an upsurge of new wineries after Prohibition, but many went out of business in the sixties. Almond trees still do well in the county and oil fields cover many an acre. Today, the low, scrub-covered hills gradually give way to broad grasslands, covered with grazing cattle, interspersed with the neat rows of new vinelands that impose order upon an otherwise wild appearing landscape.

All along the coast the mission fathers planted grapevines where they erected their temples. The missions came north to *Santa Barbara County* from Mexico: Santa Barbara and La Purisima Concepcion (at Lompoc) were dedicated by Fr. Lasuen within a year of each other (1786 and 1787, respectively) and Mission Santa Ines was built in Solvang in 1804, the year Lewis and Clark began their northwest expedition.

Santa Barbara, before the town swelled with people, was an ideal vineyard site. The fifty miles of channel shoreline--the northwest to southeast traverse from Point Concepcion to the Rincon--offered a southern exposure strikingly similar to the Spanish-French Mediterranean coastline. It is likely that vines were first planted in the bottomland of Sycamore Creek (now the Milpas district) as early as 1782, the year the presidio was finished and four years before the mission was completed.

The largest mission vineyard, some 2400 vines (probably 25 to 30 acres), was planted on the west bank of the San Antonio Creek. The padres then built an adobe winery (1804) in what is nowGoleta. Its ruins are still protected under a sheetiron roof. The vineyard and winery produced up to 6000 gallons of wine each year, with Indian neophytes harvesting and treading the grapes.

James McCafferey, a native of Ireland who had originally settled in Australia, came to California in 1849. After two years as a tailor in Mission San Jose, he came to Santa Barbara. There he rented vine and range lands from the church and built large herds of sheep and cattle. By the 1860's he was producing 8000 gallons of wine each vintage at his San Jose Vineyard.

His vineyards stood him well during the severe drought years of 1863 and 1864, when he and many others lost great numbers of their stock. The drought marked the end of the large rancheros and the beginnings of strict water conservation and agricultural diversification.

But McCafferey's most difficult test came when government tax agents attempted to confiscate his property for failing to file for the requisite bonds. It mattered not that the bonds were unobtainable. But McCafferey stood fast and, after a protracted struggle, regained full title to his lands. His port was renowned and his son maintained the winery until Prohibition.

Santa Barbara's most interesting viticultural story, however, concerns two individual grape vines. The first was planted in Montecito in 1812 by Dona Maria Marcelina Felix de Dominguez to celebrate the birth of a child. The vine grew to monstrous proportions and came to be called "La Parra Grande" (The Big Grapevine). Dona Marcelina herself was known as "La Vieja de la Parra Grande" (The Old Lady of the Big Grapevine).

Dona Marcelina made her living selling grapes and was able to do so from her one vine, generally obtaining five tons each season from it. One account tells us that the arbor covered an acre and that it was a favorite hangout of bandit Joaquin Murrietta. Another account, which at least sounds scientific, claims that the vine covered an area 115 by 78 feet (about one fifth of an acre), that it was 18 inches in diameter near the ground, and that yields were up to six tons.

When Dona Marcelina died in 1865 at 105 years, a Mr. Sarver of Canton, Ohio purchased the vine and built a dance floor under the arbor. Eleven years later the vine was cut down and shipped to Philadelphia to be exhibited at the World's Fair celebrating the American Centennial. At the time of its destruction the vine's diameter (three feet from the ground) was 14 inches and its circumference 56 inches.

La Parra Grande had competition, however, in nearby Carpinteria. In 1842 the wife of a retired presidio soldier, Crescentia Ayala, planted a vine that would surpass Dona Marcelina's vine. By 1853 the vine was an historical landmark when it sheltered the community's first polling station. Later used for social events, in 1895 it was authenticated as the world's largest vine. It then yielded ten tons of grapes, had an arbor that covered two acres, and its trunk measured nine feet around! Poetically, when Prohibition became law the vine began to wither and decay, dying in the early twenties.

Today's most significant plantings in the two county area are in the Santa Maria Valley. Areas less extensively planted but of great importance are the Paso Robles-Shandon stretch, the Edna Valley (southeast of San Luis Obispo), and the Santa Ynez Valley--encompassing Los Alamos, Los Olivos, Santa Ynez/Solvang, and the river valley towards Lompoc. Cabernet Sauvignon, with over three thousand acres, is the most widely planted variety.

A scene in the Santa Ynez Valley

Food

he geographical scope of this guide includes all of central coastal California reviewing a variety of premium winegrowing areas very well apart from each other. To visit a representative sampling of its producers is a several day proposition which will certainly introduce the traveler to unfamiliar surroundings. The following guide to selected wine-oriented restaurants was compiled specifically for wine country visitors.

As memorable meals taken en route contribute to the overall enjoyment of an excursion, some three dozen vignettes of superior restaurants follow. In many cases, restaurant recommendations were sollicited of area winemakers whose wines are served in the respective houses. In all cases, quality of food, service and atmosphere are discussed in such a way as to inform travelers of what to expect when visiting them

An appreciative way of thanking a winery for its hospitality after a visit is to buy a good bottle. If the winery has picnic facilities, the purchase can be enjoyed on the premises. Several area delicatessens purveying picnic provisions are hence included, as well as the outstanding wine merchants who stock the wines of the regions.

An increasing number of distinguished restaurants are locating in the wine country and offer travelers the opportunity to enjoy local wines in the area of their production.

In a volume of this size, it is impossible to give in any way complete coverage to the subject of food. These reviews represent merely a sampling of the many noteworthy establishments.

THE CELLARMASTER *Provisions*

After 17 years in East Bay wine retailing, Stan Freedman designed and opened an ideal wine shop in 1976 in Lafayette. All of his carefully selected California and imported wines are laid down for floor display, and warehoused in an underground cellar to the rear.

A stylish tasting room with subdued track lighting and rough sawn redwood interior accommodates 20 tasters seated around a long table for classes or catered gatherings.

The Cellarmaster, 3500 Golden Gate Way, Lafayette 94549. Telephone (415) 284-1711. Hours: 10 a.m.-6 p.m. Mon.-Sat.; Sundays by appointment. Cards: BA,

PAPA D. CARLO'S *Restaurant*

Hosts George and Barbera Morrison invite you to dine leisurely in the D. Carlo family tradition at their new northern California location in Moraga.

Prior establishments in Naples, New York and Los Angeles have proven the popularity of their hand prepared foods from international and family recipes.

Pasta entrees served with soup and garlic bread start at $4.50, while dinner entrees also include fresh vegetable, pasta and coffee. For a special occasion, the multi-course "Papa" dinner is highly recommended.

Papa D. Carlo's, 337 Rheem Blvd., Moraga. Hours: 6-9 p.m. Wed.-Sat.; 5-8 p.m. Sun.; closed Mon. & Tues. Price Range: $4.50-$8.95. Cards: BA, MC.

CHEZ PANISSE *Restaurant*

When a fine restaurant features a nightly special, they should be applauded for their interest in calling attention to seasonal, specially prepared foods. At Chez Panisse, co-owner and associate chef Alice Waters plans well in advance the single four course meal that is served nightly. The menus are then sent out to the mailing list, distributed to patrons, and posted on a small, street level marquis before the restaurant.

The resourceful menus that change nightly and seldom if ever repeat themselves are simply spectacular as to composition and execution and faultlessly served. Dinner starts with an imaginative appetizer or a distinctive soup. The entrees are usually classical or country French, followed by a battery of delightful French cheeses introduced by the captain and optional French roast coffee or expresso. The pastry chef may be responsible for the world's most delicious chocolate cake.

The cooking of associate chefs Jean-Pierre and erstwhile food editor Mark Miller is always praiseworthy, and guests heeding wine steward Tom Guernsey's timely suggestions are sure to enjoy a fine bottle from the marvelous cellar.

Chez Panisse, 1517 Shattuck, Berkeley 94709. Telephone (415) 548-5525. Hours: Lunch 11:30 a.m.-2 p.m.; Dinner 6-9:30 p.m.. Price Range: Lunch $2.00-$5.00; Dinner $11.50-$15.00. Closed Sun. & Mon. No Cards. Reservations required. Seating: 65.

NARSAI'S *Restaurant*

To acquire a reputation as one of the Bay Area's most prestigious restaurants within a matter of a few years after opening, attests to many things well done. Seasoned restauranteur Narsai David has created a palace of fine dining that ranks with the most civilized anywhere.

Of contemporary design, the restaurant interior is partitioned into two dining areas using the vertical grain staves of a virgin redwood water tower dismantled in Oakland. Several large iron statues on display were sculpted from the rods and castings that secured the tank.

The complete five course epicurean dinners served nightly are matched only in their skilled preparation by their elegant presentation. From 5 to 6:30 p.m., a 3 course "Petite Dinner" is also served for three dollars less than menu price.

Monday night at Narsai's offers an unique opportunity to explore the foods of the world. Complete five course ethnic dinners are served in addition to the regular menu and selected complementary wines are available by the glass.

The incomparable wine list spans lifetimes in its splendid array of California and European, current and older vintages.

Narsai's, 385 Colusa, Kensington (North Berkeley) 94707. Telephone (415) 527-7900. Hours: 5-10 p.m. nightly; 5-11 p.m. Fri. & Sat.. Price Range: $11.00-$18.00. All bank cards accepted. Full Bar. Reservations necessary.

BAY WOLF CAFE & RESTAURANT *Restaurant*

Erstwhile university professor Michael Wild currently exercises his culinary talents in a former Oakland residence that he and three colleagues refurnished in 1975 and dubbed the Bay Wolf Cafe & Restaurant. French and Mediterranean cooking is served year round on an inviting redwood deck with outdoor seating for 38, and indoors in the living room/cafe and parlor.

There is a choice of two entrees each evening on the weekly dinner menus which change twice a month. The imaginative three course evening meal is likely to feature a distinctive preparation or personal interpretation of a favorite dish.

Bay Wolf is very wine oriented and a favored rendezvous of Bay Area wine merhcants. Special dinners featuring newly released wines, or matching regional foods and wines are periodically held.

The regular wine list is particularly strong in French red and white Burgundies, with increasing attention to premium California varietals.

A popular Sunday Brunch is served from 10 a.m. to 3 p.m., and the weekly menu is supplemented with daily specials.

Bay Wolf Cafe & Restaurant, 3853 Piedmont, Oakland 94611. Hours: Lunch 11:30 a.m.-2 p.m.; Dinner 6-9:30 p.m., Wed.-Sun., closed Tues.. Price Range: Lunch $2.50-$4.00; Dinner $8.00-$8.50. No cards. Reservations suggested.

CURDS & WHEY *Provisions*

Curds & Whey is no less than three specialty shops cheerfully linked together offering a splendid variety of gourmet foods and wines.

Numerous baked goods scent the air every morning. A fine complement of cheeses and sausages are displayed in the Cheese Shop. Pates and terrines, low fat and triple cream cheeses and all manner of variety foodstuffs including cheeses by the wedge or the wheel are available.

The Wine Shop hosts daily comparative tastings of California and European wines and once a month a personal appearance by a noted California vintner is scheduled.

Curds & Whey, 6311 College Ave., Oakland 94618. Telephone (415) 652-6311. Hours: 10 a.m.-6 p.m. Mon.-Sat.. Cards: BA, MC.

LAKE MERRITT WINE & CHEESE *Provisions*

This multi-faceted shop is just as the name implies, Oakland's renaissance gourmet wine and cheese parlor. There is luncheon seating for 28 in the dining room entry way, where meat and cheese boards, fresh quiches and homemade soups are served all day.

Continuing on past the cheese counter and specialty food selection of pates, bakery delicacies and confections, leads to a very select wine shop and tasting bar. The weekly comparative tasting schedule and cheese and catering announcements are circulated in advance in an informative, monthly mailing list.

Lake Merritt Wine & Cheese Revival, 552 Grand Ave., Oakland 94610. Telephone (415) 836-3306. Hours: 10:30 a.m.-8:30 p.m. Mon.-Fri.; 10:30 a.m.-6:30 p.m. Sat.; 11 a.m.-5 p.m. Sun.. Price Range: $2.25-$3.75. Cards: BA, MC. 10% discount on full wheels of cheese and cases of wine.

THE CHEESE FACTORY *Provisions*

1977 marks the 60th anniversary of Greek master cheese maker Dimitrios Voultsides' arrival in Pleasanton, then a center of quality milk production. Three years later he founded the Cheese Factory relying at the time on oakwood fires under his tempering and pasturizing vats. Today, modern technology adopted to the original old world methods by second generation owner George Spiliopoulos assures higher levels of production, packaging and delivery.

A variety of imported cheeses as well as domestic cheeses produced on the premises are available for sampling and purchase. A domestic wine selection is also available and all purchases can be enjoyed on the premises are available for sampling and purchase. A

The Cheese Factory, 830 Main St., Pleasanton 94566. Telephone (415) 846-2577. Hours: 10 a.m.-6 p.m.. Cards: BA, MC.

LA VILLA ARMANDO *Restaurant*

Two doors up from the Villa Armando Winery tasting room is a stately home purchased in 1961 by Mr. & Mrs. Anthony D. Scotto, proprietors of the winery. In June of 1976, the former residence opened its doors for the first time as a formal, continental restaurant.

The interior furnishings chosen by Mrs. Scotto include crushed velvet upholstered Queen Ann chairs arranged around table settings of lenox china and French crystal. The Italian marble and tiles for the bathroom and fireplace were personally selected abroad and coordinated linen and draperies contrast handsomely in the two intimate dining rooms.

Six varied veal preparations, four beef entrees and several house specialties are served with two fresh vegetables and choice of soup or salad for dinner. For those not wishing to order a la carte, two elaborate six course meals are offered for a fixed $15.00. Diners should find some consolation for the inflated dinner prices in the attentive French service and elegant surroundings.

The wines of Villa Armando Winery are served and a nominal corkage fee is charged for guests bringing their own.

La Villa Armando, 475 St. John St., Pleasanton 94566. Telephone (415) 846-2114. Hours: 6-10 p.m. Wed.-Sat.; 5-9 p.m. Sun.; closed Mon. & Tues.. Price Range: $8.00-$15.00. Jackets required. Cards: AE, BA, DC, MC. Reservations suggested. Seating: 40.

LA ROCHELLE *Restaurant*

Of special interest at this newly established continental restaurant is the intriguing choice of daily specials in addition to the comprehensive lunch and dinner menus. Since most specials appear but once a week, diners can be assured of freshness, quality, and, of course, variety.

Hosts Signori Bruno, Bridi and Ciaibellini also take pride in the fact that all pastries served are freshly baked in their kitchen before appearing under glass in the dining room. A good selection of half bottles are available from the eight California vintners

---

La Rochelle, 348 St. Mary's St., Pleasanton 94566. Telephone (415) 846-5740. Hours: Lunch 11:30 a.m.-2:30 p.m. Tues.-Fri.; Dinner 5:30-9:30 p.m. Tues.-Thurs., 5:30-10:30 p.m. Fri. & Sat.. Closed Sun. & Mon.. Price Range: Lunch $2.75-$5.40; Dinner $6.30-$9.50. Corkage: $2.50. Cards: MC, BA. Full Bar.

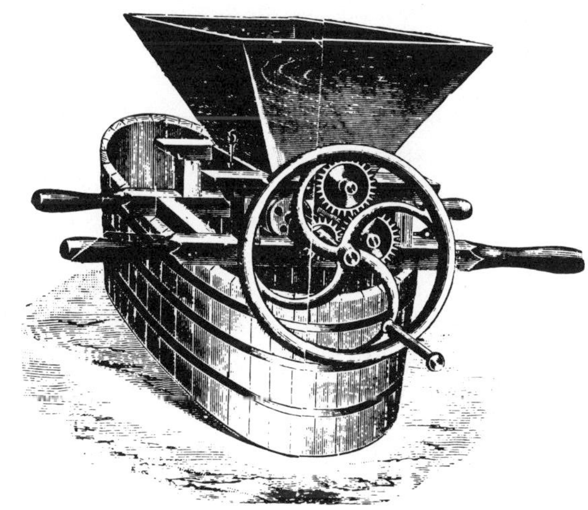

BELTRAMO'S WINES & SPIRITS *Provisions*

Walls of claret, knee deep bins of Burgundy and Hock, and the most comprehensive collection of California wineries extant make Beltramo's a one stop wine tour. Their timely selection of domestic and imported wines and spirits attracts shoppers from greater Northern California who rely on the helpful suggestions of the knowledgeable staff when in doubt.

Wine manager Tony Wood is an acclaimed authority on the wines of the world. Mr. Wood frequently conducts extra-curricular tastings and seminars for peninsula special interest groups, and periodically packs off his staff to visit North Coast and area wineries.

Beltramo's, 1540 El Camino Real, Menlo Park. Telephone (415) 325-2806. Hours: 10 a.m.-10 p.m. daily. Cards: BA, MC.

BRITISH BANKERS CLUB *Restaurant*

The remodeling of Menlo Park's most historic building - successively the City's first bank, City Hall, police headquarters and public library - was completed in 1977 and currently houses the lavish British Bankers Club. Fashioned after one of London's famed private clubs, the solid mahogany front bar and surrounding saloon area cater to the local professional crowd who find the BBC to be a most convivial gathering place. Above the main floor, there is an enclosed area for private dining, and a Victorian stairway leads to additional seating on the mezzanine.

Omelets, combination sandwiches and luncheon salads are served at mid-day, with fresh seafood when available. American cooking, pure and simple, is capably served by the young staff at dinner.

For those with unconventional hours, there is food service at the BBC from 11 a.m. to 12 p.m., 7 days a week, and a sit down Brunch is served on Sunday from 10 a.m.-2 p.m.. The outstanding all California wine selection features some 25 selections from the finest premium producers. Personally selected house wines are bottled for the BBC under their private label by a Napa Valley winery and served in fifths.

British Bankers Club, 1090 El Camino Real, Menlo Park 94025. Telephone (415) 327-8769. Price Range: Lunch \$3.25-\$5.25; Brunch \$2.95-\$4.75; Dinner \$4.95-\$9.50. Corkage: \$2.00, Cards: BA, MC, AE. Full Bar. Seating: 120.

LE POT AU FEU *Restaurant*

Owner-chef Jean Cornil was born into a restauranteur family in Vichy, France and started his intimate Bistro style restaurant in 1973 naming it after one of his nightly specials. The French provincial decor, music, staff and cuisine provide an authentic ambiance, and the dress is casual.

Monsieur Cornil culled his recipes from the classical repertoire and modified them each in his own distinctive way. His Lapin a la Moutarde (young Belgian rabbit in a mustard and cream sauce - $7.50) offered nightly, and Thursday night special, Feuillete de Ris de Veau (Sweetbreads in puff pastry, cream sauce - $7.75) are highly recommended. Prices quoted are for the full dinner including homemade soup of the day and garden salad.

Madame Cornil is the radiant hostess whose unfortunate responsibility it often is to advise weekend guests of a wait before seating. Reservations are not taken and the 50 seats in the restaurant are quickly filled.

A remarkable wine selection including eleven of California's very finest producers is offered, supplemented by a balanced selection of French wines, bien sur.

Le Pot au Feu, 1149 El Camino Real, Menlo Park 94025. Telephone (415) 322-4343. Hours: 6-10 p.m. Tues.-Sat. Price Range: $7.00-$8.75. No reservations. No cards, local personal checks accepted. Closed Sept..

THE VILLAGE PUB *Restaurant*

What a satisfying feeling to enter a favorite restaurant, and be greeted by name by a maitre d'hotel who has served his clients for years. Mr. Antoine de Vos started as a waiter the day the restaurant opened 19 years ago, and has for the past 14 years gotten to know personally his large and regular Bay Area clientele.

The building originally housed the Village Blacksmith in 1895 and is today redwood panelled, with a handsome bar, small lounge, and seating for 127 diners in two rooms.

Continental cuisine, French and Italian, is imaginatively prepared. In addition to some three dozen en trees on the extensive menu, Mr. de Vos personally prepares several dishes at the table and his commentary is equally as enjoyable as the skillful presentation. Gentlemen should note that jackets are required after 5 p.m..

The wine list features selections from a dozen California varietals prefaced with an extensive variety of European wines. Proprietor John Schutz, a native of the Pacific Northwest has included two selections from Tualatin Vineyards in Salem, Oregon, his home town.

The Village Pub, 2769 Woodside Road, Woodside 94062. Telephone (415) 851-1294. Hours: Lunch 11:30 a.m.-4 p.m. Mon.-Sat.; Dinner 5-10 p.m. Mon.-Thurs., 5-11 p.m. Fri. & Sat.; Closed Sun.. Price Range: Lunch $5.00; Dinner $7.95-$12.95. All major Bank cards accepted. Corkage: $2.50.

SCOPAZZI'S *Restaurant*

Visiting the Santa Cruz Mountain Vintners often means back roads, steep grades and much driving from one distant winery to the next. The most likely place to relax and dine when in the San Lorenzo Valley is Scopazzi's in Boulder Creek. Established around the turn of the century by one of the areas founding wine-growing families, Scopazzi's has matured into a fine dinner restaurant featuring highly reputed Northern Italian Cuisine.

The atmosphere is casual in the large redwood panelled dining room, while service is courteous and professional. Many dishes are finished at the table, wheeled from the kitchen on service carts. While being assured that pasta courses and entrees alike will be served uniformly hot, diners can also witness the last minute preparations that distinguish the restaurant's cuisine. The Fettucine Alfredo enjoyed as a side dish or as an entree is superb, and the Caneloni is homemade as expected. A variety of sauteed dishes, Calamari Saute Bordelaise and Coquilles St. Jacques Saute Bordelaise, are noteworthy items on the extensive a la carte menu. Full dinners including antipasto, soup, salad and dessert are very reasonably priced between $5.55 and $6.25.

Scopazzi's, Big Basin Way, Boulder Creek 95006. Telephone (408) 338-4444. Hours: Lunch 11:30 a.m.-3 p.m.; Dinner 4:30-10 p.m. Wed.-Sun.. Cards: BA, MC. Reservations suggested wkends. Seating: 125.

SHADOWBROOK *Restaurant*

A leisurely descent by cable car down a steep grade over lush ferns and hillside plants signals one's arrival at the Shadowbrook Restaurant overlooking Capitola River. Once a small summer home approachable only by boat, the rustic site was restored and opened in 1947.

Currently an enlarged deck over the river replete with hanging begonia arbors is outfitted with outdoor heaters to stave off the night chill. Additional seating in the enclosed Garden Room and special banquet facility with private bar, lounge and fireplace brings the capacity to 160 diners.

Broiled King Salmon ($7.95) is caught exclusively for the Shadowbrook by a local trawler, and will be fresh frozen out of season to guarantee year round supply. A healthy cut of Prime Rib ($8.95) served with creamy horseradish sauce and rice pilaf or baked potato is the most popular non seafood entree on the predominantly marine menu. Dinners include Shadowbrook salad or Boston Clam Chowder.

A special captain's wine list available on request offers numerous premium selections of limited availability from local vineyards and fine French estates.

Shadowbrook, 1750 Wharf Road, Capitola 95010. Telephone (408) 475-1511. Hours: 5-10:30 p.m. Mon.-Sat.; 2-9 p.m. Sun.. Price Range: $5.95-$10.95. Cards: BA, MC, AE. Full Bar. Reservations nightly.

SUZANNES-BY-THE-SEA *Restaurant*

The one-bedroom studio house that Shirlee Cummings and Phil McGrillis renovated now has 8 tables seating 27 dinner guests who come to enjoy the flavorful cooking of Northern Spain.

Weekend diners arriving on a recommendation or a dare slip comfortably into one of two intimate dining rooms and are served by host Mr. McGillis. Seated at one of the tables which he built, Phil summarizes the restaurant's aspiration of serving hand-prepared dishes and select wines by attentive service people concerned with the individual diner's needs.

Five distinctive regional dishes are served nightly with an additional three seafood entrees. Dinners include a trip to the buffet table and choice of gaspacho or lentil soup and salad.

Interestingly enough, the freshly baked bread served, was originally produced by a local bakery as "starter bread" simply to test the heat of the oven for an evening's baking. It is light and airy and goes down by the loaf.

An equal representation of Spanish and premium California wines are offered on the select, if moderate, wine list.

Suzanne's-by-the-Sea, 427 Capitola Ave., Capitola. Telephone (408) 476-4923. Hours: 5:30-9:30 p.m. nightly. Prix fixe: $6.50. Reservations suggested. No cards.

FELTON DELI & CHEESE FARM *Provisions*

The Carlino family have been in the Deli business in the Santa Clara Valley for 32 years, and in May of 1977 opened their new San Lorenzo Valley store.

80 cheese and 65 varieties of cold cuts are on display for service between freshly baked French bread, or specially made swirled rye. Several family recipes including Turkey and Mortadella Tortellini with fresh pesto, and Italian sausage stuffed by a fifty year old, second generation machine are favorites.

The fifteen freshly diced vegetables and fourteen dressings which make up the salad bar are available for take out.

Felton Deli & Cheese Farm, 6205 Highway 9, Felton 95018. Telephone (408) 335-2754. Hours: 10 a.m.-7:30 p.m. Mon.-Sat.; 10 a.m.-6 p.m. Sun.. Cards: BA, MC.

LA CHAUMIERE *Restaurant*

An oasis of fine dining and drinking awaits those visiting the new outcropping of Santa Cruz Mountain wineries. While vacationing in Santa Cruz in 1974, restauranteur Jacques Zadeyan found the seaside town most agreeable and reminiscent of his wife's native Menton on the French Riviera. When a telephone directory check yielded nary a French restaurant in town, he decided to one day remedy the situation.

Since opening in 1976, La Chaumiere has introduced the community to the glory that is French cooking, with indoor seating for 21 and 14 tables on the outdoor garden patio, Mediterranean style.

The French service is outstanding as certain of the dining room staff had previously worked aboard luxury liners, pampering their guests and learning to fold linen napkins 36 ways.

It is likely that a fair number of diners return repeatedly to ponder the exceptional wine list. A fine representation of premium California producers is complemented by a singular selection of French vintages dating back to the depression.

Dress is casual, ambiance is memorable and reservations are imperative on weekends.

La Chaumiere, 1314 Ocean St., Santa Cruz 95060. Telephone (408) 426-2448. Hours: Lunch 11:30 a.m.-2:30 p.m. Tues.-Fri.; Dinner 5:30-10:30 p.m. Tues.-Sun. Price Range: Lunch $3.00-$5.50; Dinner $4.95-$13.00. Sunday Champagne Brunch: 10:30 a.m.-2:30 p.m., $6.25. Corkage: $4.00. Cards: AE, BA, MC. Full Bar.

SANTA CRUZ HOTEL BAR & GRILL *Restaurant*

One flight above the Santa Cruz Hotel, the staid, premier restaurant in town (est. 1877) is the animated Santa Cruz Hotel Bar & Grill. Within, the decor is stylishly Victorian with elaborate oak fixtures, bevelled glass skylights and lots of indoor greenery. High ceilings and roomy interior, comfortable surroundings and congenial staff contribute to a relaxed atmosphere during lunch which can escalate at night as diners seem to compete with the evening piano player.

The Bar & Grill, a popular dinner restaurant, also serves brunch on Sunday mornings. Of note on the moderately priced dinner menu are a Chicken Tarragon finished in a rich, sour cream sauce ($6.50), and a memorable Seafood Saute of Pacific Shellfish ($8.50). French Onion soup and an outstanding spinach salad are served with dinner as is the variable selection of a sauteed garden vegetable.

On the predominantly California wine list are featured varietals from Ridge Vineyards and David Bruce Winery, as well as wines from other non-Santa Cruz Mountain vintners and a representative selection of imported wines.

Santa Cruz Hotel Bar & Grill, 1003 Cedar, Santa Cruz 96061. Telephone (408) 429-1000. Hours: Lunch 11:30 a.m.-2 p.m., Mon.-Fri.; Dinner 5:30-10 p.m. nightly. Sun. brunch 10 a.m.-2 p.m.. Corkage $2.00. Cards: BA, MC, AE. Full Bar. Seating: 95.

ERIC'S DELI *Provisions*

The international selection of meats, cheeses and gourmet items available at Eric's Deli can be prepared in sandwich form to go, or enjoyed at either of his two locations.

Orders phoned in for pickup at the Scotts Valley store, gateway to the San Lorenzo Valley wineries, can be carted off to the vineyards, who will supply the beverages.

Eric's Deli, King's Village Shopping Center, 222 Mt. Hermon Rd., Scotts Valley. Telephone (408) 438-4646. Eric's Deli, King's Plaza Shopping Center, 1601 41st Ave., Santa Cruz. Telephone (408) 475-4646. No Cards. Wine and beer.

STAFF OF LIFE *Provisions*

Staff of Life is a natural foods bakery specializing in a dozen varieties of whole grain breads prepared from scratch and baked daily on the premises. Owner-manager Richard Josephson recommends his apple bread as a good foil for medium dry white wines, and his ten grain for the reds.

From the vegetarian deli counter are meatless casseroles, mid-Eastern falafels, and nutritious sandwiches made to order. A nut seed taxo mix, sesame soyburger and many other preparations can also be taken out by the pint.

Staff of Life, 1305 Water, Santa Cruz 95060. Telephone (408) 423-8065. Hours: 9 a.m.-9 p.m. daily.

COURTYARD RESTAURANT *Restaurant*

Pastoral surroundings, congenial people, popular cuisine and excellent wines await patrons of the Courtyard. Recent remodeling has expanded the indoor seating overlooking Soquel Creek to 90, with additional outdoor seating for 60 on the tiled courtyard. Ample use of skylights and indoor plants, hanging and otherwise, serve to "bring the outdoors in" as intended owner-host Frank Capriotti. His careful attention to detail is reflected in the stylish, modern decor.

The dinner menu is concise, featuring a nightly special in addition to the regular offerings. Monterey Bay Salmon and Halibut appear in season, fresh Idaho trout are periodically flown in, and prime beef if used exclusively for the mid-week Prime Rib special, to name a few. Soups are prepared daily on the premises from scratch as is the complimentary loaf of freshly baked bread which accompanies the evening meal.

Mr. Capriotti's long standing interest in premium California wines is evident. The Courtyard wine list represents dozens of selected local and North Coast wineries in addition to a well balanced selection of imported wines.

Five entrees are served for the weekly Sunday Brunch and complimentary champagne is included in the $6.50 prix fixe, served from 10 a.m. to 2:30 p.m.

Courtyard Restaurant, 2591 Main Street, Soquel 95073. Telephone (408) 476-2529. Hours: Lunch 11:30-2:30; Dinner 5-10 p.m.. Price Range: Lunch $2.50-$5.95; Dinner $4.95-$9.95. Corkage fee: $3.00. Cards: MC, BA, AE. Full Bar. Reservations recommended.

FOOTHILL PLAZA DELI *Provisions*

Proprietor Harvey Veprin has been in the deli business since 1954 with operations in Los Angeles and San Francisco before opening his Los Altos store in 1972. His well balanced shop features 135 varieties of cheeses imported from a dozen countries, bagels baked fresh every day and imported coffees ground to order. His own Chopped Liver ($3.19/lb.), German Potato Salad, and Ravioli and selection of Kosher foods can also be enjoyed at the premises where the limited seating includes five tables.

Sausages hanging over the meat display are often aged for 60 days which dries out the fat and concentrates the beef and garlic flavors. Specially aging sausages in this manner is a service offered to customers.

Next door Foothill Plaza Liquors has a complete selection of complementary beverages including many premium, out of the way, California wines. The wines are well stored and displayed and certain older vintages are available on request. Owner Bramley Gardener and manager John Guynes are friendly, knowledgeable merchants, building a good business on personality, personal attention and good selection.

Foothill Plaza Deli, 2310 Homestead Blvd., Los Altos 94022. Telephone (408) 245-8082. Hours: 9:30 a.m.-7 p.m. Mon.-Fri.; 9:30 a.m.-6 p.m. Sat.; 9:30 a.m.-5 p.m. Sun.. Cards: MC, BA.
Foothill Plaza Liquors. Telephone (408) 245-8080. Hours: 9 a.m.-10 p.m. daily. Cards: BA, MC.

PACIFIC COAST WINE COMPANY *Provisions*

Peninsula residents and visitors seeking the personal attention and counsel of a superior wine merchant would do well to pay a visit to this fine wine shop in downtown Los Altos.

Managing partner Dennis Marion is an affable shopkeeper whose regular trips to the wine country at home and abroad keep him abreast of developments in the wine industry worldwide.

Dennis sends out a bi-monthly newsletter recounting recent discoveries and new arrivals, and also moderates the discussion at the weekly Wednesday evening shop tastings.

Pacific Coast Wine Company, 205 State St., Los Altos 94022. Telephone (415) 948-6300. Hours: 10 a.m.-6 p.m. Mon.-Fri.; 10 a.m. 5 p.m. Sat.. Cards. BA, MC.

MOUNTAIN CHARLIE'S SALOON *Restaurant*

"Mountain Charlie" McKiernan, first white settler in the Santa Cruz Mountains (1850), planted orchards and vineyards, blazed trails, owned the first stage coach line between Los Gatos and Santa Curz and logged together with John W. Lyndon who was one of the town's first mayors. Furnishings from the 31 room Lyndon Heights Mansion, dismantled in 1968, were reassembled by Lyndon's great-grandson Jim Farwell to grace the interior of his restaurant commemorating the two men.

Up two flights of stairs from its downtown street entrance, diners have the option of first sallying into the roomy saloon where elegant wrought iron chandeliers are suspended from the lofty ceiling. The mahogany bar is a classic running nearly the length of the room, and after dinner country swing entertainment plays nightly from 9 to 1 a.m..

Diners should arrive fifteen minutes prior to reservation to adequately study the expansive wine list. The finest Santa Cruz Mountain wineries are represented and too many other North and Central Coast producers to mention.

Mountain Charlie's Saloon and Restaurant, 15 North Santa Cruz Avenue, Los Gatos 95030. Telephone (408) 354-2510. Hours: Lunch 11:30 a.m.-3 p.m.; Dinner 5:30-10 p.m.. Price Range: Lunch $2.75-$4.50; Dinner $4.50-$12.50. Cards: BA, MC. Full Bar. Reservations nightly.

WINE CELLAR RESTAURANT *Restaurant*

Authentic in its surroundings, fair in pricing, and exhaustive in selection of wines, the Wine Cellar Restaurant in Old Town, Los Gatos is a welcome stop for wine travelers.

The cool, vaulted lower chamber of a popular complex of specialty shops provides an ideal setting. Adjacent to seating in the first chamber is a tasting bar with weekly selections of premium California wines available by the glass. Immediately beyond is the central dining area, while the far annex is an intimate arrangement of tiered tables around a performer's dais. There is acoustic entertainment nightly, Wednesday through Saturday.

An inviting roster of soups, sandwiches and quiches makes up the menu which is basically luncheon fare served throughout the day. Cheese boards and a salad bar for light eaters complete the selection of good things to eat.

On entering, many of the wines offered can be viewed in a glass display case. A supplementary selection of older vintages is also available, and all items on the wine list are priced at a very reasonable $1.50 above retail price.

Wine Cellar Restaurant, 50 University Ave., Los Gatos 95030. Telephone (408) 354-4808. Hours: 11 a.m.-11 p.m.. Price Range: Lunch $1.25-$3.00; Dinner $2.00-$4.00. Cards: BA, MC.

GENE'S COUNTRY WINES & SPIRITS *Provisions*

Larry Rugani's wine and liquor shop was established by his father in 1937 as a family grocery business. Twenty five years later when Larry purchased the store, the orientation shifted exclusively to beverages. Today the shop ranks with the South Bay's finest wine stores, as the current owner has concentrated his energies along those lines for better than a decade.

An extensive selection of the current releases from California's most sought after producers is available, while old and rare bottlings can be viewed in the temperature controlled cellar below.

Gene's Country Wines & Spirits, 217 No. Santa Cruz Ave., Los Gatos 95030. Telephone (408) 354-2772. Hours: 8:30 a.m.-9 p.m. Mon.-Thurs.; 8:30 a.m.-10 p.m. Fri. & Sat.. Cards: BA, MC.

THE CHEESE SHOPS *Provisions*

Lovers of fine things will find the very best selection of cheeses available at either of two locations on the Monterey Peninsula in Carmel and in the Santa Clara Valley in San Jose. Proprietors John and Nancy McCormack direct import a splendid array of European cheeses from the most remote areas of production. Handmade varieties and seasonal products may appear only briefly as the shops seem to supply a descriminating and demanding clientele.

The staff is quite experienced and able to make each of their customer's whims materialize with a selection of over 300 domestic and imported cheeses, fresh, locally baked croissants in the Carmel store, and an appetizing assortment of superb pates and fresh truffles and fois gras in season.

At this writing, the Cheese Shops are negotiating with some small, premium North Coast cheese producers to represent their products on a fairly exclusive basis in their respective areas. Add to the above a discriminating selection of superior California and European wines, and an educational cheese sampling program before purchase.

The Cheese Shops, Valley Fair Center, 2801 Stevens Creek Blvd., San Jose 95128. Telephone (408) 243-4435 Carmel Plaza, Ocean & Junipero, Carmel 93921. Telephone (408) 625-2272. Hours for both locations: 10:30 a.m.-9 p.m. Tues.-Fri.; 10:30 a.m.-5:30 p.m. Sat.; Noon-5 p.m. Sun.. Cards: BA, MC.

COACH HOUSE LIQUORS & CHEESES *Provisions*

In the shadow of Monte Bello Ridge down in the flat lands of unincorporated San Jose, is the La Barbera brothers' combined delicatessen, wine and liquor store.

Made to order sandwiches and festive party trays from the deli counter, and a very good selection of premium California and European wines make the Coach House a convenient stop for picnic supplies. The store is well staffed during peak business hours and service is prompt and friendly.

Coach House Liquors and Cheese Farm, 1655 Sunnyvale-Saratoga Ave., San Jose. Telephone (408) 252-7141. Hours: 9 a.m.-11 p.m.; 9 a.m.-12 p.m. Fri. & Sat.. Cards: AE, BA, MC.

EMILE'S SWISS AFFAIR *Restaurant*

Among the very finest restaurants in the Santa Clara Valley, Emile's is contrally located in downtown San Jose. Highly regarded owner-chef Emile Mooser offers a varied selection of entrees from the classical French repertoire, several Swiss Specialties and a few of his own creations.

It is very likely that midway through the meal a black tied waiter will inquire how many people in the party would care for a Grand Marnier dessert souffle. Prepared for multiples of two, these airy delights are best accompanied by a noble sauternes and are served to hundreds of patrons each week.

Arriving guests can study chef Mooser's credentials in the foyer while waiting to be seated. Adorning the entry walls are the many accolades a great chef acquires for fine work.

European wines are well stocked from vins du pays to first growths and an unique assortment of Swiss wines are offered. An admirable selection of California wines including four Santa Clara Valley producers and a dozen North Coast favorites are listed on the wine list.

Emile's Swiss Affair, 545 South Second St., San Jose 95112. Telephone (408) 289-1960. Hours: 5-10 p.m., weekends until 10:30 p.m.. Closed Mon. Price Range: $6.50-$11.00. Corkage: $5.00. Cards: BA, MC, AE. Reservations suggested.

GERVAIS *French Restaurant*

Deciding that the nation's 24th largest and fastest growing city would welcome an additional continental restaurant, chef Gervais Henrique and his wife opened their doors in March of 1977. Their stucco restaurant exterior is stylistically old California. Within, however, the decor is unmistakeably European with elegant pastel draperies, elaborate silver table service and original oil paintings adorning the walls.

Monsieur Gervais is a gifted chef and graduate of the culinary art school in his native Marseilles, France. His considered menu represents regional cooking at its finest with a distinctive, interpretive flair: the Filet de Boeuf Mistral sauteed with shallots, wine and tomatoes ($7.00); and Ris de Veau Basquaise, veal sweetbreads in a sauce of fresh mushrooms, diced tomatoes and garlic ($7.00), are nightly features.

The chef's creative ability is certainly commensurate with any imaginative request for the adjoining banquet facility.

Several Santa Clara Valley vintners are represented on the wine list which does justice to the better wines of France as well.

Gervais, Restaurant Francais, 1798 Park Ave., San Jose 95126. Telephone (408) 275-8631. Hours: Lunch 11:30 a.m.-2:30 p.m. Mon.-Fri.; Dinner 5:30-10 p.m. Mon.-Sat.. Closed Sun. Price Range: Lunch $4.50-$7.00; Dinner $6.75-$9.00. Corkage: $4.00. Cards: BA, MC. Reservations suggested. Seating: 75.

LA TERRASSE *Restaurant*

It is a welcome transition from commuting on a crowded inter-city thoroughfare, to sink deep into a canvas director's chair out of doors beneath arched grape arbors for a relaxing lunch. The enclosed restaurant patio or "terasse"' is festooned with hanging plants, and umbrellas, while indoors the decor is typically French provincial.

Veteran restauranteur Leon Sidella has assembled a fine menu of classical and innovative French dishes. Wine selections from the well stocked cellar are served in suitable 16 oz. stemware set out amidst fresh cut flowers on the smart pastel tablecloths.

La Terrasse, 3740 El Camino Real, Palo Alto 94306. Telephone (415) 494-0700. Hours: Lunch 11:30 a.m.-2:30 p.m.; Dinner 5-10 p.m., closed Sun.. Price Range: Lunch $2.50-$4.50; Dinner $6.75 $9.50. Cards: BA, MC Full Bar. Reservations advised. Seating: 120.

L'IAISON RESTAURANT *Restaurant*

As professional people keep relocating south of San Francisco, the level of sophistication of a peninsula restaurant's local clientele continues to increase. Recognizing this, an association of two talented men formed in one of San Francisco's most prestigious restaurants established the L'iaison Restaurant

Their partnership is one of contrasting, complimentary personalities. Arriving guests are warmly greeted by maitre d'hotel Franco Siccardi, a dignified gentleman whose booming voice resounds with self-assurance and good cheer. Co-owner and chef Michael Ghilarducci is a modest, young man of considerable ability who acknowledges being raised in the kitchen of his father's noted restaurant.

Vaulted arches add a Mediterranean flavor to the main dining area where the waiters are black tied, and polished silver gleams beside fine china on linen tablecloths. Among the sixteen dinner entrees, the thinly sliced Scaloppini of Veal (Wisconsin, milk fed) with fresh mushrooms in a marsala wine sauce ($8.00) and the Broiled Noisettes of Lamb, Sauce Dijonnaise ($8.50) are excellently prepared.

Pride in Santa Clara and Napa Valley wines offered is evident as these selections preface the list of imported wines.

L'iaison Restaurant, 4101 El Camino Way, Palo Alto. Telephone (415) 494-8848. Hours: Lunch 11:30 a.m.-2:30 p.m.; Dinner 5-10 p.m.. Price Range: Lunch $2.50 $7.00; Dinner $6.25-$10.50. Cards: BA, MC, AE. Reservations suggested. Full Bar. Seating: 85.

MADALENA'S *Restaurant*

Long time restauranteur Freddy Madalena's fondest wish is that patrons of his new Palo Alto restaurant feel like his personal dinner guests. To this end, fine service is indispensible, and at Madalena's service is the number one concern.

Chef Arturo Lionetti prepares some of the Peninsula's finest pasta preceeding a variety of regional Italian veal dishes among other entrees on the continental menu.

Several private and banquet rooms seating two to sixty persons can be reserved.

Madalena's, 544 Emerson, Palo Alto. Telephone (415) 326-6082. Hours: Lunch 11:30 a.m.-2:30 p.m.; Dinner 5:30-10 p.m.. Closed Sun. & Mon.. Price Range: Lunch $3.50-$6.50; Dinner $6.50-$11.50. Corkage: $3.00. Cards: BA, AE, MC. Reservations suggested. Seating: 90.

LE MOUTON NOIR *Restaurant*

Situated at the base of the Saratoga foothills along the Santa Cruz Mountain wine trail, is the elegant country chalet of Don and Marsha Duranti.

Natural light angling through skylights etched in the vaulted ceiling, gently illuminates the pastel table settings for luncheon guests. The roomy restaurant interior seats but 44 well attended patrons.

The selected luncheon and dinner entrees are imaginative, French provincial recipes, cooked to order and served with fresh, seasonal vegetables.

There are more fine wine selections than seats in the house.

Le Mouton Noir, 14560 Big Basin Way, Saratoga 95070. Telephone (408) 867-7017. Hours: Lunch 11:30 a.m.-2:30 p.m. Tues.-Fri.; Dinner 6-10 p.m. Tues.-Sat.. Price Range: Lunch $3.50-$5.95; Dinner $7.50-$10.95. Cards: BA, MC. Reservations accepted.

THE PLUMED HORSE *Restaurant*

With better than 50 years combined experience in the restaurant profession, Messieurs Klaus Pache, host, and Kurt Brinkmann, chef, are again confederates in the stylish Plumed Horse Restaurant.

Historically, the restaurant was a barn which boarded horses, later annexed to the 100 year old home of the village doctor. Today renovated as one building with two complementary dining rooms, seating is either in the former stable with lofty beam ceiling and relaxed country atmosphere, or in the smaller doctor's quarters now an elegant Victorian chamber. Custom made stained glass windows and hand crafted solid mahogany chairs enhance the restaurant's interior.

Chef Brinkmann's lengthy menu includes a dozen three course dinners, a fresh nightly special, and an impressive array of continental specialties exhibiting the full range of his culinary talents. The black tied waiters offer the finest in prompt, professional service, and regular patrons often request to be seated at one of their respective stations.

The wine list is exceptional and no less than twelve cognacs are available after dinner.

The Plumed Horse, 14555 Big Basin Way, Saratoga 95070. Telephone (408) 867-4711. Hours: 5-11:30 p.m. Tues.-Sat., closed Sun. & Mon.. Price Range: $5.95-$12.50. Corkage: $5.00. Cards: AE, BA, MC. Reservations suggested. Full Bar. Seating: 125.

ELISHA STEVENS RESTAURANT *Restaurant*

Pioneer pathfinder Elisha Stevens, first man to guide a wagon train across the Sierras, is commemorated in the Santa Clara Valley where he eventually settled, by this newly opened, fashionable restaurant

Convivial host Brenden Leary has combined a number of distinctive features ensuring a variety of dining experiences for his guests.

An old world tradition can be enjoyed Thursday nights for groups of up to six by reservation well in advance. Called the "Cook's Table", parties plan a menu of from five to ten courses with the executive chef who prepares the feast for them as they observe from a special table in the kitchen! A different wine selection accompanies every course and both are introduced by Mr. Leary; (@ $30 per cover).

From the regular menu, ten entrees including appetizer of the day and fresh loaf of cracked wheat and honey bread are served with homemade soup or salad, fresh seasonal vegetable and starch. A nightly seafood, vegetarian and chef's special are additionally offered.

Eleven premium California producers are represented on the varied wine list.

Elisha Stevens Restaurant & Bar-Room, 1655 S. Saratoga-Sunnyvale Road, Saratoga. Telephone (408) 252-4424. Hours: Lunch 11:30 a.m.-2:30 p.m. Tues.-Fri.; Dinner 5-10 p.m. Tues.-Sun.. Price Range: Lunch $2.75-$4.25; Dinner $6.25-$11.25. Corkage: One glass for the host. Cards: AE, BA, MC. Full Bar. Seating: 20

DIGGER DAN'S *Restaurant*

Ask a Gilroy winemaker for a local restaurant recommendation and chances are he will send you to Digger Dan's. Tucked away in a downtown office complex, the restaurant commemorates a colorful local miner of a bygone era.

Mining scenes adorn the walls and many of the fixtures are ingeniously fashioned from old mining equipment. Tiffany lamps and hanging green plants are suspended from the high beamed dining room ceiling, and included in the comfortable seating below are individual booths partitioned off with Santa Clara Valley fruit drying racks.

A variety of steaks, prime rib and crustaceans, and combinations of same are served in generous helpings. Dinners include fondue, soup or salad, sourdough French bread and choice of starch.

A very fine representation of Santa Clara Valley wines are offered including locally made varietals from the Thomas Kruse and Fortino wineries. The management has taken care to print the wine list on bottles nicely posed on the tables.

The adjoining lounge presents live entertainment Friday and Saturday nights, where solo artists play soft listening music.

Digger Dan's, 7793 Wren Ave., Gilroy 95020. Telephone (408) 842-0609. Hours: Lunch 11:30 a.m.-2:30 p.m., Mon.-Fri.; Dinner 5:30-10 p.m. daily, 4:30-9 p.m. Sunday. Price Range: Lunch $2.85-$4.95; Dinner $4.95-$11.50. Cards: BA, MC, AE. Full Bar.

MARIPOSA HOUSE *Restaurant*

Visitors winding up a tour of the Hecker Pass area wineries would do well to follow Highway 101 south to historic San Juan Batista for lunch before continuing to, say, the Monterey Peninsula.

A genuine air of early California surrounds this tranquil community, once the major stagecoach stop between San Francisco and Los Angeles. With restoration of California's largest mission church and periodic surroundings now near completion, mid-day visitors can also observe dozens of Indian and Spanish buildings dating from the early 1800's. And now for that lunch.

Wednesday luncheon alternatives have an international flair with daily specials prepared very imaginatively. For those domestically inclined, a particular diced breast of chicken sauteed with mushrooms and oysters, then bound with a wine based cheese sauce dotted with bay shrimp periodically appears on the menu for a modest $3.75.

Some thirty French and California wines appear on the more than adequate wine list, and a generous Sunday Brunch is served weekly form 10 a.m. to 3 p.m..

Mariposa House, 4th & Mariposa, San Juan Batista 95045. Telephone (408) 623-4666. Hours: 11:30 a.m.-3:30 p.m. Tues.-Sat.; 6-9 p.m. Fri. & Sat.. Price Range: Lunch $2.00-$4.00. No cards. Dinner reservations suggested.

VENTANA RESTAURANT *Restaurant*

Guests at the Ventana Inn will find a magnificent panorama of the Big Sur coast when seated on the terraced patio of the Ventana Restaurant. Lunches and dinner, weather permitting, are served out of doors. The serene stillness that envelops diners relaxing in directors chairs around redwood tables as red-tailed hawks hover in the distance, can easily extend a mid-day meal into an all afternoon proposition.

Indoors, tiered seating beside a great hearth extends below to orderly rows of hardwood tables draped with pastel linen and surrounded by distinctive wicker chairs.

Masterful chef Jeremiah Tower prepares seasonal menus featuring the finest in local provender superbly prepared. Bay area gourmands will remember Mr. Tower's former association with famed Chez Panisse Restaurant in Berkeley.

Consistent with the idyllic setting and excellent cuisine, General Manager Lee Ivey has assembled a superior all California wine list. Composed of the highest ranking varietals from a series of in house comparative tastings, the wine list reads like a who's who in premium California winemaking.

Ventana Restaurant, Big Sur 93920. Telephone (408) 667-2332. Hours: Lunch 11 a.m.-4 p.m.; Dinner 5-10 p.m.. Price Range: Lunch $3.50-$6.50; Dinner $8.50-$12.00. Cards: AE, BA, MC, DC. Reservations advised.

CARMEL VINTAGE SHOPPE *Provisions*

With better than thirty years combined experience in the wine industry, co-proprietors Jonathan Ables and Bart Bechtal are very knowledgeable merchants. They offer very personal service to their regular Monterey Peninsula clientele and have a widespread following elsewhere.

The staff makes regular wine country excursions and maintains close contact with the better California producers. The Vintage Shoppe has frequently been the first retailer in California to represent initial offerings from new wineries, emphasizing a selective stocking of their better varietals.

The wines are shelved by varietal appellation rather than producer which gives consumers very meaningful price comparisons.

Carmel Vintage Shoppe, Dolores between Ocean and 7th, Carmel 93921. Telephone (408) 624-3895. Hours: 10 a.m.-8 p.m. Mon.-Sat.; 10 a.m.-6 p.m. Sun.. Cards: BA, MC.

SIMPSON'S RESTAURANT *Restaurant*

Established as a luncheon Tea Room in 1946 and now a full service restaurant, Simpson's has catered to Carmel diners for more than a generation.

Soft, chandelier lighting with glowing candles, and fresh flowers on snowy linen tablecloths set a relaxed mood in the Williamsburg dining room. In addition to several fresh Monterey Bay seafood specialties, a chef presides in the dining room over flaming copper chafing dishes on the buffet table. He nightly carves roast Leg of Lamb, Prime Rib, Whole Roast Turkey and Old Fashioned Pot Roast, adding the nostalgic appeal of home style cooking to the otherwise continental menu.

A separate dessert menu is presented after the entree featuring freshly baked fruit pies, various pastry selections and a sinfully rich triple layer chocolate fudge cake. All desserts as well as dinner rolls are baked on the premises.

Mr. Little has in recent years become quite a wine buff and delights in offering his domestic discoveries on Simpson's impressive wine list. His committment to serving wines ready to drink may mean his cellaring them for many years.

Simpson's Restaurant, 5th & San Carlos, Carmel 93921. Telephone (408) 624-1238. Hours: Lunch 11:30 a.m.-2:30 p.m.; Dinner 5:30-9:30 p.m.. Price Range: Lunch $3.50-$5.50; Dinner $8.00-$12.00. Corkage: $1.00. Cards: BA, MC, AE. Full Bar. Reservations suggested. Seating: 75.

RAFAELLO RESTAURANT *Restaurant*

Owner manager Ramon D'Agliano's Raffaello Restaurant is truly an homage to northern Italy and its cuisine. Elegantly simple in decor, the restaurant offers no elements to distract from the most important element, the food itself. Amelai D'Agliano, Ramon's mother, is the chef and controls all that leaves the kitchen. Personalities promote an air of relaxation and care that all of the regular patrons have learned to expect in this fine restaurant.

From the moment that you open the menu, you might as well find yourself in Milan or Florence. The soups are always good, the vinaigretted salad just right, the vegetables never over or under done. Favorite dinners are Vitella a la Piemontese (veal with Fontina cheese and truffles) and Vitella a la Romana (veal with cheese, proscuitto, and mushroom sauce).

The cuisine is matched by one of the most impressive wine lists. Included are outstanding vintages dating from 1899, ranging in price from $7.00 to $275.00. French, German and Italian wines plus three full pages of California selections are available.

The desserts are phenomenal and who can leave without trying the Zabaglione. All of these things contribute to compose a restaurant so popular that reservations are booked months in advance.

Raffaello Restaurant, Corner of Mission & Ocean Ave., Carmel 93921. Telephone (408) 624-1541. Hours: Dinner starts at 6 p.m.. Price Range: $7.00-$30.00. Jackets are required; ties optional.

WINES OF CALIFORNIA *Provisions*

Recognized as one of the superior retailers of California wines in California, Wines of California deals exclusively in premium, domestic wines. President David Wheeler has personally selected from some 147 California producers an outstanding selection of California's finest, specializing in new offerings from smaller wineries.

An avid collector of wine related antiques, access to Mr. Wheeler's store is gained through a pair of 18th century wrought iron gates secured from an English winery. The focal point of the antechamber is an imposing 14th century wooden wine press from Spain, and the store is otherwise decorated with vintage stained glass and other period fixtures.

Active as co-chairman of the annual Monterey Wine Festival, Mr. Wheeler is also a contributing editor to several local wine publications and has inaugurated an unique program of marketing exclusive, high quality California wines. Subscribers to the Wine Guild receive two monthly samples of premium wines from noted vintners made to the specifications of Wines of California. A nationally syndicated cartoonist drafts original labels for the wines and an accompanying monthly newsletter provides specifics on samples sent.

Wines of California, #20 Carmel Center, Highway 1 & Rio Rd., Carmel 93921. Telephone (408) 624-0960. Hours: 10 a.m.-6 p.m. Mon. Sat.; Noon 4 p.m. Sun.. Cards: BA, MC.

CHEZ FELIX *Restaurant*

The intimate restaurant of Felix Roux is on Monterey's Cannery Row. His twelve tables are leisurely arranged in the elegant dining room whose French decor of the early 1900's contrasts nicely with the fine view of Monterey Bay.

A well dressed clientele, once seated by Mme. Roux, is left to consider the novel selection of French regional entrees on a menu worth studying. Several dishes are finished ablaze at the table before being subdued by their respective sauces and served piping hot.

While the wine list is predominantly French, care has obviously been taken to include some interesting California selections.

Chez Felix, 585 Cannery Row, Monterey 93940. Telephone (408) 373-0556. Hours: 5:30-10 p.m. Tues.-Sun.. Price Range: $5.75-$11.00. Cards: MC. Reservations suggested.

THE WHALING STATION INN *Restaurant*

The Whaling Station Inn is conveniently located above historic Cannery Row, and the restaurant interior has been carefully restored to capture the periodic feel of a mariner's den. The more contemporary fixtures include a full service bar and lounge, oyster bar in the dining area and the kitchen is equipped with a barbeque pit for broiling salmon and steaks alike over native live oak and grapevine cuttings.

Direct from the fleet anchored nearby, proprietor John Pisto offers the freshest sea bass, local anchovies, lingcod and salmon in season to name but a few. Prepared separately, simply accented with local herbs, spices and served perhaps with a plump artichoke dotted with mayonnaise, these fish retain their individual flavor and integrity. Combined, however, with mussels, clams and a Maine lobster and plunged into a frothing pot of bouillabaisse, the whole may be greater than the sum of its parts.

An avid wine enthusiast, Mr. Pisto cellars and serves an all California selection from some 20 premium producers, with a particularly good representation of Monterey County varietals.

Whaling Station Inn, 708 Wave Street, Monterey. Telephone (408) 373-4248. Hours: 5:30-10:30 p.m. daily. Price Range: $6.50-$14.50. Cards: MC, BA. Seating: 135.

CLUB XIX *Restaurant*

A remarkable view of golfers pitching up to the 18th green silhouetted against the placid blue waters of Stillwater Cove is enjoyed at the Club XIX by luncheon guests whose every need is seen to by Maitre d'Hotel Pierre Bain. Mr. Bain has directed dining room activities for the past twelve years and his presence at both lunch and dinner establishes the continuity that his regular clientele appreciates.

The choice of luncheon specialties varies daily, and a mid-afternoon limited menu seating from 3-5 p.m. is served. Dinner at the Club XIX is gastronomic heaven. Service is a la carte and pages of preliminaries including hors d'oeuvres, classic soups and imaginative salads preface the menu's entrees. The Mignonettes de Veau Chasseur - veal tenderloin sauteed with tomatoes, herbs and fresh mushrooms in a madiera sauce ($10.25); and Tournedos Rossini - sauteed filet of beef with foie gras and Perigord sauce ($12.00), are sublime.

The unique captain's wine list displays descriptive label copies from each of the twenty California wineries represented. A fine variety of French and sparkling wines complete the selection.

Club XIX, Del Monte Lodge, Pebble Beach 93953. Telephone (408) 625-1880. Hours: Lunch 11 a.m.-5 p.m.; Dinner 7-10 p.m.. Closed Monday. Price Range: Lunch $2.75-$7.75; Dinner, a la carte from $12.00. Cards: AE, BA, MC. Full Bar. Reservations necessary. Gentlemen required to wear jackets for dinner. Seating: 65.

EAST OF EDEN *Restaurant*

For better than 100 years a Salinas landmark, the downtown Presbyterian church now welcomes disciples of another calling. In 1972, the building was renovated to house the most congenial dinner house in the valley.

The vaulted nave now seats 100 diners around distinctive marquetry inlaid tables. In the ambulatory to the rear, a busy bar does a capacity weekend crowd.

The steak and lobster menu is reasonably imaginative, including several daily chef specials. The accompanying soups are wholesome, salads quite crisp and several Monterey County bottlings appear on the wine list.

East of Eden, 327 Pajaro, Salinas 98901. Telephone (408) 424-0819. Hours: Lunch 11:30 a.m.-2:30 p.m. Mon.-Fri.; Dinner 5-10 p.m. Mon.-Thurs., 5-11 p.m. Fri.. Price Range: Lunch $2.95-$4.50; Dinner $5.95-$13.95. Cards: MC, BA. Reservations suggested on weekends. Seating: 100.

SAN LUIS BAY INN *Restaurant*

The Castillian Room at the San Luis Bay Inn is an excellent place to dine. The tables are draped with gold linen and flanked by handsome, leather-backed chairs are leisurely arranged in the spacious dining room. A peaceful view of well maintained grounds about the terrace, and fishing pier midway across the placid lagoon sets a relaxed mood for dinner.

An array of epicurean entrees are offered including: Shrimp Marseillaise - prawns sauteed in butter with garlic, herbs, tomatoes and mushrooms, cooked in white wine and flambeed with cognac ($8.75. The chef knows numerous ways of preparing duckling as well. An inquiry of the waiter will resolve what that particular evening's preparation will be. All entrees are served with soup du jour or salad, vegetable du jour and potato or rice pilaf.

Wine Steward David Root personally finishes flambee dishes at the table while otherwise assisting patrons with the large wine list. Wines from Sterling Vineyards predominate on the domestic ledger with selections from Chappellet and a half dozen other North Coast producers and local wines soon to debut. First growth claret and Domaine Burgundies highlight an even larger selection of European wines.

Castillian Room Restaurant, San Luis Bay Inn, Avila Beach 93424. Telephone (805) 595-2333. Hours: Breakfast & Lunch 7 a.m.-2 p.m.; Dinner 6-9:30 p.m.. Price Range: Dinner $7.00-$17.50. Corkage: $3.00. Cards: BA, MC. Reservations suggested.

WINE STREET INN *Restaurant*

Adjacent to the "Old Mission" plaza and below the Network Mall in downtown San Luis Obispo is the very wine oriented Wine Street Inn. A wine bottle decorated, street level marquis directs interested diners to the cellar level where the restaurant seating for 75 people is bordered by an entourage of specialty shops.

Fondue is the specialty of the house and six pleasing varieties of this sociable repast are served for lunch and dinner. A medley of exotic sandwiches round out the luncheon fare which may include a trip to the well stocked salad bar for a slight additional charge.

More interestingly, however, next door at San Luis Obispo County's most complete wine shop, Wine Street Wines, patrons can personally choose from over 300 wines to accompany their meal. Knowledgeable proprietor Vern Meyers will cheerfully assist in the selection, and the corkage fee is a modest $1.50 over retail price.

Wine Street Inn, 774 Higuera St., San Luis Obispo 93401. Telephone (805) 543-4488. Hours: Lunch 11:30 a.m.-2 p.m. Sun.-Fri., Noon-2:30 p.m. Sat.; Dinner 5:30-9 p.m. Mon.-Sat., 5-9:30 p.m. Sun.. Price Range: Lunch $1.95-$3.60; Dinner $4.95-$7.95. Cards: BA, MC. Reservations suggested weekends.
Wine Street Wines. Telephone (805) 543-0203. Hours: 10 a.m.-7 p.m. Mon.-Wed.; 10 a.m.-10 p.m. Thurs. & Fri. Cards: BA, MC. Vern Meyers, Wine Merchant.

BALLARD STORE RESTAURANT *Restaurant*

Roughly equidistant from Santa Maria to the north and Santa Barbara, and a ten minute drive from Solvang is the small hamlet of Ballard. There, accomplished chef John Elliot and his Santa Ynez Valley born wife Alice purchased the old Ballard country store in 1970, and assisted by their two children, offer a very personal approach to fine dining in a relaxed setting.

Outwardly the Ballard Store has changed little since its establishment in 1939. But within, its rustic simplicity is accented with handsome color-coordinated table settings and hardwood floors.

Chef Elliot's thoughtful and varied menu is certain to require repeated visits to satisy his guests' curiosity. All entrees are prepared to order and served with a tureen of homemade soup and choice of salad, fresh vegetable, daily baked bread and beverage and are very fairly priced.

Several Santa Barbara County selections highlight the extensive wine list which includes European wines and a few Mexican bottlings from Baja, California.

The Ballard Store Serves dinner by reservation only and visitors planning to join them are strongly advised to phone ahead a week or two in advance.

The Ballard Store, 2449 Baseline, Ballard. Telephone (805) 688-5319. Hours: Dinner 6-9 p.m. Wed.-Sat.; 5-9:30 p.m. Sun.. Price Range: $4.50-$8.75. No cards. Local personal checks accepted. Reservations required. Seating: 50.

THE DANISH INN *Restaurant*

Under the guidance of experienced restaurant owner, Vince Evans, the Danish Inn offers the charm and warmth of an old country inn. Renowned master chef, George Peterson, formerly of the Scandia in Los Angeles, reigns over the kitchen.

The luncheon specialty is the Smorgaasbord ($4.95). Two hot dishes and an array of traditional cold delicacies are all meticulously presented, and you may return to the buffet as often as you wish. Additional luncheon suggestions include fresh seafood, omelettes, a variety of cold salads, and Danish-style sandwiches.

Dinner entrees range from Scandinavian dishes such as Medisterpolse (Danish sausage with red cabbage) to several international specialties. Both the Veal Oscar and the Veal Piccata are regular favorites. All entrees are served with Vegetable du Jour and a choice of French-fried or baked potato.

Adjoining the main restaurant is the cocktail bar where the dark wood and heavy beams continue the country-style decor. For those who wish, meals can be enjoyed here as well. With the exception of a couple of local wines, the wine list represents only the larger wineries of northern California.

The Danish Inn, 1547 Mission Drive, Solvang 93463. Telephone (805) 688-4813. Hours: Noon-9 p.m. (Fri. & Sat. until 10 p.m.). Price Range: Lunch $3.25-$5.25; Dinner $5.95 $11.00. Cards: BA, MC, AE. Full Bar. Seating: 150.

CASA DE SEVILLA *Restaurant*

Casa de Sevilla is one of the preferred restaurants of old time Santa Barbarans who often refer to it as "Pete's." In the early 1930's Pete Egus, a native of Bilbao, founded and operated his business with his mother as cook and his sister, Helen, as waitress. After Pete's death, Boyd Weiss took over operation of the restaurant but continued the Basque and Spanish traditions in the kitchen through the use of Mrs. Egus's family recipes.

The ever popular chili con queso is available a la carte for luncheon but is also served with complete dinners along with Castilian soup, salad, relishes, and a choice between rice and potato. Other a la carte items include omelettes, salads, and delicious enchiladas. Dinner entrees (several of which are available for lunch) are predominantly original recipes which require the highest grades of meat and fresh seafood to maintain the consistent quality for which Casa de Sevilla is known. Among the favorites are Salmon Vinaigrette and Chicken Pirenaos, a recipe from the Pyrenees using tomatoes.

The wine list is one of the finest in the area. It offers a lengthy selection which includes several hard-to-get wines from smaller wineries.

Casa de Sevilla, 428 Chapala St., Santa Barbara. Telephone (805) 966-4370. Hours: Lunch Noon-2 p.m.; Dinner 6-10 p.m.. Closed Sun. & Mon.. Price Range: $3.00-$11.00. Cards: BA, MC, AE. Full Bar. Reservations advised. Seating: 76.

BRINKS VINTAGE SHOP *Provisions*

For ten years, Brinks has been offering a carefully thoughtout selection of imported and domestic meats and cheeses. Once inside the door, the inviting aromas of meats cooking in the oven will tempt you to look over the entire store where you will find numerous gourmet foods, coffees and teas, and gifts for the kitchen and bar. The deli and sandwich counter is especially popular around noon.

The array of wines has been carefully selected to present both California and imported with a slightly higher percentage of California wines.

Brinks Vintage Shop, 3849 State St., #53, Santa Barbara 93105. Telephone (805) 687-3388. Hours: 10 a.m. -6 p.m. Mon.-Sat.. Cards: BA, MC.

MAY FARE WINES & SPIRITS INC. *Provisions*

For the most comprehensive selection of imported and domestic wines in the Santa Barbara area this is the place. The impressive stock of California wines representing both large and small wineries has been displayed by variety rather than by winery. Special bottlings and older vintages are housed in the cellar downstairs where tastings open to the public are scheduled every Wed. from 3-6 p.m.. The charge is $2.50.

Packaged deli and gourmet items and an attractive selection of wine books and glassware are available.

May Fare Wines & Spirits Inc, 1221 Old Coast Hwy., Santa Barbara 93108. Telephone (805) 969-2245. Hours: 10 a.m.-7 p.m. Mon.-Sat.. Cards: BA, MC.

MCCONNELL'S *Provisions*

Since 1946 McConnell's rich ice creams and delicate fruit ices have delighted Santa Barbarans and informed out-of-towners. The original, exclusive recipes of the Gordon F. McConnells were passed on to the present owners who maintain the family guarantee:

"We pledge that McConnell's Fine Ice Creams are free of synthetics, imitation flavorings or colorings of any nature. They contain no artificial stabilizers or fillers. No substitutes are used for fresh eggs, rich cream and pure flavorings in McConnell's Fine Ice Cream."

As a result, great lengths are taken to produce consistent quality. Chocolates and coffees are blended on location because no single commercial one could meet the standards.

The "batches" are mixed by hand and slowly frozen in a special batch freezer designed by Gordon McConnell in 1962. With this freezer he duplicated the "French pot" method of ice cream production. Because no air is allowed to accumulate in the ice cream, a pint of McConnell's weighs close to a pound.

The original location on State Street remains open, but production has been moved to a new plant on Canon Perdido.

McConnell's, 2001 State St. at Mission, Santa Barbara. (Second location: 815 E. Canon Perdido). Telephone (805) 965-3764. Hours: 11 a.m.-midnight; Lunch 11 a.m.-2 p.m. at Canon Perdido address. Tours of the plant by reservation Thurs. at 3 p.m..

THE TEA HOUSE *Restaurant*

Housed in a former grocery store of the 1880's, the Tea House offers vegetarian and seafood dishes along with over 50 varieties of tea.

The highly recommended Sunday brunch offers a range of omelettes, crepes and sandwiches along with the ever popular cheese blintzes. The Surprise Omelette varies with seasonal fruits and vegetables.

The dinner menu offers the best Bouillabaisse in town for $5.95, fresh fish of the day, several mouth-watering vegetable entrees, cheese fondue, and "light supper items" of the soup and salad variety.

The Tea House, 301 East Canon Perdido, Santa Barbara 93101. Telephone (805) 965-4222. Hours: 11 a.m.-11 p.m. Tues.-Sun.. Price Range: Lunch $1.35-$5.65; Sun. brunch $1.35-$5.95; Dinner $2.50-$7.50. Cards: BA, MC. Reservations recommended.

THE WINE CASK *Provisions*

President and founder of this wine shop which services the greater Santa Barbara area, Ralph Auf der Heide, personally purchases his wines from small producers throughout the winegrowing regions of California. The selection found in this shop is varied and interesting and strong on California vintages.

A newsletter is published regularly which lists the newest finds from Mr. Auf der Heide's travels.

The Wine Cask, 813 Anacapa Street, Santa Barbara 93101. Telephone (805) 966-WINE.

Lodging

hen visiting the wine country, it is best to plan plenty of time between appointments, and free time for the unexpected. Winemakers can be a very gregarious lot whose good nature is often only exceeded by their generosity in opening more bottles than expected. An open ended schedule allows the flexibility to savor those shared moments without having to hasten off to another committment.

As often as can be arranged then, planning to lodge in the wine country for the duration of the visit will spare an unnecessary commute and afford more time for leisurely wine touring.

Visitors to California Central Coast wineries can alternately enjoy the variety of the Bay Area, the serenity of the Santa Cruz Mountains and the myriad vacation possibilities of Monterey, San Luis Obispo and Santa Barbara Counties. Accommodations reviewed herein range from economical, Spartan comfort to luxurious full service resorts.

Each inn surveyed was considered on the basis of cleanliness, hospitality and convenience to area wineries. When planning a several day excursion, reservations well in advance are in order, especially during the busy spring and summer months.

In conjunction with the preceding restaurant guide, this chapter should anticipate the balance of the traveler's needs. The hospitality industry in the ten counties considered in this publication is very extensive, so not being able to secure reservations at suggested inns should have travelers checking other peripheral accommodations.

BURLINGTON HOTEL *Hotel*

What was once an animated port town as shipping center of California's turn-of-the-century grain trade, has all but been commercially forgotten. Today, much of the flavor of those reckless early days of Port Costa can now again be savored by passers-by due largely to the restorative efforts of one Bill Rich.

Mr. Rich in rehabilitating the waterfront Burlington Hotel to recapture the spirit of its day, has outfitted the 19 rooms with periodic photos, antiques and Victorian furnishings. Central coast travelers find this a convenient stop over before continuing to the Napa Valley due north.

———

Burlington Hotel, 2 Canyon Lake Drive, Port Costa 94569. Telephone (415) 787-9973. Rates: Single $12.00; Double $15.00-$17.00. Cards: MC, BA.

HOTEL CLAREMONT *Hotel*

Surrounded by 22 acres of landscaped gardens, the palatial Hotel Claremont is something of a modern day Versailles. This stately resort hotel was constructed in 1911 in such a grandiose fashion as to prompt leading architects of the day to comment on its warmth, charm and character.

Today recreational facilities include six new tennis courts and an olympic size swimming pool. Certain of the Bay View rooms have a particularly fine vista of the San Francisco skyline 20 miles away by car or public transit.

Hotel Claremont, Domingo & Ashby Avenues, Oakland/Berkeley 94705. Telephone (415) 843-3000. Rates: Single $26.00-$32.00; Double $32.00-$38.00; Suites $50.00-$175.00. All major credit cards accepted.

TOWN HOUSE MOTEL *Motel*

Since there are no accommodations in Pleasanton, those visiting the Alameda County wineries would do best to lodge in Livermore, seven miles east. The Town House Motel is a Friendship Inn affiliate, and membership in that organization is a good guarantee of comfort and cleanliness.

The motel is downtown and reasonably quiet. Rooms have air conditioning, telephone and color T.V., and guests can enjoy swimming in the modest pool. Advance reservations for Friendship Inns can be made at any member motel

Town House Motel, 1421 1st St., Livermore 94550. Telephone (415) 447-3865. Rates: Single $16.00; Double $18.00-$20.00. Cards: BA, MC, AE.

BOULDER CREEK COUNTRY CLUB *Lodging*

High in the redwoods, well above the fog line, are several complexes of modern luxury houses on the grounds of one of the finest recreational facilities in the county. Some 45 of the 150 privately owned Villa-Condominiums are available for year-round rental, and are ideal for family vacationing in a tranquil mountain setting.

The deluxe 1, 2, and 3-bedroom villas have exposed beam ceilings, wall to wall carpeting and all modern conveniences in the kitchen and dining rooms. All units have outdoor terraces extending the length of the house, which provide a particularly good vantage point for watching the sunset through the redwoods.

The units are alternately situated by golf course fairways and bridged lagoons formed by damming Boulder Creek, which meanders through the grounds.

Villa guests receive special rates and preferred starting times on the championship 18 hole golf course and 6 tennis courts. Resident golf and tennis pros offer lessons and swimming instruction is available at the pool. The Redwood Room restaurant serves 3 meals a day but unfortunately offers no locally made wines.

Boulder Creek Golf and Country Club, 16901 Big Basin Way, Boulder Creek 95006. Telephone (408) 338-2111. Rates: 1-2 persons $30-$45, 3-4 persons $45-$50; $5-$10 for each additional person up to six. Cards: BA, MC. One day's deposit required; refunded on 48 hour notice.

HENRY COWELL REDWOODS STE. PK. *Campground*

A proliferation of coastal redwood trees, Sequoia Sempervirens, can be observed from the self-guided nature paths which loop through the park, and fifteen miles of trails are open to hikers and horseback riders.

The park's two overnight areas are located in a stand of Ponderosa pine. Piped drinking is provided close to all campsites, and there are hot showers, laundry tubs, and flush toilets. The picnic grounds have tables, stoves and ample parking and overlook the eastern bank of the San Lorenzo River.

Henry Cowell Redwoods State Park, Highway 9, Felton 95018. Telephone (408) 335-4598. Campsites: $2.00-$4.00 per night. Dogs $1.00 each. Trailor hook-ups $5.00. Reservations required.

CAPITOLA VENITIAN HOTEL *Hotel*

Three miles south of Santa Cruz on Highway 1 and down to the ocean, lies the village of Capitola. On the beach next to the wharf is the landmark Capitola Venitian Hotel. Built in 1924 and recently fully restored under new ownership, the Hotel has 22, one and two bedroom suites with kitchens, queen size beds, fireplaces and balconies.

A distinctly Mediterranean flavor pervades the hotel whose room doors are decorated with original redwood carvings depicting literary, musical and historical Venitian themes.

Capitola Venitian Hotel, 1500 Wharf Road, Capitola 95010. Telephone (408) 476-6471. Rates: Single $34.50-$39.50; Double $39.50-$44.50.

BIG BASIN REDWOODS STATE PARK *Campground*

Located on the ocean facing slopes of the Santa Cruz Mountains, the Big Basin Redwoods State Park includes about 12,000 wooded acres within the Waddel Creek watershed. Having been first visited by the Portola expedition in 1769, establishes Big Basin as the oldest park now in the California State Park System.

Thirty-five some odd miles of hiking and riding trails follow tranquil streambeds through the deep redwood forests interrupted by several spectacular waterfalls. A centrally located nature lodge houses a collection of area historical and natural science exhibits and is often frequented by Columbian black-tailed deer.

Each of the 190 individual family campsites has a table, stove and food locker with nearby restrooms and hot showers. Also scattered throughout the park are 158 picnic sites with table and stove available on a first come, first served basis. Campsite reservations should be made from 10-90 days in advance of arrival date.

During the summer and at other times when there is sufficient demand, guided Redwood tours and an occasional Ranger hike are offered.

A day-use area for individual and group picnics is located amidst the tallest (285 feet) and most impressive grove of redwoods in the park.

Big Basin Redwood State Park, Highway 9, 20 miles North of Santa Cruz, Big Basin 95006. Telephone (408) 338-6132. Camping $2-$4/night. Dogs not permitted on trails. No trailer hookups in the individual campsites; trailer sanitation station provided.

THE DREAM INN *Inn*

The Dream Inn on the beach in Santa Cruz monopolizes a once unfettered stretch of sand, offering visitors 164 units with ocean view and private lanais.

The view from the balconies over the volleyball courts in the sand below, extends from the boardwalk amusement complex to Pacific Lighthouse Point whose beacon will hopefully not fall onto any further area coastal development.

The Dream Inn is just a short stroll to the wharf with its seafood restaurants, fresh fish markets and fishing and crabbing from the pier.

The Dream Inn, 175 West Cliff Dr., Santa Cruz 95061. Telephone (408) 426-4330. Rates: Single $32.00; Double $38.00. Cards: BA, MC, DC.

PASATIEMPO INN *Inn*

Up in the redwoods just north of Santa Cruz on Highway 17 and adjacent to the Pasatiempo Golf Course lies this established, resort motor hotel. Guests can enjoy the heated pool and mountain air while lodging in handsome one and two bedroom redwood panelled suites.

Host Ray Nazari's Continental Restaurant on the grounds serves nightly. There is evening entertainment in the rustic lounge, and the Cellar Night Club below packs them in on the weekends.

Pasatiempo Inn, 555 Highway 17, Santa Cruz 95060. Telephone (408) 423-5000. Rates: Single $20.00-$22.00; Double $22.00-$24.00. Major credit cards honored. 58 Units.

MISSION TRAIL MOTEL *Motel*

There are no resort hotels in Gilory, but satisfactory accomodations with standard conveniences can be found at the Mission Trail Motel minutes from Highway 101. The 25 units have cable TV, queen size beds and direct dial telephones. A large swimming pool for those frequent summer days when the mercury climbs into the 90's is also heated for spring and fall enjoyment.

Tony and Ann Margherita have recently assumed the management of the motel and aim to please. They welcome winery pilgrims but discourage bringing their pets.

Mission Trail Motel, 5530 Monterey Rd., Gilroy 95020. Telephone (408) 842-6464. Rates: Single $14.00-$18.00; Double $20.00-$24.00. Cards: BA, MC.

LOS GATOS GARDEN INN *Inn*

The designer of this highly recommended hostel must have spent a very favorable time in Southern Europe, because this attractive inn is infused with a genuine warm, Mediterranean feeling.

The Los Gatos sun shines on the terra cotta roofs of the 25 adjoining units year round. Colorful tile mosaics around fountains on the secluded patios reflect the profusion of domestic and exotic plants growing at hand.

Los Gatos Garden Inn, 46 E. Main St., Los Gatos 95030. Telephone (408) 354-6446. Rates: Single $18.00; Double $19.00-$20.00; Suites (sleep six) $30.00. Cards: AE, BA, MC.

LA HACIENDA INN *Inn & Restaurant*

Back when Los Gatos was only a whistle stop on the Inter-Urban railroad, a small inn was founded in the Santa Cruz Mountain foothills. The year was 1901, and to this day the La Hacienda Inn retains the same welcome air of early California hospitality.

All 18 units are snugly arranged around a heated pool. The guest rooms have private patios, are air conditioned and comfortably furnished with natural wood ceilings and adobe brick walls. Adjoining suites are available, some with fireplaces and all with color television and stereo music.

A short walk across the manicured grounds redolent of fragrant garden flowers and herbs is the La Hacienda Restaurant, noted for Sunday Brunch and gracious dining seven days a week for lunch and dinner. The European lunch and dinner menus include daily specials, and for guests of the Inn, continental breakfash is complimentary.

The La Hacienda Restaurant has ample dining facilities for larger groups by reservation. Four distinctive dining rooms on the main floor, and three private rooms seating 15-65 persons on the second floor welcome guests year round.

La Hacienda Inn, 18840 Saratoga-Los Gatos Blvd., Los Gatos 95030. Telephone (408) 354-9230. Rates: Single $19.00-$22.00; Double $24.00-$30.00. Cards: AE, MC, CB, DC. Reservations required.
La Hacienda Restaurant Hours: Lunch 11 a.m.-2:30 p.m.; Dinner 3-10 p.m.. Price Range: Lunch $3.10-$5.75; Dinner $8.25-$11.50; Seating: 210.

LE BARON HOTEL *Hotel*

San Jose is the hub of the populous Santa Clara Valley and those that visit San Jose with any regularity are likely to lodge at the Le Baron. Conveniently located near the junction of two major arteries with prompt, free transportation to and from the nearby municipal airport, the Le Baron is the logical starting or stop over point for valley visitors.

In house features at the Le Baron include an elegant, continental restaurant situated on the ninth floor penthouse level serving buffet lunch, dinner a la carte and Sunday Champagne Brunch. There are two shows nightly at the lively discotheque on the same floor, and quiet entertainment is provided in a separate den by the Fireside Lounge.

The stylish, color coordinated decor and furnishings in the modern guest rooms include thick shag carpet, radio and television and digital clocks. Alternate floors are designated as "non-smoking" as a very considerate gesture. Certain units also havd adjoining "parlours", or suites with conference rooms, and all are comfortably furnished. Queen and king size beds and waterbeds are available.

Le Baron Hotel, 1350 No. First St., San Jose 95112. Telephone (408) 288-9200. Rates: Single $29.00-$33.00; Double $34.00-$38.00. Cards: AE, BA, MC, CB, DC. Reservations suggested. Units: 325.
Restaurant Hours: Lunch 11:30 a.m.-2 p.m.; Dinner 6:30-10:30 p.m. Mon.-Fri.. Price Range: Buffet Lunch $3.95; Dinner $7.25-$20.00. Sunday Brunch: 10 a.m.-2 p.m., $6.95.

SAN JOSE HYATT HOUSE *Hotel*

Visitors de-planing at San Jose Municipal Airport, the most convenient "point de depart" for visiting the Santa Clara Valley wineries, will find the Hyatt House just three minutes away. San Jose's downtown business districts are less than two miles from the Hyatt from where there are 22 vineyards within a half hour ride.

The 500 comfortable units are air conditioned, and a continental restaurant and 24 hour coffee shop are based at the Hyatt.

San Jose Hyatt House, 1740 N. First St., San Jose 95112. Telephone (408) 298-0300. Rates: Single $31.00-$34.00; Double $38.00-$41.00. Cards: BA, MC, AE, DC, CB.

CABANA HYATT HOUSE *Hotel*

The avenue of fountains leading from a busy peninsual thoroughfare, signals one's arrival at the 200 room Cabana Hyatt House in Palo Alto.

Big city service and efficiency are enjoyed by the Cabana's many guests, who may congregate around the large pool or exercize and sauna in the hotel's health club.

Sister hotel Ricky's Hyatt House, directly across El Camino Real, has additional accommodations numbering 350 units.

Cabana Hyatt House, 4290 El Camino Real, Palo Alto 94306. Telephone (415) 493-0800.

Rates: Single $32.00-$40.00; Double $40.00-$48.00. Cards: AE, BA, MC, CB.

DEL MONTE LODGE *Lodge*

One of the world's finest resort hotels, the Del Monte Lodge is located within the private Del Monte Forest overlooking Carmel Bay and the Santa Lucia Mountains in Pebble Beach.

A multitude of sporting activities are available to Lodge guests. World famous Pebble Beach Golf Links, regarded as one of the top five courses in the world is open on a preferential basis to Lodge guests. Two other demanding courses are similarly available as are thirteen championship tennis courts, a heated freshwater pool and saunas. Equestrian, hikers and marksmen alike will find excellent grounds and facilities nearby to enjoy their respective interests as well.

The luxurious accomodations in the stately Lodge include rooms and suites bordering the fairways with magnificent ocean views. Three fine restaurants, several Pebble Beach Shops, and an excellent wine merchant, The Company Store, can make the Del Monte Lodge a charming insular retreat, healthful and relaxing.

As Pebble Beach annually hosts such well attended events as the Bing Crosby Pro-Amateur Golf Tournament and the Concours d'Elegance classic car exhibit to name but a few, guests are well advised to make reservations as many months in advance as possible.

Del Monte Lodge, Pebble Beach 93953. Telephone (408) 624-3811. Rates: European Plan, double or single occupancy; Fairway Rooms, $55.00-$85.00; Fairway Suites, $100.00-$145.00 - One bedroom, $230.00 - two bedrooms. Cards: BA, MC, AE.

QUAIL LODGE *Lodge & Restaurant*

Some three miles inland from coastal Highway 1, and forever away from the inhibiting Monterey Peninsula fog line, is the Quail Lodge at the Carmel Valley Golf and Country Club. Acclaimed as one of the finest quality resort hotels on the west coast, the Lodge is a self-proclaimed "delightful California retreat".

Situated in the lush green trough of serene Carmel Valley amid ten sparkling lakes, the unique cottage units were designed for privacy or entertaining. Four individual guest rooms per cottage with separate entrance, patio and bath are so arranged as to share a larger, central sitting room with fireplace and bar, itself convertible to a bedroom with bath and patio. This practical arrangement for family vacationing also has many possibilities for friendly groups and business associates.

By reservation, Lodge guests can obtain a courtesy card granting the privileges of swimming pool, tennis courts, resort golf shop and club house enjoyed by members of the Country Club.

The elegant Covey Restaurant located on the lake at Quail Lodge serves continental dinner every evening at 6:30 p.m.. Reservations are necessary and gentlemen are required to wear jackets.

Quail Lodge, 8205 Valley Greens Drive, Carmel 93923. Telephone (408) 624-1581. Rates: Patio, Terrace and Balcony rooms: $64.00-$68.00; Center Lounges: $61.00. Third person: additional $6.00 per day. Cards: BA, AE, DC, MC. Reservations required.

NORMANDY INN *Inn*

Designed and decorated by Mr. and Mrs. Robert Stanton in 1936, the Normandy Inn is a model French Provincial country house located just below the Carmel Shops and galleries, a short walk up from Carmel beach.

Accommodations include modern guest rooms, apartments with wood burning fireplaces, and a covey of family thatched cottages with such old world furnishings as down pillows and antique tables and chairs.

Guests are served a complimentary continental breakfast in the common pantry adorned with French antiques and accented with fresh flowers in season.

Normandy Inn, Ocean Avenue at Casanova, Carmel 93921. Telephone (408) 624-3825. Rates: Single $29.00-$37.00; Double $33.00-$43.00; Suites $53.00-$59.00; Cottages $60.00-$75.00. No credit cards or pets. Units: 48.

CASA MUNRAS *Hotel*

The Casa Munras was one of the first residences built outside the walls of the old Presidio, first occupied by Spanish diplomat Don Estaban Munras in 1826. Some of the original adobe structures still remain on the 3 and one-half acre garden estate when in 1941 the historic home became the Casa Munras Garden Hotel.

Today the "Casa" is in the very center of Monterey's historic and recreational area. Thrifty golf packages are offered year round on championship Monterey Peninsula courses and resident facilities include a sheltered freshwater pool.

Attractive contemporary furnishings can be found in the 130 units in two story, early-Monterey style buildings. Several new suites for entertaining are available, and many units are equipped with gas burning fireplaces and some with waterbeds.

Breakfast and lunch are served daily in the Coffee Shop, dinner in the Monterey Room and live entertainment and dancing nightly in the intimate lounge. Banquet and meeting rooms for groups of 20 to 200 are on hand and the helpful staff can assist in making all necessary arrangements.

Casa Munras, Munras Ave. and Fremont, Monterey 93940. Telephone (408) 375-2411. Rates: Single $30.00-$34.00; Double $38.00-$44.00; Suites $75.00. Cards: MC, BA, AE, CB, DC. Reservations required. No charge for children under 12 in same room as parents.

VENTANA INN *Inn*

The natural beauty of Central California's rugged coast is nowhere more striking than at Big Sur, 28 miles south of Carmel on Highway 1. Situated 1200 feet above the crashing surf, with an equally impressive vista on the golden, convoluted peaks of the Santa Lucia Range, is the luxurious Ventana Inn.

Only 24 guest rooms are available, each with individual terraces. Many units have Franklin fireplaces and others adjoin to form suites, while a few townhouses are available with separate bedrooms.

An adjacent spa houses sociable Japanese therapy hotbaths and saunas with a 90 foot heated swimming pool outside. Rates based on the European Plan include complimentary continental breakfast served in the handsome guest lobby.

Ventana Inn, Big Sur 93920. Telephone (408) 667-2331. Rates: Double $52.00-$87.00; Townhouses to $140.00. Reservations required. Cards: BA, MC, AE.

PASO ROBLES INN *Inn*

Two years after a disastrous fire destroyed the historic Hotel El Paso De Robles (est. 1891), the new Paso Robles Inn was constructed in 1942 on the same site. Much of the original red pressed brick was salvaged and used to build the new inn.

Situated on a beautifully landscaped nine acre estate, oak shaded footpaths past running streams wind to the Monterey style bungalow accommodations. The grounds are further arrayed with lily and fish ponds and many rare and beautiful flowers and trees.

In addition to its close proximity to the area mission sites, the Inn is but a leisurely drive to seaside Morro Bay, gateway to Hearst Castle thirty miles to the north. Reservations can also be made at the Inn to visit the local mineral baths, hot and cold soda springs, and the celebrated mud waters.

Paso Robles Inn, 1103 Spring St., Paso Robles 93446. Telephone (805) 238-2660. Rates: Single $12.50-$14.00; Double $15.50-$20.00. Cards: BA, MC, DC.

SAN LUIS BAY INN *Resort Hotel*

Quiet elegance is the theme at this luxurious, all year resort hotel. There is ample opportunity for activity on the Inn's tennis courts and championship 18 hole golf course, or relaxation by the heated pool or sandy beach lagoon. Meeting facilities are available and a wealth of central coast sightseeing is immediately accessible.

The guest rooms all have private balconies overlooking either the ocean or the lagoon and golf course. All guest rooms also have color T.V., queen or twin beds and spacious bathroom with sunken tub. Reservations must be made at least one month in advance and visiting guests whould plan to set aside a few days on their itinerary to experience all that the Inn has to offer.

San Luis Bay Inn, P.O. Box 188, Avila Beach 93424. Telephone (805) 595-2333. Rates: Single $36.00-$42.00; Double $40.00-$46.00. European plan. Reservations required. Cards: BA, MC.

SAN YSIDRO RANCH *Resort*

Nestled in the peaceful foothills of the Santa Ynez mountain range in Montecito, this ranch hideaway has been a favorite retreat for authors, actors and vacationers since its opening as a guest ranch in 1893.

The guest cottages are scattered among twelve acres of foliage and flowers. No two rooms are alike in size, shape or furnishings, and because each one is secluded, a map is sometimes necessary to navigate. With the help of the one provided, you can easily locate trails for hiking, badminton and tennis courts, swimming and wading pools, the ranch stables, or one of the lounges.

The Hacienda Lounge provides complimentary coffee, tea and hot chocolate twenty-four hours a day; morning newspapers; and an "Honor Bar" where you can mix your own drinks beginning at 11:30 a.m.. The Plow and Angel Bar, the original ranch wine cellar, opens daily at 6 p.m. and provides music until 1:30 a.m.

The Plow and Angel dining room (where gentlemen are requested to wear jackets) is housed in the original citrus packing house. The buffet luncheon consists of two hot entrees and a salad bar.

San Ysidro Ranch, 900 San Ysidro Lane, Montecito, Santa Barbara 93108. Telephone (805) 969-5046. Rates: Rooms $42.00-$59.00; Studios $54.00-$73.00; Suites $89.00-$93.00. Restaurant hours: Lunch 11:30 a.m.-2 p.m. Mon.-Sat.; Sunday brunch 11 a.m.-2 p.m.; Dinner 6-10 p.m.. Price Range: Lunch $4.95; Dinner $7.95-$13.25. Cards: BA, MC, AE. Reservations recommended. Units: 39.

SOLVANG INN MOTEL *Motel*

Whether journeying to Solvang in the Santa Ynez Valley for the Summer Theaterfest or Autumn folk festival, any stopover visit to this charming Danish community will highlight a central coast wine tour.

The picturesque Solvang Inn Motel built in 1972 of traditional Scandinavian design is a modern inn conveniently located in the heart of the downtown, old world shopping area.

Robert and Elli Nielson manage the 45 units, all air conditioned with queen size beds, sound proof rooms and heated swimming pool.

Solvang Inn Motel, 485 Alisal Road, Solvang 93463. Telephone (805) 688-3248. Rates: Double $20.50-$28.50. Cards: MC, BA, DC, CB, AE. Reservations required.

THE ALISAL RANCH *Ranch Resort*

Within 10,000 acres of oaks and sycamores is a self-contained world of ranch life. Guests at the Alisal will find not only the comfort and seclusion of their bungalows but also a seemingly endless list of recreational opportunities. This winter feeding ranch for cattle, now owned by the Petan Company, offers horseback riding for all levels of experience and on more than thirty trails, boating and fishing on the 90-acre lake, golf, tennis, swimming, croquet, volleyball, and many other diversions.

The spacious ranch-style accommodations range from double rooms and studio suites to private bungalows with covered porches. All rooms are decorated in tasteful simplicity to include a wood-burning fireplace.

The Alisal facilities and Ranch dining room are reserved for registered guests. The rates include breakfast and dinner on a modified American plan. The Sycamore dining room, however, is open to the public for lunch and dinner, and American plan guests using the Sycamore Room for their dinner are allowed credit. The wide ranged choice on the menu features mahi mahi saute′ and top grades of meat, cooked ranch style.

The Alisal Ranch, Alisal Road, P.O. Box 26, Solvang 93463. Telephone (805) 688-6411. Rates: Single $45.00-$60.00; Double $80.00-$92.00. Public restaurant hours: Lunch Noon-2 p.m.; Dinner 6-8:45 p.m.. Price Range: $5.95-$9.00. Cards: AE. Reservations recommended. Total # of units: 60.

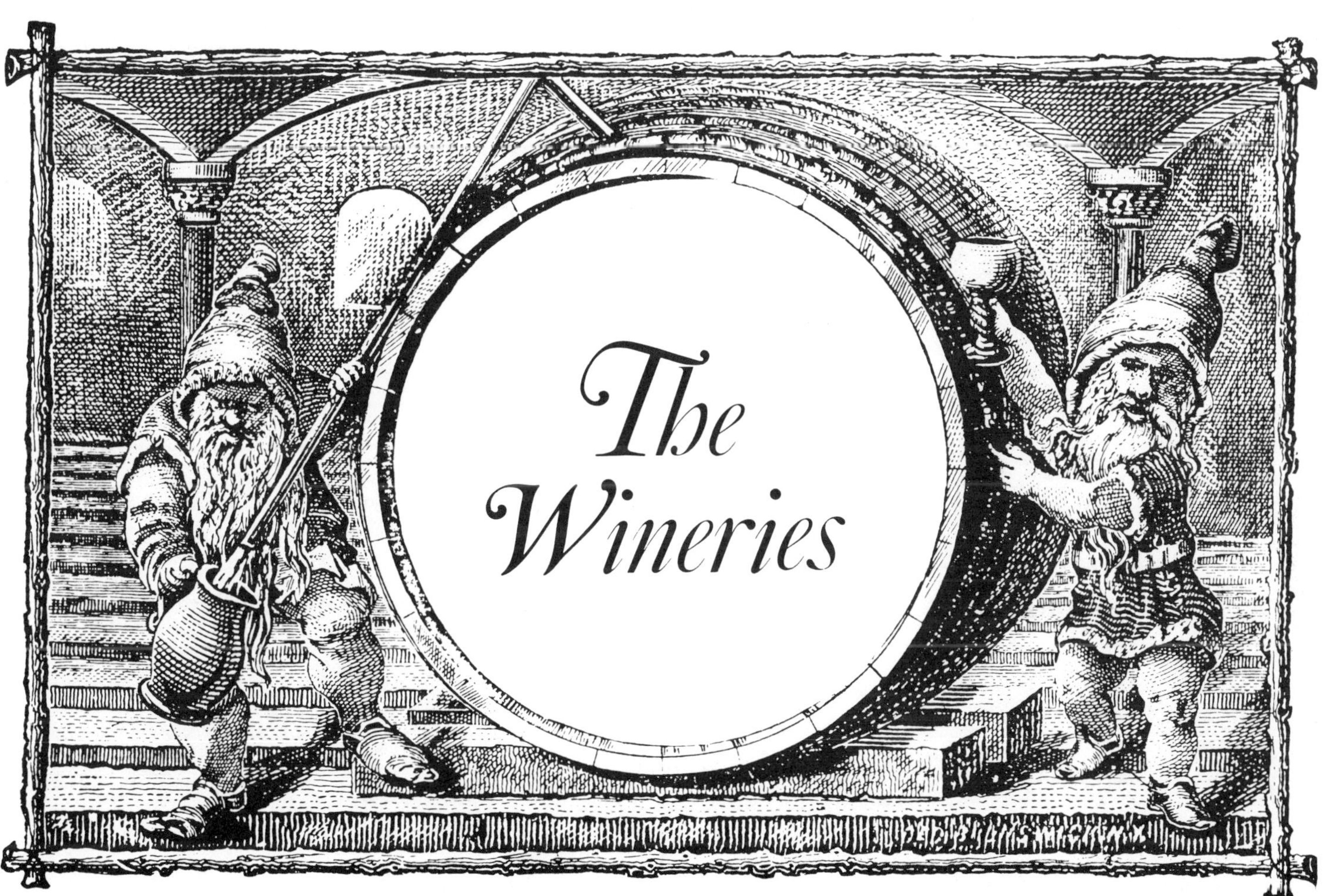
The
Wineries

San Pablo Bay
Benicia
Carquinez Strait
Pittsburg
West Pittsburg
Antioch
San Joaquin
Martinez
J.E. DIGARDI WINERY
CONRAD VIANO WINERY
Concord
Oakley
JULIUS FIRPO WINERY
Knightsen
Rodeo
Hercules
Pinole
El Sobrante
San Pablo
Richmond
Pleasant Hill
Clayton
Brentwood
El Cerrito
Walnut Creek
Albany
Orinda Village
Lafayette
WINE AND THE PEOPLE
OAK BARREL WINECRAFT-WINERY
Berkeley
Tiburon
Sausalito
Rheem Valley
Rossmoor Leisure World
Alamo
Diablo
Emeryville
J.W. MORRIS PORT WORKS
Moraga
Piedmont
Danville
Oakland
Tassajara
Alameda
CHANNING CELLARS
MONTCLAIR WINERY
San Leandro
Contra Costa County
Alameda County
CHATEAU VINTNERS
San Ramon
Altamont
Castro Valley
Dublin
Springtown
Livermore
Brisbane
San Lorenzo
Hayward
CONCANNON VINEYARD
VILLA ARMANDO
Pleasanton
WENTE BROTHERS
STONY RIDGE WINERY
So. San Francisco
San Bruno
Alameda County
San Mateo County
Mt Eden
Union City
Millbrae
Burlingame
Sunol
Scotts Corner
Hillsborough
San Mateo
Foster City
Fremont
Newark
Belmont
San Carlos
Redwood City
LLORDS & ELWOOD WINERY
WEIBEL CHAMPAGNE VINEYARDS
Alameda County
Santa Clara County
MILES
KILOMETERS

Contra Costa -
Alameda Counties

Conrad Viano Winery

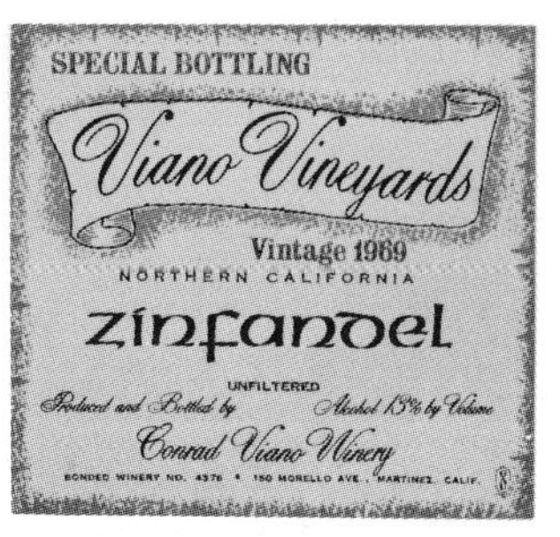

In the shadow of pastel colored oil refineries and housing developments like "Sun Hill Manor," the only commercially producing winery left in Contra Costa County actually contemplates expansion. The man behind the winery is Clem Viano, a barrel-chested man with a warm smile who is the image of the farmer that he is.

"I'm not interested in being a businessman," says the man who is not so sure he wants anyone to know the size of his winery. "I'm just interested in growing grapes and making wine. You see, we're for the family farm. My dad and my mom, my wife and I, and our children are all involved in what goes on here. And I want to give my kids the same opportunity I was given."

To that end, Clem anticipates planting another 25 or 30 acres of vineyards someday. "It'll have to be after a year or two of rain, though," he cautions. "We're sure lucky we didn't plant two years ago!"

Clem contends that pollution from the refineries is actually less today than it once was. The prevailing winds blow toward the west and the Vianos are east of the refineries. Also, air pollution controls are more stringent today, requiring collectors to filter the plumes of smoke that billow skyward from tall stacks.

Clem's grandfather purchased the farm in 1920. Some grapes had been planted there in 1888. Clem's father, Conrad, added to the vineyard, did some replanting, and also planted apples and apricots. When times were difficult in the thirties, Conrad worked for nearby Shell Oil, as did Clem during school vacations.

"Grape prices were so high in the early twenties that dad was almost able to pay off the farm with one year's harvest," remembers Clem. Indeed, because the demand for grapes for home wines was so high in the early years of Prohibition, grape prices reached highs that were not equalled until the early years of the present decade.

Conrad did not begin making wine in this country until 1946. The operation was never a bulk one. The wines were sold retail and wholesale from the winery, mostly in gallon jugs, a custom that continues today. Viano is what Clem refers to as a "Mom and Pop" winery.

Around 1962 the emphasis began to change toward the fifth trade, and sales of gallons gradually took a back seat. Clem's premium wines, made from the fruit of non-irrigated hillside vines, aged longer, and all bottled in fifths, are mostly in the two dollar price range. The jug wines are around four dollars a gallon.

Clem Viano has a degree in viticulture from U.C. Davis. He hopes that his four children (two boys, two girls, aged 8 to 13) will follow in his footsteps. In the meantime, he is doing his darnedest to keep the ranch a going operation until they are old enough to decide their own futures. The winery is nine-tenths of a mile north of Highway 4, on Morello Avenue.

J. W. Morris Port Works

For those lovers of port who have been grousing about the relative paucity of fine dessert wines, take note: there is a new, small winery whose winemaker is dedicated to making Vintage Port in the Portuguese style.

The winery is the J.W. Morris Port Works, located in Emeryville's warehouse district. The space leased is the back and basement of what used to be the People's Bakery, built in 1913. The walls are foot-thick brick and the beams supporting the basement ceiling appear adequate for a four story building.

The winemaker is Jim Olsen, a quiet, bespectacled young man whose interest is English Literature and experience is marketing and sales. The winery's first crush was 1975 and it's first wine was released in October of '76 (at $4.75). Ninety percent of the grapes came from the northern coastal counties and the blend was as follows: 40% Zinfandel, 30% Carignane, 20% Ruby Cabernet, and 10% Petite Sirah.

Why the unusual combination of coastal areas and table wine varieties? "I steadfastly refuse to use central valley grapes," offers Olsen, "hence the absence of Tinta Madera. If someone would plant that variety in Sonoma, or someplace like it, we'd buy the grapes. The area the grapes are grown is the most important thing in regards their quality. Then the varieties themselves. The Portuguese use up to fifteen varieties in their ports. I'm like an artist with a full palette of colors; it is by blending that great works can be created."

The fruit is harvested at table wine ripeness and the stems are left in during fermentation to boost tannin so as to balance the high residual sugar. "With most California ports," says Jim, "the grapes are picked overripe to get high alcohol. Thus, they are too low in acid and make an unbalanced wine." He has purchased most of his grapes from Napa and Sonoma counties, but has also gone to Amador County for Zinfandel.

Jim ferments each variety separately to the desired sugar level, then halts the process (at 14% residual sugar) with a wine spirits addition. The varieties are then aged separately. Sample blends are made and the final blend is usually made the following summer. Individual samples are retained for later tasting and evaluation. Among the new varieties crushed in 1976 were Barbera and Pinot Noir. The latter, tasted out of oak, would have made an outstanding port on its own.

Jim plans on making two ports and an occasional angelica. One port will be his Vintage Port, a selection of his biggest and most fruity ports, which should sell for $6.75. The other will be a "Founders," or Wood Port, meaning a blend of several vintages, selling for $4.75. He anticipates handling between forty and forty-five tons each crush, or roughly in the three thousand case production range. He crushed but thirteen tons in 1975, and double that amount in '76.

J.W. Morris Port Works is a partnership. In addition to Jim and his wife Teri there is a third partner, Teri's father. His name? J.W. Morris.

Villa Armando

Villa Armando is not a common name in California, but in New York it is well known. It's a case of putting the cart before the horse, or in this instance, the label before the winery.

Anthony D. Scotto's family grew grapes and made wine on the islands of Ischia and Procida in the Bay of Naples, dating well back into the last century. In 1903 Anthony's father brought his family to New York, where the elder Scotto started in the wholesale wine business. During Prohibition he sold grapes, but once the ill-advised experiment was over he went back to wine sales on the retail side as well. Anthony, who grew up in the business, took a history major at St. Francis College in Brooklyn. He dates the demise of baseball from the day Ebbets Field was torn down.

The Scottos had been selling wine under the Villa Armando label (for Armando Colluci) since the late thirties, when the wines were made by Cesare Mondavi, first in Acampo (near Lodi) and later at his St. Helena winery (Charles Krug). In 1953, when Anthony started Siena Wines, an import house and distributor, he acquired the Villa Armando label. Eight years later, feeling the need to protect his supply, he purchased a winery that had been built in 1902 by Frank Garatti. In 1962 the winery began producing Villa Armando Wines

Fully ninety percent of Villa Armando's production still travels east to satisfy the demand for basic, down-home, Italian-styled wines. They are the kinds of wines his customers made themselves, from California grapes, during Prohibition, and they are not forgotten. Scotto's most popular wine is a healthy red called Vino Rustico, which he calls "wine of the countryside." It's not surprising, then, to find that it is high in alcohol, very fruity, and possesses some residual sugar.

This wine, like many of Scotto's reds, is made by a distinctive fermentation process called, in the old country, "vinificatore." Here, Scotto has patented the idea under the name "Autovin." Essentially, it is a system whereby the must is heated and circulated over and about the skins before fermentation begins for color extraction. The fermentation then proceeds without skin contact. Scotto estimates that there is a ten to twenty percent loss of color with his method, but then tannin extraction is almost non-existent. "This way," he smiles, "in six months you have a wine that is as smooth as if it were aged for years."

The winery itself stands behind a bright, new, Spanish-styled tasting room. It is an old winery, with several square, concrete fermenting tanks. Most of the cooperge, however, is redwood or oak, and there are some particularly exquisite old ovals. One holds nearly 5000 gallons. Another, dated 1850 (from Bavaria), carries the inscription: "Sunbeams condensed from nature's holy shrine/Are gently housed in every drop of wine."

Scotto's three sons--Anthony, Jr., Dominic, and Gregory--are all active in the business. "If my sons weren't interested in it," he says softly, "I'd sell the winery. Just like that."

Stony Ridge Winery

In 1887 Lou Crellin built an imposing three story brick winery east of Pleasanton on a 450 acre ranch. With a capacity of 300,000 gallons, it was sold in 1921 to Ernest Ferrario, who brought fame to the winery, known then as Ruby Hill.

Today, the palm tree lined driveway directs one to a different sort of operation. The winery and its 225 acres of surrounding vineyards (unirrigated) had nearly been abandoned since the Southern Pacific Land Company bought the property in 1973.

In September of 1975 a group of young people, headed by Harry and Len Rosingana, took a two year lease on the winery. Six months later they secured a bonded winery license and two months after that they leased the vineyards as well. That fall they crushed their first grapes, yielding a Nouveau Zinfandel, a Zinfandel Rose', a Semillon, a Malvasia Bianca, a Pleasanton Johannisberg Riesling, and a Pinot Chardonnay.

There is a light-hearted, yet serious, communal atmosphere about the rehabilitated, rustic winery now. Harry describes it as an ''extended family.'' Several employees live at the house. All are encouraged to purchase shares in the corporation and employer employee barriers seem nonexistent.

Harry Rosingana has acquired the Ruby Hill label for the winery. It will be used for special wines. One such wine will likely be a sweet, rich table wine, to be called Chateau Ruby Hill.

The three hundred acre property is still for sale by Southern Pacific. In the meantime, the Rosinganas and their partners will continue to restore both vineyards and winery. They hope to be able to extend their lease until they can raise enough money to purchase the property outright.

Two hundred acres of vineyards are still usable. The group expects to use 125 to 150 acres of it (pruned and thinned to less than one ton per acre) for the winery's crush and lease the remainder, in one to five acre parcels, to amateur winemakers.

The group has also purchased bulk red, white, and rose' wines for three and one gallon ''bag-in-box'' cartons. The large containers are sold to the restaurant and bar trade; the smaller ones retail at $4.49.

Harry Rosingana took his CPA from San Jose State College and worked for three years with Arthur Anderson in Los Angeles. He later spent three years as controller at Mirassou. Len Rosingana, Harry's brother, comes to the winery from the electronics business.

Stony Ridge's winemaker is Lanny Replogle. A chemistry professor at San Jose State, Replogle has been an amateur winemaker for years.

Concannon Vineyard

Both major wineries in the Livermore Valley share a common founding date: 1883. And, like the Wente story, that of the Concannons began a continent and an ocean away.

James Concannon was born in 1847. In 1865 he left his native Aran Islands (on Galway Bay) and emigrated to Boston. He spent two years in Maine, working in a hotel, rising from bellhop to management and attending night school to improve upon his meager education.

He joined the westward migration in 1875, moving to San Francisco to sell Bret Harte novels for Anton Roman, the book publisher. Itchy feet and the urge to travel led Concannon to the burgeoning rubber stamp business, a franchise that took him from Canada to Mexico City by horseback and stage coach.

Once, in Tombstone, he very nearly joined the legions entombed on Boot Hill. In a hotel saloon he was approached by a cowboy, who ordered, "Drummer. Buy drinks." "I don't drink," Concannon protested. "Then I'll buy and you drink," growled the cowboy. Whereupon Concannon dispelled the tension, saying, "If I don't have the courage to say 'No,' pull the trigger."

In Mexico City, he offered dictator Porfirio Diaz a plan for a complete sanitary system and walked off with the sole franchise for horse-drawn street sweepers. But James Concannon was becoming disenchanted with constant travel. His family was well on its way to a full complement of five sons and five daughters and he was ready to foresake travel and city for the good life of the countryside. A card-playing partner, San Francisco's Bishop Joseph Alemany, suggested that a decent living could be made by the production of altar wines and offered an introductory letter to the local priests. By selling his street-cleaning franchise, James was able to purchase 47 acres and build himself a winery.

A year after the land was acquired and the winery built, Joseph Concannon was born at the winery. A breed apart, Joe forswore the collegiate direction of his brothers and chose, instead, a career in the military. A superb horseman who ran cattle on the ranch, he joined General Pershing to chase Pancho Villa. Concannon was known to speak highly of the Mexican folk hero: "He was like a coyote; he could see you from behind a hill."

James Concannon died in 1911. After World War I, Joe, who had attained the rank of Captain--a title he carried to the end of his life--returned home to run the winery with brother Thomas. Joe eventually outlived or bought out each of his brothers. The winery outlasted Prohibition by the production of altar wines. Even with the help of the winery's many priestly friends, however, only fifty percent of normal production could be achieved.

In 1947 Captain Joe changed the winery from a sole proprietorship to a family corporation. He hired winemaker Katherine Vajda from Cresta Blanca. A

Barrel aging cellars

temperamental, hard-nosed, soft-hearted artist, she later instructed Joe's son Jim in the fine art of winemaking. A ballerina in her native Hungary, after retirement from the winery she embarked on yet a third career, in interior decoration.

Both of Captain Joe's boys took to the business. Joseph, Jr., a Notre Dame graduate and Korean veteran, took over the vineyard and administrative functions. Jim became production man and winemaker. He speaks with gratitude of his mentor:

"Katherine had no degree in enology, but had great natural abilities. She had a *feel* for wines. She knew what wine was in each of a hundred seventy tanks and what its condition was. There was some initial resistance to her from the men, but they couldn't stand up to her. She was just too strong."

The brothers Concannon have been great innovators in a constantly changing business. The plunge they are most known for is their initial bottling in America of Petite Sirah as a varietal. The first release, from the 1961 vintage, came in 1964. (The wine was not vintage dated.) Since then they have honed their Petite Sirahs to a fine mixture of softness and character, in sharp contrast to the many harsh, rough wines which bear the name.

The Concannons have the only plantings of White Rielsing and Cabernet Sauvignon in the Livermore Valley. They were the first to label a light, sweet table wine as Muscat Blanc, perhaps the correct name of a variety that carries different titles according to where it is grown. Their first Muscat Blanc came with the 1975 vintage and has been such a hit that the following vintage was virtually sold out before it was released.

In 1970 the Concannons accomplished the first American planting of a Russian variety called "Rkatsiteli." Obtained from the Vivilov Institute, the variety is native to the Caucasus and over 60,000 acres of it are planted in the USSR. Another 18 acres were planted by Joseph Concannon in 1975 so that, in a few years, more of this unique wine will be available. A medium bodied white, Rkatsiteli reminds me of something between a French Colombard in the nose and a Sauvignon Blanc on the palate.

Among the other distinctive wines offered by Concannon are their Chateau Concannon and Zinfandel Rose′. The former is a sweet Semillon, late harvested, that brings out the finest characteristics of the variety. The latter is a fruity, cherry colored wine, made from Amador County grapes, that is also a winner with consumers.

Perhaps the most pleasing thing about Concannon is the atmosphere about the winery. Though a half million dollars were invested three years ago for new equipment, the winery and its people retain an old world charm that is hard to believe. The mood is informal, to the point of having the tasting room situated between the laboratory and the bottling line. The tasting bar is simply a table, covered with a red and white checked tablecloth. In a very basic sort of way, substance prevails over form.

Wente Brothers

Carl H. Wente came as a young pioneer to Illinois from Hannover, Germany, along the Leine River. He dug post holes and did other ranch work from there to Missouri and thence to Lake County in California. He served an apprenticeship with Charles Krug, who taught him the differences between Old World winemaking and that of California. In 1883 Carl acquired a third interest in a fifty acre plot in the Livermore Valley.

In 1896 Carl purchased the Hayes Ranch and, by the turn of the century, had bought out his partners in the first ranch, upon which the current Wente Brothers winery stands. In 1890 and 1892 two of his seven children were born. They were Ernest A. and Herman L. Wente, the brothers who would later firmly establish the winery's reputation.

Ernest was the farmer. He was also among the five students who made up the first class at the University of California at Davis in 1908. There were nine teachers. Ernest's interests were in grape growing, cattle, and dairy farming. Those interests were vital in keeping the winery intact through the scourge of Prohibition. To this day, Ernest plays an active role in vineyard and winery management of the family business.

Herman was the winemaker. Both his technical skills and essential humanity are legendary in the industry. A bronze plaque, which hangs on the winery's office wall, attests to his imprint: "impatient with the commonplace, seeker of the best...ever willing to help those less endowed, to encourage those more timid, inspire those less sure..." and so on.

The third brother was Carl F. Wente. According to his brother Ernest, Carl F. didn't like the feel of a hoe handle. While hoing in the vineyards one sweltering day, he declared that there had to be a better way of earning a living. He decided that banking would be a fitting means, and began working at Livermore's First National Bank. After a time, he began working for the Gianninis and eventually became president of Bank of America. In that position he was able to assist many growers through the trials and surpluses of the Great Depression.

Wente had been a bulk winery before Prohibition. And, during the thirteen years of near ruination, the winery supplied one customer with altar wines: Beaulieu Vineyard.

"Georges de Latour was a devout Catholic," remembers Ernest Wente. "Because the government required the wines to be shipped directly from the selling winery to the churches, we had to be bonded as 'Beaulieu Winery Number Two.' Georges liked our wines so much that he wanted to buy the winery."

After Prohibition the brothers Wente began to establish the winery identity, based on their sibling relationship. Ernest tended the fruit of the gravelly, often rocky soils and Herman continued to make the

The Tasting Room

outstanding white wines that are associated with the Livermore Valley.

It was Ernest's son, Karl L. Wente, who would take the reins at his uncle's death (1961) and guide the winery for the following fifteen years until his own untimely death in January, 1977.

Karl Wente has left a legacy of innovation for his two sons to carry on. From an era when wineries the size of Wente were almost forced to produce a complete line of wine types, Karl directed Wente Brothers to a position where they make not only just table wines, but where their white wines account for over ninety percent of winery production.

"We seem to do the best job with white wines," he once said. "We have planted several red varieties in our Monterey County vineyards (Arroyo Seco), but that was partly because of our certified nursery there. We have to live with the image that red wines can't be made in Livermore, but that's not true. Except for Cabernet, most red varieties do well here. But, the public won't believe that, so we're kind of stuck with whites. But that's not bad."

Karl was one of the first vintners to make a full commitment to Monterey County. It was a matter of survival. He purchased land in Greenfield in 1961 and began planting vineyards the following year. (Five hundred of the winery's 1300 acres are located there.) He would have moved the winery to Greenfield had California's legislators not passed the Williamson Act in the middle sixties, protecting land set aside for agricultural uses.

In 1969 *botrytis cinerea* was discovered in the Johannisberg Riesling and Karl made the first in a series of German-styled wines that bore the handwritten label of "Riesling Spatlese." Botrytis is a capricious mold, requiring a fixed sequence of weather conditions. It was not until 1972 that a second spatlese was made, thereafter made again in 1973 and 1974. None was made in 1975 and 1976.

It was just as well that the "noble mold" was present in the Monterey vineyards, for Johannisberg grown there is too acidic if made dry. The wine needs the residual sugar that is so much a part of late harvested wines.

The Arroyo Seco Vineyards of Wente Brothers are probably unique in Monterey County. They are likely the only vineyard in the county to have been planted on resistant root stock. While others who have planted in the area are convinced that the combination of its phylloxera-less past and its native light soils will discourage the influx and spread of the destructive louse, there are those who feel that it is only a matter of time before an invasion will bring woe to Monterey growers.

Philip R. Wente is following in the vineyard footsteps of grandfather Ernest. He manages all viticultural operations for the winery. Eric P. Wente takes after his great uncle and is the winemaker. The two young Wente brothers have a long and sound tradition to uphold, but indications are that they are well-equipped to do so.

Llords & Elwood Winery

If you look closely at the crest that appears on the Llords & Elwood label, you will note that the right side of the shield depicts a cluster of grapes and the left side three kernels of grain. This logo was designed to represent the refined approach to selling wines and spirits carried on by the late J.H. "Mike" Elwood and his son, Richard.

The Elwoods had been serving a select clientel of Hollywood stars and professional and business leaders, in Beverly Hills and West Los Angeles, since the end of Prohibition. Originally known as "Mike Elwood's," the name was changed in the late thirties when a second store, by the name of "Llords" and located but a mile away, was purchased.

In the process of compiling a chain of stores and a renowned selection of the finest wines and spirits, Mike Elwood's frequent trips to California and European wineries had convinced him that far better wines could be made in California, wines that could be equal in quality to the finest that Europe had to offer.

In the course of presenting this view to Rudolf Weibel, the founder of Weibel Champagne Vineyards cut Elwood off in mid-sentence and told him, in effect, "If you're so smart, why don't you prove it!?" Weibel backed his challenge with an offer to lease a small portion of his land to Elwood.

As Mike had already been selecting imports for his label and the cuvee for his stores' "Monseigneur Champagne," he took up the challenge and the offer. In 1955, after some hassle with the state government and a threatened injunction, he acquired the necessary licenses and set to work.

Elwood decided that the most obvious improvements could be made with sherries and port. "Dad was intent on having his first wines be appreciably superior to any then on the market," says Richard Elwood. It wasn't until the middle of 1961 that Mike Elwood was ready to sell his first wine. By that time, he was so committed to his winery that he sold his stores and retired from the retail field.

Llords & Elwood sherries are made only from the traditional Palomino and Pedro Ximenez grapes and are aged in outdoor oak soleras. Surface and submerged flor processes are employed. In the mid sixties the winery entered the table wine field.

Llords & Elwood is distinguished in the marketplace by its unusual labels. In the first instance, they are printed in West Germany and have a glittering gold leaf border that couldn't be duplicated anywhere else. Secondly, many of the wines bear what seem to be whimsical titles: Castle Magic Johannisberg Riesling, Velvet Hill Pinot Noir, and The Judge's Secret Cream Sherry.

Llords & Elwood, the winery, has a split personality. The business office is located in Beverly Hills, where the retail stores once flourished, but the production and aging facilities are presently in four separate locations: three in the Santa Clara Valley, one in Fresno.

Weibel Champagne Vineyards

The name itself gives away the essence of the operation. Though the widest possible variety of wines are bottled under the Weibel label, Weibel maintains its identity through its sparkling wines. And, though many recognize Weibel's Brut and Blanc de Blancs, fully half of the winery's production is sold under a myriad of other labels.

Fred Weibel Sr. estimates that in the late fifties he produced wines under 800 different labels, which created the necessity of the winery acquiring its own printing plant (still in operation). The demand for private labeling is not as great as it once was, but Weibel still bottles 250,000 cases a year (mostly sparkling wines) under other labels. There are two keys to look for: the bottling address at the bottom of the label (which will read variously as Warm Springs, Mission San Jose, or Fremont) or the bonded winery number 4372 (not usually on the label, but always on the case). Wines bearing such labels originate at Weibel.

The Weibel winemaking story goes back at least to 1904, when Fred's father, Rudolf, began making wine near Berne, Switzerland. Rudolf was a lover of travel, and would combine business with pleasure on his post-Repeal trips to the United States as an importer of cordials and brandies. When a burdensome excise tax was placed on brandy production in Switzerland and made retroactive, Rudolf moved his family to San Francisco. In 1939 he began making sparkling wines for other wineries at Clay and Montgomery, later moving to larger quarters in a four story building at Folsom and 2nd Street.

As World War II ground to a close, Rudolf felt the increasing need for better control of production. He began looking for a winery site where he could also plant vineyards. He hired a realtor and, three days after looking at the former Leland Stanford Winery south of Mission San Jose (today a part of Fremont), he purchased the property.

Fred's son, Fred E. Weibel Jr., has been with the winery since 1968, when he finished his degree in Business Administration. It was at that time that they began planting vineyards in Redwood Valley (Mendocino County), which now total 300 acres.

"The move was an obvious one to make," says Fred Jr. "It had become increasingly more difficult to buy grapes and we couldn't buy any land for planting here (Fremont). The subdivisions were just crowding us out. It was Monterey or Mendocino. Charlie Barra, one of our growers in Mendocino, suggested Redwood Valley, an area we had been buying grapes from already."

The early seventies saw the new winery facility and tasting room go in alongside Highway 101, six miles north of Ukiah. The winery itself is a crushing, fermenting, and aging facility, with all of the wines being transferred to Fremont for bottling.

The tasting room, which opened in July of 1973, is one of the most spacious and elegant in the state.

Other Wineries

CHANNING CELLARS

John Channing Rudd is making a carefully planned move into the wine business. An art director for importer/distributor Browne-Vintners for five years, Rudd has been a home winemaker for eight. His winery has been bonded under the tentative name of Channing Cellars for the 1977 crush and will have cooperage enough to make one thousand gallons of wine.

Rudd believes in going slowly: "Small production makes it possible to produce *artistic* wines. I intend to stick with big, long-lived varietals and possibly a vintage port. I won't be in any rush to sell a wine before it's ready."

Long term plans are for gradual expansion, with the hope of an eventual move to Sonoma.

Chateau Vintners
Produced Exclusively from Premium
California Grapes
California
Semillon
Made and Bottled by
Chateau Vintners
San Leandro, Calif.
Alcohol 12.4% By Volume

Chateau Vintners was founded in 1971 by a trio of Bay Area engineers in an unlikely industrial setting in San Leandro, immediately south of Oakland. A just-larger-than-hobby winery, it stands between a tool-and-die shop and a monstrous sign advising "STOP CASTING POROSITY." The noisome Nimitz Freeway completes the incongruous backdrop.

When one of the partnership was transferred, the remaining partners chose to sell the winery. In May of 1977 plant physiologist Richard Carey bought the concern. Though he will continue to use the existing label, Carey plans to eventually change it to Torosa Vineyards. "Torosa is one of the common Spanish names for the California poppy," he explains. "I am a native Californian; I am a bontanist; California wines are unique. We should promote that uniqueness."

The winery is operated by Carey, his wife June, Sue Rice (June's sister), Rick Rice (Sue's husband), and environmentalist Mark Wexler. The winery markets several generic reds and whites, a Semillon, and a Chenin Blanc, all from $1.90 to $2.50 the metric fifth. Carey plans to add Zinfandel, Gamay Beaujolais, Sauvignon Blanc, Sylvaner, and Moscato di Canelli with his 1977 crush.

The J. E. Digardi Winery, built by the Joost family in 1886, was purchased by Frank Digardi in 1912. It remained bonded until 1930, when the main floor was used for a corn husk packing operation. "My father and I made tamale wrappers from a special corn hybrid, King Phillip," says Frank's grandson

Francis Digardi. "The corn was grown in the San Joaquin Delta and we shipped some of the husks as far as Iowa!"

Re-bonded in 1933, the winery was primarily a bulk operation until its last commercial crush in 1964. "The bulk business had become dog-eat-dog and there was no longer any money in it," recalls Digardi, who now runs a liquor and wine shop at the winery.

Though he occasionally bottles a little wine for his own label, the winery's main function today is the storage of sparkling white wine stock for the Weibels. Weekend visitors who make an appointment may be shown the sandstone block cellars and the main winery rooms, whose aging walls are insulated with redwood shavings.

Edward Firpo and his late father, Julius, bonded the Firpo Winery in 1934. They had been farming grapes, cherries, peaches, walnuts, and almonds on the fertile delta soils of eastern Contra Costa County since 1919. Firpo's son-in-law now farms the eighty acre ranch.

Today, Ed Firpo crushes only enough grapes in his 32,000 gallon basement winery to maintain his permits. Most of his wines are purchased from Barengo Cellars (near Lodi) and none is sold wholesale. Firpo only offers his wines to family and friends from his home on Sellers Avenue, situated almost equidistant from Oakley, Knightsen, and Brentwood.

If you've never seen the Oak Barrel label on the retail shelf, don't feel too badly about it. Though it has been in existence for nearly twenty years, the winemaking aspect of the operation has often been overlooked. Oak Barrel's prime function and reputation lies in its sale of wine and beer making equipment and supplies. Also, according to owner Ivo Gardella, "advice, tastings, sympathy, praise, and problem solving."

The winery was begun in 1958 by John Bank, an Hungarian refugee and graduate of the University of Budapest. Before starting Oak Barrel, Bank worked at Schramsberg, Charles Krug, and Buena Vista. Though some wine is made at Oak Barrel, most of the wines bottled under the label (and sold at the winery and some local restaurants) are made elsewhere. They are aged, blended, and bottled by Oak Barrel.

Housed in a new, cream-colored, Spanish-styled building at the corner of University and Curtis in Berkeley, Oak Barrel claims to be the nation's largest supplier of presses, stemmer-crushers, bottling and corking equipment, European oak ovals, American and Limousin oak barrels, and filters for home winemakers and small wineries, at both wholesale and retail. Also available at the winery is a fine selection of premium wines from top north coast wineries.

As the name might imply, this operation is concerned with several aspects of the relationship between wine and people. At its inception, it was felt that nowhere in the United States was there a "village winery" as is common in Europe. As sales manager Denis Kelly noted in the winery's delightful newsletter: "The (village) winery supplied the needs of the community for everyday drinking wine and for more special wines that you could age and bring out for christenings, funerals, weddings, saints' days, birthdays, when Uncle Jules returned from the colonies, seductions, feuds, or any other excuse you could dredge up for cracking open a bottle of the five year old Cabernet."

Wine and the People originally limited its operations to guiding home wine and beer makers through the chemical intricacies of those processes. Advice and equipment were offered and grapes brokered. The home winemaker could get the books, tools, and grapes (stemmed and crushed, if desired) at a single stop in downtown Berkeley.

Since 1975, under the direction of president and winemaker Peter Brehm, Wine and the People has become bonded as a winery and now offers wine in addition to its other functions. The home winemaker may now purchase bulk wines--to age, barrel, and blend at his own discretion--or simply purchase some of the company's premium wines, already bottled, corked, and labeled.

Big Foot Industries was the fanciful name first used by the group who founded Montclair Winery. Ultimately, however, they concluded that "Bigfoot" (sometimes one word, often two) just didn't have a premium ring to it. So the colorful name was shelved, temporarily, though there is a possibility it may be used someday as a secondary label.

Rick Dove is listed as president, general manager, and winemaker for the youthful winery whose first crush was in 1975. For those who were involved, October 7, 1975 was a day not to be forgotten.

"We received our bond that day," recalls Dove, "just in time to crush our first grapes. That in itself was a little hairy, but my wife delivered our daughter Jennifer on the same day!"

Montclair Winery is located in a leased building not far from the Oakland-Alameda County Coliseum, home of several winning athletic teams. The winery is set up to be a simple operation, capable, says Dove, of being run by "one man and a small boy." The 3000 square foot space includes a cold room, used for fermenting white wines in small stainless steel barrels and bottle aging.

All new oak was used to start the winery and four wines were made in 1975. French Colombard (from Teldeschi Vineyards, Healdsburg) was aged in Yugoslav oak and sells for $2.99. Zinfandel was aged in air-dried American oak ("It's an American wine."). Their Cabernet Sauvignon saw Nevers oak and the Chardonnay (from Rene di Rosa's Winery Lake Vineyards) Limousin.

"Four wines were just too much for us," says Dove. "It posed a real clean up problem. Reds are easy to make, so we'll probably drop the Chardonnay next year."

Like most new professional winemakers, Dove has had a career as an amateur. His first wine was a blackberry wine, which he still considers one of his best creations. He made several fruit wines and also tried Zinfandel and French Colombard. In fact, his use of Yugoslavian oak for the winery's Colombard came about because he had accidentally used it in his amateur days and the wine had turned out well.

The decision to go commercial was helped by the fact that better equipment could be afforded and that a tax write-off never hurt anyone. The plant is run by Jim Burkhard and the chemist is Mary Jo Dorie. Mary Jo's husband, Larry, heads up the marketing effort.

The group originally hoped to restrict sales to a private mailing list, but later felt that good will would be served by at least one retail outlet. Thus, Montclair wines are also available at the Lake Merritt Wine & Cheese Revival in Oakland. The wines may also be ordered by mail or phone: 1149 Yorkshire Drive, Cupertino, CA 95014 (Dove's home); (408) 446-4841. He promises home delivery anywhere in the Bay Area (Napa to Gilroy), but notes that deliveries may not be quite so prompt in Napa.

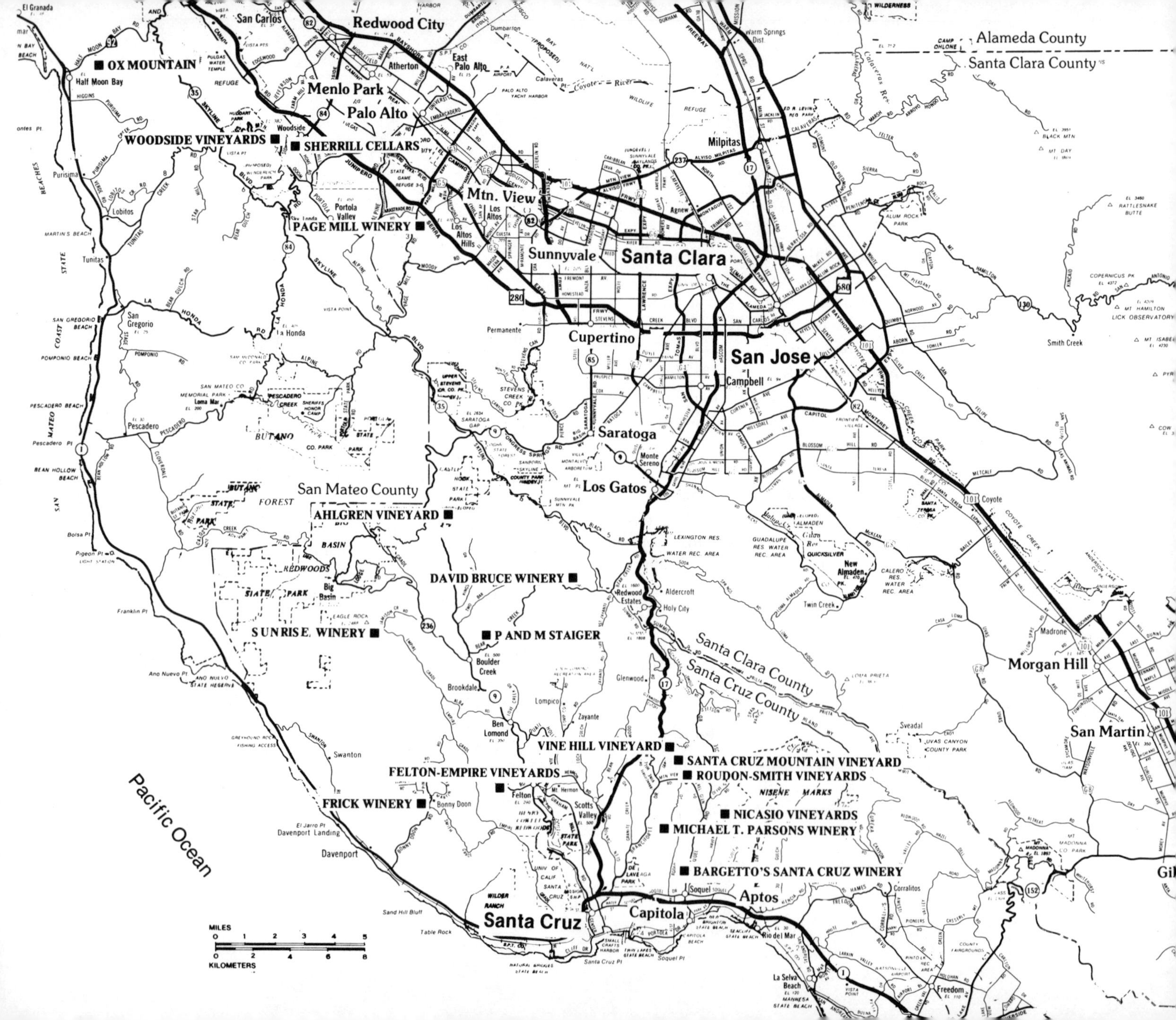

OX MOUNTAIN
WOODSIDE VINEYARDS
SHERRILL CELLARS
PAGE MILL WINERY
AHLGREN VINEYARD
DAVID BRUCE WINERY
SUNRISE WINERY
P AND M STAIGER
VINE HILL VINEYARD
SANTA CRUZ MOUNTAIN VINEYARD
ROUDON-SMITH VINEYARDS
FELTON-EMPIRE VINEYARDS
FRICK WINERY
NICASIO VINEYARDS
MICHAEL T. PARSONS WINERY
BARGETTO'S SANTA CRUZ WINERY
Alameda County
Santa Clara County
San Mateo County
Santa Clara County
Santa Cruz County
Pacific Ocean
Redwood City
San Carlos
Menlo Park
Palo Alto
Atherton
East Palo Alto
Half Moon Bay
El Granada
Woodside
Milpitas
Mtn. View
Los Altos
Los Altos Hills
Sunnyvale
Santa Clara
Cupertino
San Jose
Campbell
Saratoga
Monte Sereno
Los Gatos
Portola Valley
Purisima
Lobitos
Tunitas
San Gregorio
La Honda
Pescadero
Permanente
Big Basin
Boulder Creek
Brookdale
Ben Lomond
Lompico
Zayante
Glenwood
Redwood Estates
Aldercroft
Holy City
New Almaden
Twin Creek
Coyote
Madrone
Morgan Hill
San Martin
Sveadal
Felton
Mt Hermon
Scotts Valley
Bonny Doon
Swanton
Davenport
Davenport Landing
Santa Cruz
Capitola
Aptos
Soquel
Corralitos
Rio del Mar
La Selva Beach
Freedom
Smith Creek
Pescadero Pt
Pigeon Pt
Franklin Pt
Ano Nuevo Pt
Sand Hill Bluff
Table Rock
Santa Cruz Pt
Soquel Pt
MILES
0 1 2 3 4 5
0 2 4 6 8
KILOMETERS

San Mateo -
Santa Cruz Counties

Woodside Vineyards

Woodside Vineyards probably held claim to "California's Smallest Winery" until it doubled the size of its cellars in 1973. Now the winery measures 24 by 48 feet, safely out of the home winemaking category.

Bob and Polly Mullen, as many newcomers to the industry, began as home winemakers in 1960. Bob, who is Western Regional Manager for Armstrong Cork Company (his field is ceiling tile), was transferred to California in 1954. He had never been exposed to wine previously.

A few years later, the Mullens chanced to meet Bob and Bev Groetzinger, zealous home winemakers. The two couples went into partnership and, in 1960, Bob and Polly made their first home vintage of a typical old vineyard blend: Carignane, Petite Sirah, Zinfandel, and Alicante Bouschet.

In 1962 the Mullens purchased a few acres on Kings Mountain Road and began building a home. The plans featured a small winery underneath the carport. The property had an acre and a half of mixed reds, planted in the late twenties or early thirties by the Avenali family. Two acres of Pinot Noir and Chardonnay now surround the house.

The bond was acquired in 1963 and the tiny winery was open for business. The first vintage was crushed in the carport. The must was funneled through a trap door to fermenting tanks below. The winery's press once graced the cellars of Hallcrest Vineyards, (in Felton), and had to undergo major reconditioning several years ago. After searching high and low for a cooper or carpenter willing to undertake the delicate task, the Mullens found their man in fellow churchgoer George Warden. The press is still in use.

In addition to the vines on their own property, the Mullens have exclusive rights to part of the former Rixford property (La Questa Vineyard). There, they maintain three acres of Cabernet Sauvignon (on four separate parcels), which they bottle under the La Questa label. Emmett H. Rixford had begun winemaking on the property in 1883, achieving an international reputation for his Cabernets. The Mullens do not have an easy time of it, though. The growing season is quite cool for the variety. "It's hard to get sugar in that location," laments Bob. "If we don't have twenty-two Brix by the end of October, we pick!"

Only three wines are now made at Woodside: Cabernet, Pinot Noir, and Chardonnay. Volume is in the neighborhood of 600 cases a year and, after each crush, some of the wine is used for communion at the Woodside Village Church. As you might imagine, the wines are difficult to come by, usually obtained by the bottle rather than the case. The Cabernets are velvety, with a mixture of chocolatey, almost pepperminty aromas.

When asked about his winemaking philosophy, Bob responded: "We try to let the wine make itself. We used to fine, but found that it really didn't make any difference in the wines. Filtration? We don't even own a filter!"

Sherrill Cellars

There are those who refer to winemaking as a holy trinity, comprised of equal parts of science, art, and luck. One who agrees with the characterization is Nathaniel D. Sherrill. Nat, by trade, is an electronics engineer with the United States Geological Survey. Jan Sherrill, his wife and partner, coordinates financial aide for the School of Education at Stanford University.

Nat is not tied to any particular means or philosophy of winemaking. "We try to combine the best of the old and the new," he says, "whatever is best for the wine. I would say that we are neither crude and archaic nor ultra modern. We have a small operation, so we are able to stay close to everything."

Being small and maintaining a distance from any strict orthodoxies has given the Sherrills the opportunity to do different, exotic things. The label, for example, is both unusual and somewhat impractical. "We have trouble in printing them, in placing them on the bottles, and in keeping them stuck," observes Jan. "The narrow corners, in particular, keep coming loose. But we like them too much to change now."

Also distinctive is their use of wax to protect the cork. "First of all," says Nat, "I don't aesthetically care for plastic. Secondly, lead foils can transfer a metallic quality to the wines. Finally, wax is as simple and as cheap to use as any other method. And," he smiles, "we like its look."

The wines are equally distinctive. They make a Zinfandel from vines planted in Pleasanton prior to the turn of the century. The 1975 vintage was dark and exhibited a strong peppercorn nose, which carried over into its taste.

The Sherrills have also made a huge, late harvested Zinfandel. Of the 1974 vintage (see label), the grapes came from the Okahara Vineyard near Lodi and were picked on October 29, 1974. Brix was 27 degrees (there were many raisined berries mixed in) and acid was 0.65. The wine was fermented straight through to 18.1% alcohol, leaving 1.7% residual sugar, and was released at $8 the fifth.

"Everybody assumes that I had to add high proof," notes Nat. "Not true. It was a completely natural fermentation, though we had to wrap the barrel with an electric blanket to keep the temperature up and bubble air into it to keep the yeast alive. The apparent sugar (brix) actually rose steadily during the week of violent fermentation--due to the raisins slowly releasing their sugar--and got as high as thirty degrees. It was sort of like grabbing onto the tail of a comet and hanging on for the ride." The wine has a port-like nose, rich with fruit, and is huge, sweet, and heady.

The winery is presently located underneath the Post Office in Woodside, about a mile west of Interstate 280. Plans are in the works to move to larger quarters in 1978. Tastings are held on some Sundays in the summer, by invitation. Write the winery for their newsletter and you will automatically reserve a spot at one of them.

Page Mill Winery

Richard E. ''Dick'' Stark describes himself as a refugee from the electronics industry. As such, he knows he's not the first to leave that field for his present one, but feels that twenty years in marketing at Spectra Physics (the world's largest laser company) was quite enough. It was time to get closer to his family and to the earth.

He got closer to both family and earth in a hurry. When Dick left his job at the end of May, 1976, several tasks presented themselves to him almost simultaneously: an addition to the house needed finishing, an acre of vineyard needed planting, and the basement winery needed work to be ready for the winery's soon-to-be first harvest.

Dick and Ome (pronounced ''Owe'-mee'') Stark will not soon forget that first harvest. ''If you want to get premium grapes,'' says Dick, ''you've got to make it very easy for the grower to part with his crop. So we hauled all of our own grapes. We took boxes, spread them out in the vineyards for the pickers, and loaded them onto the truck ourselves. My oldest son, Eric, and I literally had to sleep in the vineyard one night. All of the kids worked hard to help.'' The Starks have three boys and a girl, aged nine to sixteen.

The Starks used 450-gallon fiberglass cube fermenters and are aging all of their wines in small oak cooperage. They hope to keep cellar treatment to a minimum in hopes of obtaining maximum character from the grapes.

''We had a particularly long fermentation with our Chenin Blanc,'' notes Dick. ''We used a special slow yeast to retain as much fruitiness as possible.'' The yeast was developed at the Institut Pasteur and is called ''Prise de Mousse.'' The fermentation of the Starks' Chenin Blanc had just finished the day before I interviewed them (in January), after eighty-eight days!

Four varieties were crushed in 1976 at Page Mill: Chardonnay, Chenin Blanc, Zinfandel, and Cabernet Sauvignon. The Starks had to cover a wide range of territory to secure those grapes: Clements (east of Lodi) for Zinfandel; Chiles Valley (near Lake Berryessa) for Cabernet Sauvignon and Zinfandel; Napa to obtain Chardonnay and Chenin Blanc; and finally Greenfield (Monterey County). ''Finally'' doesn't fully state the case: they picked Cabernet Sauvignon there on December 13th at 25 degrees Brix.

Dick has planted one acre of vines behind the winery/residence. ''It's not so much a source of grapes as it is an experimental plot,'' offers Dick. ''It stands to benefit me, as a winemaker, more than anything else.'' Planted there are: Chardonnay (primarily), White Riesling, Zinfandel, Merlot, and Cabernet Franc.

David Bruce Winery

Dr. David Bruce is another of those professionals who have become so enamored of the mysteries of winemaking that they have pursued home winemaking with a vengeance, to the point of picking up a second profession. Bruce is a practicing dermatologist in San Jose, specializing in contact allergies and the seborrhea-acne spectrum. He enjoys both sides of his dual career: "They keep me busy. I enjoy the intellectual stimulation of winemaking and the people I work with in my practice."

A graduate of Stanford University's Medical School, Dr. Bruce purchased land high in the Santa Cruz Mountains in 1961. With his family, he planted twenty-five acres to what some call the "high varietals": Pinot Noir, Chardonnay, White Riesling, and Cabernet Sauvignon. The largest blocs were in the first two varieties.

In 1964 the winery was bonded and David began making wines so distinctive in style and quality as to warrant occasionally outrageous prices. In 1968 a new winery building was completed, a concrete block edifice encompassing 6000 square feet. An additional fifteen acres of vineyards were also acquired.

In the winery's first vintage, Dr. Bruce found that he had more Zinfandel grapes than he had cooperage for. Necessity, always the mother of invention, caused him to make a white wine from those grapes, something that could be bottled without aging. Thus was born Bruce's Zinfandel Blanc de Noir, an idea in winemaking that has gained increasing popularity in the midst of the white wine boom of the middle seventies.

David Bruce's wines are characteristically huge in body and long on flavor. This is the result of what David calls "traditional Burgundian techniques and a truly personal approach to winemaking." Translation: most of his wines are not sulphured at crush; fining and filtration are rarely used cellar practices; the wines undergo long fermentation with longer than normal skin contact; and they are aged in small oak cooperage. As a result, most of David Bruce's wine labels bear the warning: "This wine must be hand decanted."

Dr. Bruce is most known for his generous Zinfandels and mouth filling Chardonnays. The latter typically receive eighteen hours of skin contact during early fermentation and possess intense, orange-like noses. Bruce believes that low-yielding vines grown at a high elevation (2000 feet) have a lot to do with it, along with limited cellar handling. "Air is wine's primary enemy," he reminds. "When you can reduce the processes, the handling of the wine, you reduce the possibility of oxidation."

Steve Millier has served as assistant winemaker to Dr. Bruce since the crush of 1975. A graduate of Fresno State, Steve echoes Bruce's attitudes, adding, "The better the equipment and the more knowledge we have, the better the wines will become."

P and M. Staiger

P AND M STAIGER
ALAMEDA
CHARDONNAY
PLEASANTON VINEYARD
1975
PRODUCED AND BOTTLED BY P AND M STAIGER
BOULDER CREEK, CALIFORNIA
PICKED SEPTEMBER 27TH
THIS HARVEST PRODUCED 825 BOTTLES
ALCOHOL 12.9% BY VOLUME
BOTTLED SEPTEMBER 19, 1976

North of Boulder Creek, Hopkins Gulch Road runs off up into the hills and ridges of the Santa Cruz Mountains. Two miles up Hopkins Gulch from Bear Creek Road lies a small hillside vineyard. Situated just above, so as to be almost theatrically imposing, is a futuristic wood and concrete structure. This is both home and winery to Paul and Marjorie (she prefers "Em") Staiger.

The structure, at once simple and elegant, is yet in the process of being built. Started during the summer of '73, the winery, which occupies the lower level, was the high priority item. A small concrete room, it has storage space for less than five thousand gallons.

Paul, who grew up in Portland, Oregon, came to enjoy wines after a summer of study in France. He and Em first made wines as home vintners in the late sixties. For three harvests, starting in 1971, they leased the Novitiate's abandoned vineyards further up Bear Creek Road, near Highway 17. Harvesting White Riesling, Cabernet Sauvignon, and Grenache, they bonded a winery called Bear Creek Vineyards with Hans Kobler and John Dach (who has since begun his own winery in Philo, Mendocino County). The winery operated for two years, but none of the wines were ever sold commercially.

In 1973 Paul and Em bonded the P and M Staiger Winery and made a White Riesling, which was sold entirely to a single retail store. The following year they began purchasing Zinfandel from the eighty year old Sandahl Vineyard in the Santa Lucia Range, west of Templeton. Production is barely one ton per acre on the five and a quarter acre chalkstone plot, and the wines are big and pepperish, yet intensely fruity. "The grapes have high acid, but little of it is malic acid," says Paul. The 1975 vintage is soft and well balanced, while the 1976 edition is robust, pepperish, with ample fruit and flavor.

The Staigers have four acres of their own vineyards on a south facing slope that had been planted to Zinfandel prior to Prohibition. Chardonnay, Cabernet Sauvignon, and Merlot now occupy the slope. The latter two are planted in an 85:15 ratio for the Staiger Cabernets. The Cabernet vines, of an early ripening clone, came from the David Bruce vineyard along with the Chardonnay. The Merlot cuttings were purchased from Ridge Vineyards. Paul and Em have also densely planted a third of an acre (over six hundred vines) to a Pommard Pinot Noir clone, just to see how it does. They hope to make a barrel a year of Pinot Noir.

P and M Staiger wines are not sold from the winery, in fact the Staigers do not encourage visitors. The winery is tiny, the road partially unpaved, and there is almost no parking space on their craggy, hillside hideaway. But the wines, unfiltered and unfined, are available in a few stores from Carmel to Palo Alto. They are in the $4.00 to $5.50 price range.

Sunrise Winery

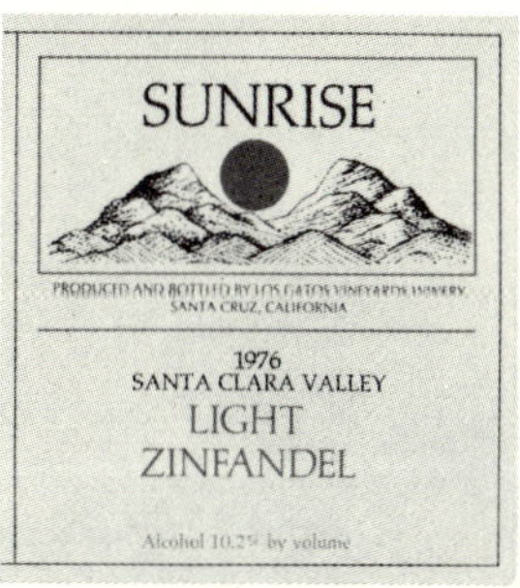

The old Vincent Locatelli Winery is back in operation again. On July 1, 1976, R. EuGene Lokey and Keith Hohlfeldt leased the lower level of Mr. Locatelli's secluded ranch house and began making wine for money.

Lokey is a consulting health care specialist who is likely to be in Sacramento one day and in San Diego the next. An amateur winemaker and bee keeper, Gene has leased vineyards both for his own wines and to sell grapes.

Hohlfeldt, a slender, soft-spoken young man, is a biochemist by training. From 1973 to 1976 he was microbiologist at Paul Masson, making sparkling wines, taking charge of yeast cultures, and doing malolactic studies. Since August of 1976 he has been employed by the Stanford Research Institute, doing cancer research on anti-leukemia agents.

The pair had made wines together before undertaking their current project. They originally intended to fund the winery by starting a bottle washing and recycling operation. They found, to their dismay, that there was an insufficient supply of glass. Then their investors dropped out. So Keith suggested, "Let's pool our assets and just do it!"

Between savings and a couple of small loans, the duo began operations. Locatelli's winery had been out of production, but he had used the cooperage to store wines and had maintained the licenses. The winery was built in 1933 for no other reason than that the lumber business, the Locatelli family's main source of income, was slow. The wines were sold under the Eagle Rock label, named for a rocky outcropping across from the vineyards, now a Forestry station.

Lokey and Hohlfeldt lease 35 acres, spread out between Morgan Hill and Santa Cruz. At the winery they had to bring in stainless steel and wood cooperage and rebuild their open redwood fermenters, which were then set inside the old, square, concrete fermenting tanks.

Hohlfeldt, who has also done consulting work for David Bruce, Greenfield Vineyards, Thomas Kruse, and a couple of Canadian wineries, is the winemaker. He began his program of making several batches of each wine with the first crush.

"I want to do a lot of experimentation. I hope to combine the elements of technology and artistry, using limited treatment and natural settling to finish the wines. It's a funky sort of operation, without any fancy equipment, but we expect to be able to market our wines at reasonable prices. I'm thinking the two and a half to four dollar range."

Hohlfeldt emphasizes that he and Lokey intend to make the winery a full-time, commercial operation one day. He also echoes the increasing sentiment of wanting to make "The Great California Pinot Noir."

The first crush at Sunrise Winery included three batches of Cabernet Sauvignon, two styles of Zinfandel, one lot of French Colombard, and double batches of Petite Sirah, Pinot Blanc, and Grenache.

Felton-Empire Vineyards

Less than a quarter of a mile west of Felton, back off the road and adjacent to old, closely pruned vines, are two small winery buildings of grcy brick. This was the Hallcrest Winery of the late San Francisco attorney, Chafee Hall. The vineyards were planted by Hall in 1941, with the assistance of U.C. Davis people, and the winery started in 1945. For nearly two decades Hallcrest earned a reputation for fine Cabernet Sauvignon.

The winery was developed by Hall as a retirement plan, but events didn't follow his expectations. The winery was closed in 1964 and Chafee Hall died five years later.

In May of 1976 two young men got together to plot the winery's revival. They intitially planned on calling it Two Friends Winery, but shortly thereafter they were joined by a third partner. Finally it was named for the road of the winery's address, Felton-Empire Road.

The first two planners were Jim Beauregard and John Pollard. Beauregard is the scion of an established Santa Cruz Mountain grape growing family which also happens to own Shopper's Corner, the major independent grocery store in Santa Cruz. Pollard is a veteran pilot for Western Airlines who has a love for the fruit of the vine.

The third member of the team is winemaker and partner Leo McCloskey. After schooling in biochemistry, Leo has done lab work, analysis and consultation for several wineries, including Ridge, David Bruce, Calcra, and Vine Hill.

The group owns or leases 45 acres of grapes. Fourteen acres are the Bonny Doon ranch owned by Beauregard's father, comprised of Cabernet Sauvignon, Zinfandel, and smaller amounts of White Riesling and Chardonnay. The leased fifteen acre plot at the winery has an additional eleven acres of White Riesling and four of Cabernet. Grapes are also purchased from Sonoma and San Luis Obispo Counties. Grapes were purchased from Dick Smothers' Vine Hill Vineyard until he decided to start a winery. Beauregard manages the Vine Hill Vineyard.

The trio plans to concentrate on one variety: White Riesling augmented with Santa Cruz Cabernet Sauvignon. It will have a "Santa Cruz Mountain" appellation and will be bottled under the Hallcrest & Santa Cruz label. Says McCloskey, "In a bad year the Hallcrest Cabernet will be blended with the Bonny Doon, but in a good year the wines are inky black and sturdy."

Just 3000 gallons were made from the 1976 vintage, including a botrytised White Riesling. Hopes are that that figure can be doubled for the 1977 harvest for a typical production of about 5000 cases.

"German wines are my favorites," says McCloskey, "so I intend to make them in that style. My object is to aim for excessive fruitiness, then tone it down a little with judicious aging and racking."

Roudon-Smith Vineyards

Robert "Bob" Roudon is a native Texan and Jim Smith is a farm boy from Wisconsin, where his parents were dairy farmers. The pair met in 1971 when they worked as mechanical engineers at Amdahl Corporation. Bob's enthusiasm for wines, prompted by bis German (Pfalz) born wife, Annamaria, quickly infected Jim and June Smith. The following year the two couples made their first wine--a Sauvignon Blanc from Hollister that was later aged in French and Canadian oak--in a rented building.

By the spring of 1973 they had begun building the Roudons' home over a basement winery. That fall they crushed at their new 800 square foot winery. Early on, they experimented with several varieties that were later to be discarded: the Sauvignon Blanc, Chenin Blanc, Pinot Noir, and Barbera.

Now the two families are going to concentrate on crushes of three red varieties and but one white. As Bob Roudon says, "We're doing everything ourselves, so four wines is enough."

Though their 1973 Cabernet Sauvignon came from a Vine Hill vineyard, their later Cabernets will come from Dry Creek, north of Healdsburg. Zinfandel grapes will come primarily from Glen Ellen (north of Sonoma) and about 20% from Livermore. The third red slot will be alternated: one year a Gamay Beaujolais will be made, the other a Petite Sirah will be tried. The Petite Sirah will be made with lower alcohol to avoid the roughness that most Petites are plagued with. The Chardonnay will come from Healdsburg, Monterey County, or anywhere else good Chardonnay can be found.

Roudon is a self-taught winemaker. After extensive reading and attendance of seminars offered by U. C. Davis, Roudon believes in winemaking by doing. He seeks to avoid the overprocessing that he feels Davis recommends: "They teach you to stabilize the wine rapidly through whatever means are available. We're trying for natural stabilization, no matter how long it takes." Roudon-Smith wines will not be filtered and, if unfined the label will so state. The winery's cooperage is all small American and French oak.

Smith is the vineyard man, a natural inclination for a man "who likes to drive tractors." Jim raises chickens on his ranch at Scotts Valley and has horses for his four children. Two acres of White Riesling were planted in 1976 on the twelve acre parcel surrounding the home/winery. An additional two acres of Chardonnay were planted in early 1977, though Roudon feels that the county tax structure and zoning policies militate against vineyards.

Roudon-Smith wines are sold through thirty retail outlets and restaurants from Monterey to Napa. Annamaria Roudon, a commercial artist, designed the winery's label. The two families hope to eventually make enough wine to support themselves, doing all the work necessary, with the occasional help of their friends.

Bargetto's Santa Cruz Winery

Though many people know Bargetto's for their outstanding fruit and berry wines the winery also produces distinctive table wines. They range from fruity, dry, well-finished Chablis to big, acidic flavorful Barberas. Also included are such wines as a 1976 Greenfield (Monterey) Chenin Blanc--harvested at 27 Brix--possessing a lush, peach-like nose, and a Nevers aged Cabernet Sauvignon that is 90% 1974 Napa and Sonoma and 10% 1975 Santa Clara Valley.

The winery also produces a line of what is conventionally referred to as ''bulk'' wines, less expensive table wines that are bottled in fifths, half gallons, and gallons for everyday use. In addition, the winery offers dry and sweet vermouths, sherries and a port, sparkling wines, red wine vinegar, and a selection of imported, flavored Marsalas (almond, coffee, cherry, etc.).

Bargetto's was started in 1933 by brothers John and Philip Bargetto. Philip and his father, Giuseppe, immigrated to the United States in 1887 from Asti, in Piedmont. They went to work for the Delmas Winery in Mountain View. Giuseppe left after five years to return home, but Philip continued until the turn of the century, when he moved to San Francisco to start his own winery.

John Bargetto came to the U.S. in 1909. He worked with Philip for a short time, then left for Soquel to start a small farm and produce business. He continued that business until the early thirties, when he and Philip began building a winery on a five acre parcel alongside the Soquel Creek. The winery was owned by John until his death in 1964.

Meanwhile, John's sons, Larry and Ralph, were growing up in the business. Both attended Santa Clara University, Larry in biology, Ralph in business administration. After graduation in 1949, Larry turned down an acceptance to Creighton Medical School to work full time at the winery. He has been there ever since. His oldest son, Martin, is a college chemistry major. Ralph, on the other hand, worked at the winery until 1963, when he decided to go into real estate. He still serves as winery vice president, however.

When asked what the three casks on his label signified, Larry answered, ''They're symbolic of barrels.'' He wasn't being facetious. The winery is full of small American, Nevers, and Yugoslavian oak cooperage, added this decade, and more is on order. Out of 70,000 gallons a year, over seventy percent are grape wines.

Bargetto owns no vineyards, but must purchase grapes from growers in several counties, primarily Santa Cruz, Santa Clara, and Monterey. He buys some wine in bulk, which may account for between 15 and 40 percent of a year's crush.

Bargetto operates two tasting rooms. At the winery, overlooking the creek, the tasting room is open daily from 10 until 5:30. The second tasting room is located on Cannery Row in Monterey (10 Prescott) and is open daily from eleven to seven. It stays open until ten in the evening during the summer months.

Other Wineries

Ahlgren Vineyard started out as a joint affair. In 1972 Dexter and Valerie Ahlgren purchased ten acres--seven miles north of Boulder Creek--with another family. The plan was this: each family would have two and a half acres to use as they pleased and there would be a common parcel of five acres for vineyards.

So Dexter, a consulting civil engineer, with the design of California State Architect Sim Van der Ryn, began to build an airy, low energy, post and beam house for his family. When the other couple decided to drop out of the winery project, the Ahlgrens decided to incorporate the winery into the house (as a full basement) and plant what they could of their own property along with their share of the common land.

So they are planting two and a half acres to Chardonnay. ''Chardonnay will be the main thrust of our winery,'' says Dexter. ''We'll make both table and sparkling wines from Chardonnay and White Riesling, and possibly from Chenin Blanc. Zinfandel and Cabernet will be our primary red varieties, although we're interested in Petite Sirah if the vineyards are right.''

With their 1976 (first) crush, the Ahlgren family made a Cabernet Sauvignon Rose′ from Santa Clara County grapes, a Monterey Chardonnay (from grapes crushed in November), and a big, but soft, late harvested Zinfandel (17.6% alcohol) from Glen Ellen.

FRICK WINERY

Add the Fricks, William and Judith, to the list of those seeking the elusive California Pinot Noir. Not to mention an estate bottled rose petal wine!

The Fricks have converted an old gas station in Bonny Doon into a tiny (600 square foot) winery, which will make do until their new home and new winery are built on a former quarry site on Smith Grade Road. They had hoped to inaugurate the winery with the 1976 crush, but local red tape prevented that. So 1977 will be the official beginning of Frick Winery.

The couple hopes to be in local stores and restaurants by the end of the decade and are planting two acres of their property to Pinot Noir, Gewurztraminer, White Riesling, and roses. Offered Bill, ''We intend to experiment a lot. I know it's a chancy sort of thing, and perhaps not the most economically sound course to follow, but it's certainly the most interesting.''

Mike Parsons is a graduate of Marquette Dental School, with specialty training as a periodontist from the University of California at San Francisco. A small scale grape grower and home winemaker since 1964, when he made Ruby Cabernet from the first commercially planted vineyards of that variety, he bonded a small winery at his parents' home near Soquel in 1976.

"I got the idea for bonding a winery after seeing the Roudon-Smith layout a couple of years ago," he says. "The main reason was so I could afford some new oak, stainless steel tanks, and other sophisticated equipment."

His 1976 crush consisted of a Cabernet Sauvignon and a Pinot Noir, both from vineyards east of Gilroy. He has an acre of Pinot Noir at his parents' place and has ambitions of making only Pinot Noir. He also has his eye on a couple of other Pinot Noir vineyards: one in Evergreen and another in Monterey.

Designed to be just a 500 case winery, Parsons admits that it's an avocation. He enjoys his Sunnyvale dental practice, and puttering in his own winery is a satisfying change of pace.

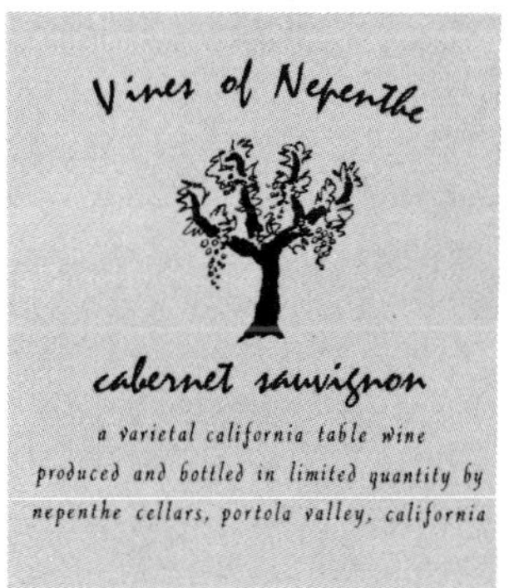

George L. Burtness began making wines at his Portola Valley home in 1962. By 1967 the hobby had escalated and become bonded. The business was later moved to Woodside.

Burtness favors heavy, full-bodied wines made from single varieties, without filtering or chemical treatments of any kind. His wines, bottled under the Vines of Nepenthe label, are as highly regarded as they are difficult to find. (Nepenthe is the ancient Greek word for a potion, like wine, which relieves pain and sorrow.)

A native of Santa Barbara, Burtness is a Stanford University graduate and now manages the university's real estate holdings. He flies and scuba dives for relaxation.

Burtness temporarily suspended Nepenthe's bond in December of 1976. He is in the process of moving from Woodside to Scotts Valley, in the Vine Hill district of the Santa Cruz Mountains. He is planting ten acres to vines there and building a home and winery. He was unable to make wine in 1977, but feels certain that he will be producing again in 1978.

Dan Wheeler is a bit like pro football coaches who prefer to draft the best players available, regardless of position. "Well made, any wine is terrific," he says. "The point is to get good grapes, though. If you get the best grapes you can buy and just make whatever varieties you get, the wines will be good."

Wheeler has several firm beliefs about how wine should be made. He feels that they lose their natural fruitiness if they are fined or filtered, or if sulphur dioxide is added after the fermentation. He believes that wines should be made wholly from single varieties and that they should be aged at a constant temperature. He gives most of his wine pre-bottle bottle aging in five gallon carboys, before they age in fifths. For his sparkling wines he uses only aged wines, uses a mutant champagne yeast that he developed himself, and uses only the traditional French method ("this bottle fermented"), without dosage.

After growing up on a wheat and cattle ranch in northeastern Montana, Wheeler acquired a degree in radio engineering in just three years from Tri-State College in Indiana. He has been an electronics engineer since 1950 and currently puts in a highly charged three day week as senior design engineer at Wiltron. He flies to Palo Alto from Watsonville Airport, then bikes the last three miles to work.

He used to have a short, hilltop runway on the winery property, but a few years ago he crashed on takeoff when a small piece of crud lodged over the main fuel jet and starved the engine. He managed to put the plane down (upside down) in the trees at the end of the runway. The craft was ruined, but Dan walked away with only a black eye.

OX MOUNTAIN

A local landmark not on many maps, Ox Mountain lies alongside Highway 92 two miles east of Half Moon Bay. Across the road, in a field of daisies, is the thousand case winery of the same name.

Paul Obester, an executive with a small electronics company in Palo Alto, and his wife Sandy are the founding partners. But it was Sandy's 95 year old grandfather, John Gemello, who provided the inspiration for their vinicultural adventure. Gemello, who lives with the young couple, founded the Mountain View winery that bears his name.

Ox Mountain was initiated with a crush of 16 tons of Zinfandel, Petite Sirah, and Cabernet Sauvignon in 1977. Grapes are purchased, but Paul notes that an extra acre at the winery may be planted to "some variety that does well in the fog."

Ken Burnap is one of those tortured, demented, souls who is searching for the perfect California Pinot Noir. So intent is he, that he spent four years looking for the right vineyard and intends to make only the one wine at his new winery in the Vine Hill district.

"I decided a long time ago that I would like to spend the rest of my life making the best Pinot Noir in the state," says the husky walrus-mustachioed Burnap. "I did a little home winemaking and some intense, lengthy research. This is the result of research more than practical experience, but I had over a dozen criteria for what I wanted in a vineyard."

After stopping in to buy some wine from David Bruce while on one of his many trips through the vineyard regions of California, Burnap ended up purchasing a vineyard that Bruce himself had planted just east of Highway 17 in the Santa Cruz Mountains. "Bruce had considered the spot so ideal for Pinot Noir that he had actually pulled out Zinfandel to plant it," says Burnap. "He even called it the Romanee-Conti of California!"

The son of a boomer in the construction business, Burnap purchased the vineyard in the fall of 1974. The following season Burnap made his first wine in a 20 by 36 foot cinder block building that will eventually be an implement shed. Tasted in early 1977, it had an unmistakable Pinot Noir nose and was a big (15% alcohol), heavy wine, as yet unbalanced in acid (it's high). Aged in French (Limousin) and American (Wisconsin) oak, it was bottled in January, 1977, and will be released in January of 1980.

Burnap worked for the Atomic Energy Commission while in the Air Force and later studied mechanical engineering at the University of Southern California. In addition to running a sandblasting and coating business he co-founded the popular Hobbit Restaurant in 1972. He refers to the restaurant as a labor of love, much as his winery venture is, and was chagrined when he was legally required to sell it in order to continue with the winery. He has since sold the sandblasting company as well so as to devote his full energies to his vines and wines.

Though he intends to plant a smattering of Chardonnay to make for his family, Burnap is realistic enough to admit that he may one day make other wines. He knows that the two varieties come early enough in the season that he'll be out looking around to see what others are going and may well end up purchasing more grapes.

The vines were planted on their own rootstocks, after Bruce tested the soil for phylloxera and the results came back negative. That was fine with Burnap, who contends that there is a noticeable degree of difference between bare root vines and grafted ones. He also wants to exploit all that is distinctive about his geographical location, so he is using the natural yeast present on the berries. Without any backup! He also thins to a one ton per acre maximum. As he says, "I want to be able to stand in a room someday, unknown, and hear somebody smell a Pinot Noir and say, 'That's from that crazy fellow, Burnap's place!'"

VINE HILL VINEYARD

A half mile east of Highway 17 lies the new winery operation of former entertainer Dick Smothers. Smothers retired to his thirty acre ranch in the Vine Hill district of Santa Cruz in 1976.

Acquired from Ridge Vineyards, the ranch had thirteen acres of thirty year old vines, mostly White Riesling. In past years the fruit had gone to Ridge, Bargetto, and Roudon-Smith wineries. Beginning with the 1977 vintage, Smothers cleared space in his garage for a small winery. It will produce about 4000 cases by 1978.

To say "garage" is a bit misleading, for it used to house eight automobiles, part of Dick's vintage car collection. Smothers has raced on the Formula 5000 circuit and also driven the 24 hours of LeMans.

Winemaker-consultant Leo McCloskey says that Vine Hill will concentrate on White Rieslings in the German style. He will also make Chardonnay and Cabernet Sauvignon from Smothers' ranch and Cabernet from the Robert Young Vineyard in Alexander Valley.

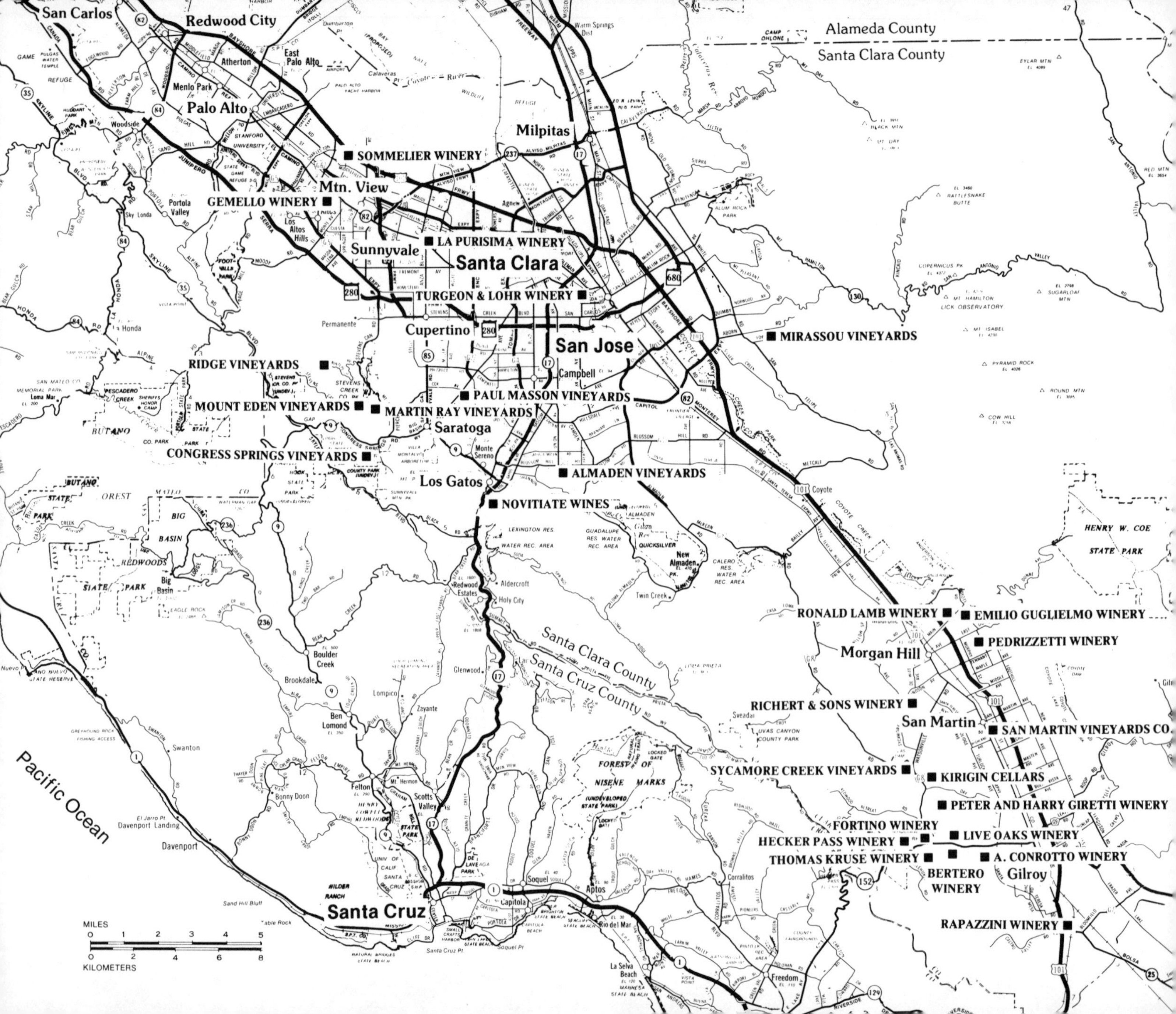
Alameda County
Santa Clara County
San Carlos
Redwood City
Atherton
East Palo Alto
Menlo Park
Palo Alto
Woodside
Milpitas
SOMMELIER WINERY
Mtn. View
GEMELLO WINERY
Portola Valley
Los Altos Hills
LA PURISIMA WINERY
Sunnyvale
Santa Clara
TURGEON & LOHR WINERY
Cupertino
San Jose
MIRASSOU VINEYARDS
RIDGE VINEYARDS
Campbell
PAUL MASSON VINEYARDS
MOUNT EDEN VINEYARDS
MARTIN RAY VINEYARDS
Saratoga
CONGRESS SPRINGS VINEYARDS
Monte Sereno
Los Gatos
ALMADEN VINEYARDS
NOVITIATE WINES
HENRY W. COE STATE PARK
BIG BASIN REDWOODS STATE PARK
New Almaden
Redwood Estates
Holy City
RONALD LAMB WINERY
EMILIO GUGLIELMO WINERY
PEDRIZZETTI WINERY
Morgan Hill
Santa Clara County
Santa Cruz County
Boulder Creek
Brookdale
RICHERT & SONS WINERY
San Martin
SAN MARTIN VINEYARDS CO.
Ben Lomond
Swanton
Pacific Ocean
SYCAMORE CREEK VINEYARDS
KIRIGIN CELLARS
Felton
Bonny Doon
FOREST OF NISENE MARKS
Scotts Valley
PETER AND HARRY GIRETTI WINERY
Davenport
FORTINO WINERY
HECKER PASS WINERY
LIVE OAKS WINERY
THOMAS KRUSE WINERY
A. CONROTTO WINERY
BERTERO WINERY
Gilroy
Soquel
Aptos
Corralitos
Capitola
Santa Cruz
RAPAZZINI WINERY
Rio del Mar
La Selva Beach
Freedom
MILES
KILOMETERS

Santa Clara
County

Gemello Winery

In 1934 the El Camino Real (Spanish for "The King's Highway") was little more than a two-lane, paved roadway. There, just south of San Antonio Road, in Mountain View, John Gemello laid the foundations for a small, family winery. A native of Italy's famed Piedmont, John was born to vineyards and winemaking. So, too, was his son Mario.

"When I was a boy," says Mario, "we were ashamed of our way of life. Part of it was the stigma of being called 'bootlegger' by our classmates. Also, having to bring our plough horse home from the vineyards was hardly chic. It was so bad, I used to plead with my father not to put the winery sign out on the highway." He chuckles. "Now, wine is such a romantic thing that any kid would give his right arm to have a father in the business."

Mario took over the family operation in 1944. Two years later, the end of World War II precipitated a vast demand for new housing. The El Camino became busily travelled and vineyards gave way to tract homes and shopping centers. Today the winery is tucked away behind a massive bowling alley.

Gemello owns no vineyards today, so grapes are purchased in small lots from the nearby Saratoga foothills, Carmel Valley, and Amador County. "My dad used to tend grapes and make wine for the old Monte Bello Winery, where Ridge is today," notes Mario. "At one time, we had eighteen acres of vineyards just off the El Camino. We bring all of our grapes in in fifty pound lug boxes. Actually, they're forty pound boxes, but you can get fifty pounds in if you fill the corners. But a lot of workers are lazy, and they get paid by the box, not by the pound. When the grapes come in in lug boxes, you avoid unnecessary juicing and oxidation."

Louis Sarto bought into the winery in 1969. He had owned and operated the retail liquor store immediately in front of the winery since 1956 and had directed the marketing of Mario's wines as well. He initiated the use of back labels and vintage dating, and imported Limousin and Nevers oak for the winery's justly known Cabernet Sauvignons and Zinfandels.

By 1974 Mario was growing tired of working and thought seriously of retiring. In July he and Louis sold the corporation to Mike Felice Sr. and his family. Mario was retained as winemaker, which turned out to be a fortunate circumstance. Just two years later Gemello and Sarto realized that the Filice organization was on shaky ground, being then six months in default. They soon regained control of the winery.

Mario Gemello believes in staying close to his wines. "I buy my grapes by the soils. Where grapes are grown makes all the difference. I ferment in wooden tanks and age in small cooperage. Every single bottle is *touched* by me!"

In all of this, Mario decries the modernization of winemaking practices. "They (the universities) send us push-button winemakers today," he moans. "You can't get people who'll shovel pomace any more."

Turgeon & Lohr Winery

While most wineries are set in the midst of idyllic greenery and rolling hillsides planted to vines, Turgeon & Lohr Winery lies in the middle of one of California's largest cities. With 280 acres of vineyard in Greenfield (Monterey County, between Soledad and King City), the winery is just off The Alameda near downtown San Jose.

"Out winery may be in the middle of a city, but we'll be flagwavers for Monterey as an appellation of origin," declares partner/winemaker Peter Stern. "We believe strongly in Monterey as a grape growing area producing grapes with strong varietal character."

The winery itself was purchased in the summer of 1974 by the fledgling company. The building formerly housed the tapper keg filling and quality control operations of the Falstaff Brewing Company. Only forty tons of grapes were crushed that year. Over three hundred tons were crushed in each of the following years, over six hundred tons are expected this year (1977), and an optimum of 1500 tons is aimed for by 1983.

Founding partners of the winery are Bernard Turgeon and Jerome Lohr. They are also partners in the design and construction of custom homes with their Saratoga Foothills Development Company. They hired Peter Stern to consult for the first harvest. He came aboard as a partner in early 1975.

Stern was born in St. Helena and holds both Bachelor's and Master's degrees from U.C. Davis. He worked for Gallo and did some vineyard consulting for a few years before becoming involved with the new winery.

"One of the things I like most here," he says, "is that we have vertical control of the product. I have control over the vineyards, the grapes, and how the wine is made, aged, and sold."

"We had originally planted some Petite Sirah," notes Stern, "but found that it is not suited to the area. We're going to pull it out and graft Gewurztraminer to the stocks."

Stern believes that it is more difficult to grow grapes successfully in Monterey County, because of the problems peculiar to the area, but that the results of patience and hard work will pay off in great wines.

"We have very deep topsoil in Greenfield. There is limited rainfall and the wind is a major problem. The Salinas River takes up the slack in rainfall and we must prune much more severely and achieve lower crop levels to overcome the wind problem. Four tons per acre is about the maximum we can expect from Monterey County."

"But look what you can get out of, say, Cabernet Sauvignon. Where Napa Valley Cabernets are so aromatic, with that cranberry quality, we're obtaining wines with a more hay-like, soil-like character, similar to those of Bordeaux. It's a combination of the soil, the climate, and the youth of the vines. But it makes Monterey distinctive."

Mirassou Vineyards

"The oldest winemaking family in America," says the literature. But the Mirassous are not of a disposition to rest on a promotional claim. Their present is every bit as vibrant as their history is long. The current crop of Mirassous (with an Alexander thrown in for good measure) is equal in number to their generation: they are the fifth generation; they are five strong.

It is a tribute to the wisdom of the fourth generation, Edmund and Norbert Mirassou, that they have so gracefully stepped aside to allow their offspring to take the ball and run. Though Ed and Norb still own the winery and its bulk operation, the fifth generation has purchased the "Mirassou" label and bottled inventory. They own some of the vineyards and lease most of the winery and the remaining family vineyards.

The fourth generations's judgment was sound. The younger troops immediately charged ahead to create a public identity for the Mirassou name, previously entrenched in the bulk (interwinery) trade. Thus, for the five young men, September 10, 1966 became a benchmark: on that day the first "Mirassou" wines were released to commercial channels.

"Our parents didn't want to market the label," says Daniel Mirassou. "It had been sold at the winery since the forties, but never to the trade. We're happy to have the success or failure of the venture on our own shoulders. We'll either be heroes or bums, but it's our responsibility. We anticipate purchasing the winery as time goes on. It's the only sensible thing to do. The government is wiping out family businesses. Inheritance taxes alone could ruin us."

The Mirassou family history unfolds as a microcosm of Santa Clara Valley's viticultural history. The first generation began with the arrival of Pierre Pellier from France circa 1850. His brother, Louis, a LaRochelle nurseryman, had preceeded Pierre to California. On arriving in 1848, he sent for his younger brothers (Pierre and Jean), asking them to bring vine cuttings from Bordeaux. The exact date is uncertain, but by 1852 the brothers had begun farming the western slopes of Mount Hamilton, south and east of San Jose.

Pierre had an event-filled voyage returning to California on his second trip. He brought not only cuttings, but a bride as well: Henriette Renard. At one point in the voyage the winds stopped and the ship lay still in the water. As drinking water became precious, Pierre's equally valued cuttings began to dry out. In a bold move, he purchased all of the potatoes in the hold, slit them open, and inserted the infant plants into them.

The original quarter section (160 acres) was part of the Rancho Yerba Buena in the Evergreen District, originally a Spanish land grant. By 1869 Pierre had over 300 acres of vineyard. In 1881, Henrietta, one of Pierre's four daughters, became captivated by a suave young French immigrant. He was Pierre Huste Mirassou, a well-educated gentleman from the Basque town of Pau. They were soon married. Three of their sons-- Peter, Herman, and John-- were to carry on the

Inside the Tasting Room at Mirassou

family's winemaking traditions after their father's death in 1889.

At the same time, phylloxera had become a menace to California viticulturists. The vineyards were replanted onto 20,000 St. George rootstocks, brought from France by the three brothers' new step-father, Thomas Caselagno, who had been Pierre's ranch foreman. A new 500,000 gallon winery was constructed on Quimby Road after the 1906 earthquake, only to be dismantled thirteen years later at the onset of Prohibition.

At that time, Peter traded the Quimby Road site to his brothers for the Aborn Road ranch and vineyards. John and Herman went into the orchard business on family land in what is now the city of Campbell. Though he made no wine during Prohibition, Peter did well, as grape prices were high until the middle twenties.

Peter's sons, Norbert and Edmund, the aforementioned fourth generation, began taking over their father's operations after Prohibition. Beginning in early 1937, they uprooted the old vineyards and replanted them to premium varieties, including Cabernet Sauvignon, Johannisberg Riesling, and Chardonnay. Even so, virtually all of the wines sold were sold in bulk to other wineries.

In 1941, to help the faltering Villa Vista Winery, Mirassou acquired a winemaker and perpetual grandfather to the fifth generation: Max (affectionately "Mackie") Huebner. Born in Germany in 1899, Huebner came to California in 1928 to work for Albert Haentze at Villa Vista. It wasn't long before he acquired a reputation as a champagne master. Officially retired, he now only puts in 20 hour weeks at Mirassou.

It is the fifth generation which sets the pace at Mirassou today. Norbert's son Steve is in charge of sales and son-in-law Don Alexander is the winemaker. Edmund's sons are James, Daniel, and Peter. Jim is president, Daniel handles marketing, and Peter is the vineyardist.

Peter must be given a great deal of credit for the development of "field crushing." With a good portion of the winery's vineyard acreage in Monterey County, it became vitally important to find a means of maintaining freshness in grapes that would have to be hauled a distance for crushing.

The answer came in eliminating both time and distance between harvest and crush. With the aide of mechanical harvesters, a small crushing unit was devised that could be run along an adjacent row. The grapes could then be crushed immediately, placed under a bed of inert gas, and be removed to the winery in prime condition. A small experimental lot of Chenin Blanc was field crushed in 1969. The following year 70% of Mirassou's Monterey vineyards were field crushed and that vintage's Chenin Blanc will remain a standard for fruitiness and flavor.

The Monterey experience has been a good one for the Mirassous. It has given the wine world such treats as Fleuri Blanc (a sweet Gewurztraminer), Monterey Rielsing (Sylvaner), and Chenin Blanc.

It won't be too many years before the sixth generation of Mirassous and Alexanders will begin to exert their influence on the winery. It will be interesting to see if they can keep up with their predecessors.

Paul Masson Vineyards

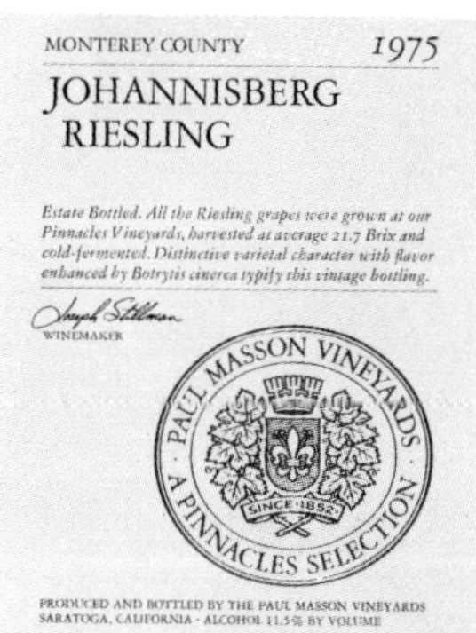

Paul Masson claims to be the oldest California winery in continuous operation. The path to proving that claim is tortuous, but plausible. Historical waters are muddied, for example, around Frenchman Etienne Thee (pronounced somewhat akin to 'Tay'). Some reports have him in California seeking gold before gold was even discovered. It seems far more certain that in 1852 he purchased 350 acres alongside Guadalupe Creek, eleven miles south of San Jose (in Los Gatos), from the Narvaez family. The land had once been part of the San Juan Bautista Rancho.

Thee bought cuttings of the Mission variety (a poor grape for winemaking) to start what some contend was the first private vineyard in the state. It was certainly one of the earliest of any stature. Thee later made wine and sold some of his fruit as table grapes.

Another Frenchman, Charles Lefranc, joined up with Thee circa 1857, acquiring half interest then and full interest after he married Thee's daughter, Adele, and inherited her father's property.

The winery's permanent name came from yet a third Frenchman who, like Lefranc, married into the business. Paul Masson was born on St. Valentine's Day of 1859 in Beaune. A big, broad-shouldered, outgoing man, he came to California at age nineteen, took additional schooling in business, and signed on as bookkeeper at Lefranc's winery and vineyards.

Masson married Lefranc's daughter, Louise, in 1888, took a wedding trip to France, and within a few years had bought out brother-in-law Henry's interests. The Lefranc-Masson Wine Company became the Paul Masson Champagne Company. In the latter name is the key to Masson's greatest legacy, for it was he who gave sparkling wines commercial importance in California.

In 1884, on one of many voyages to his homeland, Masson brought back special equipment for the production of sparkling wines: basket presses with the feather touch necessary for the sensitive crushing of delicate grapes, corking and disgorging tools, pupitres--the riddling racks--as well as cuttings from Reims and Epernay in the Champagne district. By 1892 he was producing sparkling wines on a large scale.

The wines suited his style, for Masson was a *bon vivant*. A gourmet cook and elegant entertainer, he loved nothing more than being surrounded by friends at his mountain chateau, "La Cresta." "Good wines make good friends," he would say, and bottles of chilled champagne were never wanting at his *soirees*. The reputation was such that he was widely rumored to have given entertainer Anna Held, of Ziegfeld fame, a bath in the bubbly. While many have attempted to defend or discredit the story (or point to the particular bathtub), there was little question but that Paul Masson Champagnes showed a corresponding spurt in sales.

In 1905 Masson planted what came to be called the "Vineyard in the sky" in the thin air of the Santa

Masson Champagnery at Saratoga

Cruz Mountains. Caves were dug for cellars and thousands of bottles of sparkling wine were placed therein for aging. The following April the earth shook and the sky burned in San Francisco and thousands of those bottles encased in that Saratoga hillside were demolished.

Masson rebuilt the sandstone winery and capped the project by constructing the winery facade from the ruins of St. Patrick's Church in San Jose, a 12th century portal which had been brought around Cape Horn from Spain. The new winery, which later survived a fire in 1941 (one year after Masson's death), became State Historical Landmark Number 733 in 1960. The building is now used for the aging of Paul Masson's Rare Flor Sherry and as the site for the popular musical productions, Music at the Vineyard and Vintage Sounds.

Masson retired in 1936, selling the winery to stockbroker Martin Ray, a combative proponent of California wines. Ray kept the winery only seven years before selling it to the international liquor company of Joseph E. Seagram & Sons.

Paul Masson is now one of the ten largest wineries in the country. It produces as wide a line of grape wines as can be made, including table, sparkling, and dessert wines, vermouth, and brandy. The major exporter of American wines, Paul Masson ships to more than 60 countries.

In 1955 the winery began to look beyond the confines of the Santa Clara Valley for a place to plant needed, supplementary vineyards. Following the research of U. C. Davis professors Amerine and Winkler, Paul Masson initially purchased 750 acres in Monterey County in 1960. Planting began two years later and a new winery complex was erected in 1967 in Soledad, next to Masson's vast Pinnacles Vineyard. Nearly 4500 acres of Paul Masson vineyards now occupy Monterey County soils.

Masson recently began to visibly display their confidence in their Monterey holdings by adding vintage-dated, Monterey County appellation, varietal wines to their program. President Arthur Palombo: "As out Monterey County vineyards have matured, we have selected small, special lots of varietal wine. Those which have developed the most intense and complex varietal character are being released as 'Pinnacles Selection' wines in limited bottlings of approximately five thousand cases. The drinker of varietal wines is very discriminating--and his numbers are growing. We believe that the varietals of today will be the generics of tomorrow. Witness the number of varietals being sold in bottles larger than seven hundred centiliters."

June of 1959 saw the completion of Paul Masson's main winery in Saratoga. A spacious visitors center and tasting hall is showcased by a stunning "champagne" fountain, reflecting pool, and spiral ramp. A 153 foot long mosaic mural, conceived and executed by Jose Moya del Pino, depicts the history of wine. Inside, guests are invited to tour the building and taste a selection of Masson wines, including their proprietary favorites--Emerald Dry, Rhine Castle, Baroque, and Rubion.

Ridge Vineyards

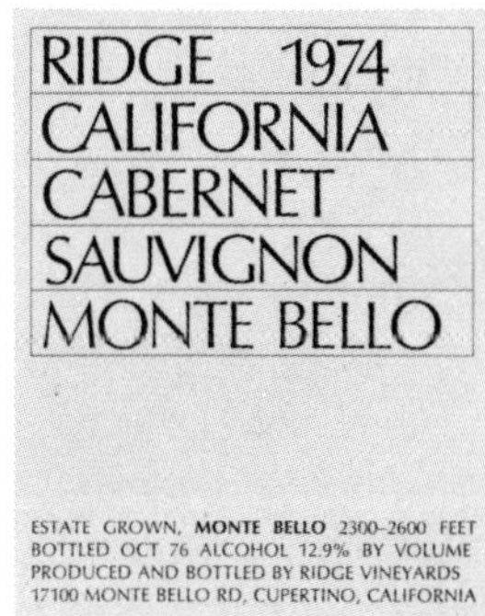

If your palate craves gutsy, filled out wines, then Ridge is your winery. Ever since president and co-founder David R. Bennion made his first Cabernet Sauvignon at home (1959) the Ridge style has been clearly defined: natural winemaking practices and limited handling.

While that sounds idealistic and familiar, few wineries who preach the method practice it as well as Ridge. Winemaker Paul Draper:

''We are one of the few wineries in this country to use the natural fermentive yeasts. Two strains usually develop. One starts the fermentation; the second, which is more tolerant to alcohol, carries the fermentation to completion. Because of this, we need only use thirty-five parts per million of sulphur dioxide to retard the non-fermentive (wild) yeasts. The only time we'll use a commercial yeast is if we've gone twelve to twenty-four hours without the fermentation beginning. With this method we feel that we get a cleaner fermentation, better fermentation curves, and more moderate temperatures.''

Draper and Bennion agree that once fermented, the wines should be handled as little and as carefully as possible. They aim to achieve clarity and stability by racking alone. Draper estimates that a light fining is necessary for a third of the wines he makes and that only a tenth of them require rough filtration.

''We have no centrifuge and do not polish filter,'' he says. ''Wait a minute. We did sterile filter a wine once. It had not undergone its malo-lactic fermentation by the time we were ready to bottle, so we had to.''

A practice that is rarely found today, though it is an old technique, is ''submerged cap fermentation.'' By means of a latticework, the cap is prevented from being pushed to the surface of the wine by the carbon dioxide resulting from the fermentation. A hardwood lattice was used at Ridge until Draper designed a stainless-steel grid sepcifically for use in Ridge's Mueller tanks.

The lower vineyard property was purchased as an investment from William Short in 1959 by David Bennion, then with the Stanford Research Institute, and three co-workers. Two of the other three founders are still major shareholders: Hewitt D. Crane (secretary) and Charles A. Rosen (treasurer). The winery was established and bonded in 1962 and the first vintage crushed, with Bennion as winemaker. Following incorporation in 1967, the group purchased the old Monte Bello Winery further up the ridge (at 2600 feet) and began the work of rennovating the building and gradually moving all winery operations there. Draper joined the team in 1969.

Ridge owns about fifty acres of vineyards and produces Zinfandel and Cabernet Sauvignon for the most part. Because the winery also purchases grapes from diverse areas (including Geyserville, Lytton Springs, York Creek, Fiddletown, the Shenandoah Valley, and Paso Robles), specific vineyard appellations are almost always listed on the label along with more detailed information about the wine.

Martin Ray Vineyards

The redoubtable Martin Ray is dead, his ashes scattered among the vines he tended so carefully. But the essence of his winegrowing philosophics will not die, on his beloved and much-fought-over Mount Eden, or anywhere else. For, though an Englishman would (with justice) accuse him of "bad form," the man's winemaking abilities and determination produced still and sparkling wines that were, for the longest time, without equal in the United States.

A stockbroker as a young man, Martin Ray dreamt of following in the footsteps of Paul Masson. He did. In 1936, when Masson retired, it was Ray who purchased the Paul Masson Champagne Company. In 1943 he sold to Seagrams and later purchased two quarter sections on Mount Eden, just north of Masson's hillside domain.

In 1959-1960 Ray put together the Mount Eden Group, composed of twenty-five well-to-do investors (mostly doctors, but including actor Burgess Meredith). The Mount Eden Group was to control one quarter section (160 acres) and the chateau house and winery. Wines made by Ray from their grapes were to have been sold under the label "Martin Ray: Mount Eden Vineyards, Prop." There never were. Conflict over control of the Mount Eden enterprise led to charges and counter-charges and the eventual court battles that nobody could win. Much of the litigation terminated with a Sheriff's Sale in 1971, which had the effect of splitting the assets between Martin Ray and the Mount Eden Group, leaving each side with a winery premises.

A subsequent sale by Ray of his own holdings led to additional litigation. The winery was locked up by the courts during the 1975 vintage. Then, a few months after Ray's death in January of 1976, a new corporation was formed and the winery reopened. Prime movers in the new venture are Peter Martin Ray (Ray's stepson) and Kenton Brooks, a research associate at Stanford University.

Peter Martin Ray has emerged as president, viticulturist, and winemaker for the reborn Martin Ray Vineyards. It is not a new role for the University of California and Harvard educated botanist. He has been supervising crushes at the winery almost continuously since 1959. Peter had to juggle the rain-threatened 1976 vintage between his lectures at Stanford, where he has taught plant physiology since 1968.

"There is a tremendous feeling in producing something out of nature," says Ray, who will follow most of the winemaking precepts laid down by Martin Ray. "I don't think it is *absolutely* essential to make wines that are a hundred percent varietal, but the only excuse for blending is to improve the wine, not stretch it. We will continue to pick at maximum ripeness and extract maximum flavor and color by multiple crushings."

During the summer of 1977 the winery released Martin Ray's 1970 Cabernet Sauvignon, the wine the late winemaster considered his finest effort. An incredibly intense and concentrated wine, in nose and flavor, it sold for $22.50.

Mount Eden Vineyards

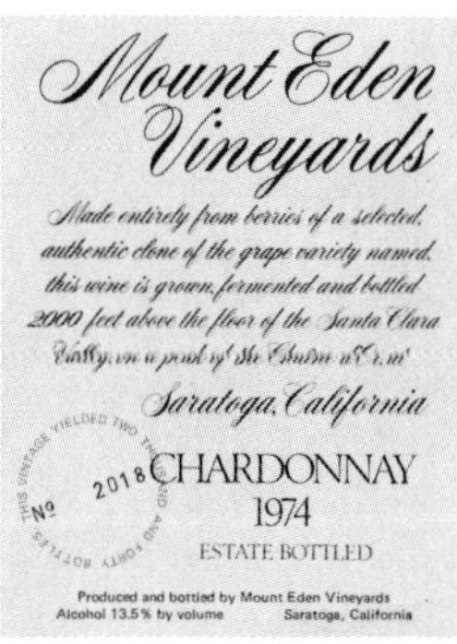

Mount Eden's tortuous path to its existence as a winery began over thirty years ago when the iconoclastic Martin Ray first planted vineyards on the steep, rugged, 2000 foot slopes of Mount Eden, in the range Paul Masson dubbed the ''Chaine d'Or,'' or Chain of Gold. Today Mount Eden Vineyards--which encompasses four of the five vineyards originally planted by the late Martin Ray--is operated by many of the same shareholders who were once in partnership with Ray.

Getting to that point, however, was not easy. A prolonged court battle between Ray and his shareholders, referred to as the Mount Eden Group, dragged on through the late sixties. It was finally settled in 1971. Ray retained the winery's equipment and inventory (at the lower, or main winery). The Mount Eden Vineyards (MEV) Corporation purchased the original (upper) winery and two of the five vineyard parcels. Mount Eden shareholders bought two of the other vineyards. Thus, the MEV Corporation now owns or controls four of the five original parcels. Richard ''Dick'' Graff (Chalone Vineyards) was hired as consulting enologist.

In February of 1974 Meredith ''Merry'' Edwards became the winemaker. Her husband, Bill Miller, whose prior experience was as Assistant Budget Officer at the Pentagon (for the Army), signed on to handle accounting and general management responsibilities.

In April, 1977, Ms. Edwards left Mount Eden to eventually become winemaker at a new Sonoma County winery. Mount Eden's new helmsman is Bill Anderson, a Stanford graduate in psychology. After working at Stanford Hospital and taking science courses at a nearby junior college, the former home winemaker entered the master's program in enology at Davis.

Anderson spent the 1976 crush working with Ed and Phyllis Pedrizzetti at their Morgan Hill winery. Bill then decided to forsake his enology degree when he was offered the Mount Eden job. Born in San Francisco but raised in Los Altos, Bill says that he can almost see the house he grew up in from the winery's hilltop site. Dick Graff will be back as consultant.

Perhaps the main thread of continuity between Ray and the current Mount Eden operation has been the selfless dedication of vineyard manager Bonifacio ''Boni'' Zarate. ''It's a mistake to call Boni the vineyard manager,'' says Merry Edwards. ''These are *his* vineyards! Though his home is in Mexico, he tends the vineyards nine months a year to put his son through medical school. He's been a fixture on Mount Eden for fifteen years.''

Twenty-two acres of vineyards flank the winery. Four acres are planted to Chardonnay, ten to Cabernet Sauvignon, and eight to Pinot Noir. The wines from these stringently pruned vines are bottled under the Mount Eden label and rarely fail to measure up to the prices asked for them. Wines made from grapes purchased elsewhere are bottled under the ''MEV'' label. As when the vineyards were controlled by Martin Ray, they continue to produce what have to be considered among the finest wines made in California.

Congress Springs Vineyards

Another of a score of new wineries in Santa Clara County lies on the crest of a small rise, hidden from the road by tall trees and protected from the casual visitor by a rutted dirt road (soon to be paved) reminiscent of Mount Eden and Martin Ray.

Congress Springs Vineyards, however, is not three miles away from paved roads. It is, in fact, just three miles northwest of Saratoga and only a couple of hundred yards off of Highway 9.

The building the winery is housed in dates to 1923. The date and name of the home are inscribed on its west face: "Villa De Monmartre, May 1, 1923." The estate was logged in the 1890's. It was further cleared and settled by a French immigrant, Pierre Pourroy. It was he who built the house, a barn (winery), and planted 25 acres of vineyards.

When the house was built, part of the downstairs was also used for winemaking. Though today both stories are exposed, half of the lower story was originally an underground basement. One has the feeling that this information, coupled with the fact that there was a tiny trap door (one man) leading from underneath the master's bed to the concealed basement, indicates that that part of the winery was quite illicit.

In 1974 a young couple began coming up to the property regularly to rehabilitate a vineyard whose sucker growth was out of hand. Dan Gehrs was working at Paul Masson at the time and had visions of a small, self-sustaining winery. His wife, Robin, a native of Seattle, grew up with wines. "My father made sauerkraut and wine as long as I can remember," she says. "It was a family project."

After meeting up with Vic Erickson, a San Jose industrialist, they were able to secure a lease on the house and vineyards.

They moved into the house in February of 1976 and planted four acres of Chardonnay to go with three acres of Zinfandel that had been planted in the early thirties. A corner of the lower level has been turned into a small winery, with plastic fermenters and small oak cooperage. Dan's brother, Jim, has joined the concern as vineyardist.

Dan Gehrs believes firmly in the distinctiveness of the Santa Clara side of the Santa Cruz Mountains. "This is the warmer side of the hills. We get higher sugar, acid, and pH. The wines, therefore, are bigger, richer wines. We are using no pesticides or herbicides in our vineyards and will strive to accentuate the regional distinctiveness of our wines."

The Gehrs are purchasing some of their grapes now, but hope to gradually plant another twenty acres and become a self-contained winery. Those that are purchased, however, are all from the immediate vicinity. Two unusual red wines Dan has made as a home winemaker are Grenache and Cabernet Franc.

The 1976 crush for the winery totaled only 400 gallons (of a projected 1200) and was made up of a dry and a sweet Sauvignon Blanc, a Semillon, and a pepperish Zinfandel that shows great promise.

Almadén Vineyards

The site of Almaden's Los Gatos Winery was first planted a century and a quarter ago by a French *vigneron* from Bordeaux, Etienne Thee. Said to be one of the earliest commercial plantings of European wine grapes in California, the early harvests were, interestingly enough, sold as table grapes.

Thee built an adobe and stone winery and a home on a knoll with a sweeping view of the valley on the property he had acquired from Jose Augustin Narvaez, along the Guadalupe Creek. (The winery building still stands, but the home was destroyed by fire in 1974.) Oak casks were brought around the Horn from France. Another French import was Charles Lefranc, an ambitious young man who had been a tailor in Passy (near Paris).

Lefranc joined Thee in 1857*, purchased a half interest in the vineyards and winery, and married Thee's daughter, Adele, insuring his inheritance of the remainder. It was Lefranc who would give the operation the name of the quicksilver mine a few miles south of the winery, Almaden. (The mine was called New Almaden, for the mines in Ciudad Real, Spain.)

* There is much controversy over this date. Most give it as 1852, but Lefranc himself, under oath in a court of law, said he came to California and associated himself with Thee in 1857.

Lefranc loved to entertain lavishly. Some of his famous guests included Civil War heroes Admiral David Farragut, General William Sherman, and General (later President) Ulysses S. Grant.

Curiously, both Lefranc and his only son, Henry, met tragic deaths. Charles died in a wagon accident at the winery in 1887; Henry died in an electric trolley accident in 1909. After Henry's death, the winery was held in trust until its sale to Charles Jones, who opened it briefly after Prohibition. Almaden's modern history, however, didn't begin until its ownership passed to Louis Benoist.

In 1941 the San Francisco socialite purchased Almaden for $125,000. Benoist enlisted the assistance of the renowned importer/wine writer Frank Schoonmaker to run the operation. Schoonmaker, in turn, lured master winemaker Oliver Goulet from Martin Ray's Paul Masson Winery to bring Almaden back into prominence. A former Jesuit Brother (and winemaker for The Novitiate), Goulet distinguished himself for twenty-one years at Almaden.

It was at Schoonmaker's suggestion that Goulet took Grenache grapes that had been used in ports and burgundies and made, in 1945, the first Grenache Rose in California. Two decades later it became a staple in the collegiate ranks, known as much for its lively flavor as for its distinctive packaging. Goulet, like the Lefrancs before him, died in a traffic accident, an auto collision with a freight train.

When the wine market tumbled after World War II, Almaden effected a short term merger with Madrone Vineyards, which lasted only until 1950. When the

Almadén Cienega Valley Winery

merger was dissolved, Hans Peter Jurgens, who had headed Madrone, took charge of Almaden.

By the early fifties it became obvious that the vineyards and orchards of the Santa Clara Valley were doomed to a slow death by urban development. Benoist had the foresight to begin puschasing land in San Benito County in 1955. After some experimental studies, large tracts were planted to prime varieties. Today, nearly four thousand acres of vines make up the Paicines Vineyard, one of the largest single plantings in the world. An additional five hundred acres at nearby Cienega make for a total of over two million vines in Almaden's two San Benito County vineyards, requiring over 3000 miles of trellis wire.

In 1967 Benoist, who also owned the Lawrence Warehouse Company, sold the winery. National Distillers, which had previously owned wineries in California, purchased Almaden for a reported $14 million.

Almaden has grown immensely since its acquisition by National Distillers. When William Dieppe assumed the presidency in 1969 Almaden's annual sales were $18 million. The figures for 1976 approach $70 million.

By the close of the sixties Dieppe and Jurgens saw the viticultural promise of Monterey County and secured the services, as a consultant, of U.C. Davis' renowned A.J. Winkler. By the harvest of 1973 the first grapes began to arrive at the winery from plantings in King City and San Lucas, a total of two thousand acres in all.

The separate moves toward San Benito and Monterey counties have combined, over a period of time, to raise both the quality and the image of Almaden as a producer of fine wines. Yet each is a different growing area, according to winemaster Klaus Mathes: "San Benito is warmer and has heavier soils. The wines are generally a little heavier. The whites are lighter and more fragrant in Monterey. Monterey's soils are sandy and gravelly; there's more boron and lime in San Benito."

In recent years Almaden has begun releasing vintaged wines under a new, "Special Selection" label. Many of these also indicate the specific regional appellation of the wine. The whites are clean, fresh, and fruity. Some of the reds are highly distinctive. The 1974 Monterey Zinfandel is a rich, yet lively young wine with a perfumed nose and lots of flavor.

Almaden is one of the largest producers of premium wines in the country. It now has four winery facilities (at Los Gatos, Paicines, Cienega, and Kingsburg) to process the fruit of its nearly 7000 acres of owned and leased vineyards and 8000 acres of contracted vineyards.

Though the home winery (with its new bottling facility of 89,000 square feet on two levels) does not have a tasting or retail room, it does offer tours (including the original, vine-lamp lighted cellar) Monday through Friday from 10 AM to 3:30 PM. Almaden does, however, have a tasting room that is regularly open to the public. It is located at 8090 Pacheco Pass Highway (at the junction of California Routes 152 and 156), twelve miles east of Gilroy and six miles north of Hollister.

Novitiate Wines

Father Nicholas Congiato, Society of Jesus, was, from all accounts, a determined man, a seasoned patriarch. Several times Superior of the California Jesuits, he had also been rector of St. Ignatius College in San Francisco (later the University of San Francisco) and Santa Clara College. By the end of 1886, with the assistance of a fine harvest from the Society's Villa Maria Vineyard in Cupertino, Congiato had convinced the Jesuit General in Rome that a new training facility for Jesuit seminarians should be built at Los Gatos. In 1887 he began construction of the Sacred Heart Novitiate, known today as Sacred Heart Jesuit Center.

The Jesuit Fathers and Brothers had two important needs in those days: financial support and legitimate sacramental wine. By Church canon law, altar wine must not exceed eighteen percent alcohol and must be made solely of grapes. The solution was obvious: make the sacramental wine themselves and sell the excess to the public. In the fall of 1888 the first vintage took place at the new Novitiate, under the direction of winemaker Brother Constantine Valducci.

Since that time the Novitiate has been making fine sacramental wines with such names as ''L'Admirable'' (a sweet angelica) and ''Santa Rosa'' (a dry rosé). The first frame winery building was abandoned for a newer concrete facility in 1893. This building has since been surrounded by later additions, all of which have survived the 1906 earthquake and the devastation of fire in 1934.

The Novitiate no longer caters to the training of seminarians. That task was shifted to a new seminary in Montecito (a suburb of Santa Barbara) in 1967, though the novices still return in the fall to assist in the harvest. The buildings at the Novitiate now serve as a Jesuit residence, administrative center, and retreat house.

Father Francis Silva is president of Novitiate Wines and general manager Father Louis Franklin oversees winery operations. Winemaker is Brother Lee Williams and the winery's 650 acres of vineyards (in Santa Clara, Stanislaus, and San Benito counties) are managed by Father Henri Charvet.

The winery took on Stanford Wolf & Associates in 1976 to handle the Novitiate's national marketing. The move was made because the winery is shifting and increasing its production to give greater emphasis to premium table wines.

The Novitiate lies in a glorious sylvan setting, with an old, non-producing vineyard gracing the hilltop behind the winery. If you like the serenity of an untraveled place, take the Los Gatos exit from Highway 17 and look for Los Gatos Boulevard, which runs into Main Street. College Avenue runs south off of Main (there's a winery sign on the lamp post at the corner) and up to the winery. The tasting room is cold (it's part of the cellars), but a brisk tour or a sample of the excellent Muscat Frontignan will warm you up.

Emilio Guglielmo Winery

Emilio Guglielmo (the second "g" is silent) was one of the many who emigrated from their native Piedmont to seek the fabled prosperity of California. He reached the United States in 1908. After working as a miner in New Mexico ("That got old in a hurry," says his grandson), Emilio moved to San Francisco and a tannery job. After seventeen years of hard work and thrift he was able to purchase fifteen acres of vineyards in the Santa Clara Valley.

As the "Noble Experiment" was still in force, Emilio and his wife Emilia were forced to haul their grapes to San Francisco for crushing and the production of sacramental wines. But when Repeal became a reality, they were ready to build and bond Emile's Winery and earn that prosperity on their own merits.

In 1945 Emilio was unsure of his son George's intentions and considered selling the winery. George, stationed in London at the end of the war, returned home immediately to take over the business. Since then, Emilio's grandsons have grown up into the business and now operate the winery.

George Jr. is a graduate in viticulture and enology from Fresno State and oversees all winemaking and viticultural practices. Brother Gene, a University of Santa Clara business grad, handles marketing and sales for the expanding winery.

"My grandparents had both worked in France as children," observes George Jr. "I guess it was the French influence--they both spoke the language fluently--that caused him to use the French version of his name for the winery."

The winery uses several labels. A special Claret (a blend of Zinfandel and Petite Sirah) comes out under the "Emilio Guglielmo Winery" label. An aged Burgundy is sold as "Emile's Cavalcade Brand" and most of the generics sport a simple "Emile's," as do the sparkling, dessert, and aperitif wines. The best varietals, however, are sold under the "Mount Madonna" label. Leading the line is a Petite Sirah that is spicy, complex, and full-bodied.

Like other wineries in the Santa Clara Valley, the Guglielmos are feeling the pinch of urban sprawl that has all but eliminated the county's fruit orchards and is severely limiting its vinelands.

"The area has grown, with more and more people from the San Jose area wanting to get away from the city," says George, Jr. "The minimum parcel for single homes is two and a half acres, but even that hasn't stopped construction."

The growth has become painfully obvious. The foothills are now spotted with houses and a high school has been thrown up directly across the street from the vine-covered winery.

The operation remains a close family one. "We don't have a distributor," says Gene, "but we do have a broker in the East. We still deliver most of the wine ourselves to our customers, stores, and restaurants. We like to keep the family touch. Most of our business is by word of mouth."

Pedrizetti Winery

There are several instances in the wine industry where warm, open, friendly people make fine wines and sell them for reasonable prices. The circumstance exists because winemaking is, for these people, more than just a living. It is, rather, a way of life. Phyllis and Ed Pedrizzetti typify it.

The Pedrizzettis are vital people who make what the industry is now, somewhat euphemistically referring to as "honest" wines. They've been doing it for a long time, though.

The winery itself was founded in 1923 by a young *Peimontese*, Camillo Colombano. After building the small winery, he sent back to Italy for cuttings of the most noted variety grown in his home district: Barbera. Today it remains the mainstay of the Pedrizzetti production.

Another native of Piedmont, John Pedrizzetti, purchased the winery in 1945. In 1963, son Ed took over the operation and acquired full ownership by 1968. Ed nearly died that year in a freakish accident that all winemakers dread. He had gone into a tank that had not been sulphured and was overcome by what must have been methane gas, formed by mold that had accumulated in the tank. Many factors combined to save his life: Ed was in excellent health and had never smoked; his son Dan was near enough to administer mouth-to-mouth breathing; and the ambulance crew, doctor, and emergency room staff were all efficient and effective in treating the stricken man. When Ed regained consciousness five hours later, he had no recollection of what had happened.

By August of 1973 Ed and Phyllis had decided to retire. The sold the winery to Varietal Vintners, a Delaware Corporation. As part of the deal, Ed stayed on as winemaker. By the end of the following year the new owners were in default, but it took until November of 1975 for the Pedrizzettis to regain ownership of their winery. As general manager Dave Tatro says with a smile, "We made a lot of 'late harvest' wine that year!"

Though the winery had been expanded in 1932 and 1938, increasing sales had caused the Pedrizzettis to store case goods like chipmonks. Late 1976 saw a concerted move of expansion and modernization at the winery. A new case goods warehouse was erected and new stainless steel fermenters were introduced.

The Pedrizzettis are active in promoting their own wines as well as those of the Santa Clara Valley. In 1976 Phyllis served as president of the Santa Clara Valley Wine Growers Association.

Phyllis and Ed are proud of the wines they make, often labeling them "Grown, Produced & Bottled By" to indicate that the grapes used came from the vineyards immediately surrounding the winery. "That is what 'Estate Bottled' really means," contends Ed.

The tasting room is located on U.S. 101, just north of Morgan Hill, in a restaurant/gift shop complex called "The Courtyard."

Richert & Sons Winery

When we think of a winery we often conceptualize the ideal: an old stone building surrounded by rolling hills, teaming with vines that turn glorious colors in the fall. The Richert & Sons Winery offers just such a building. And, it is surrounded by gently rolling hills. But there are no vines in sight, for the winery owns no vineyards and buys no grapes.

Richert & Sons has been a blending winery, specializing in sherries and ports. Table wines and fruit wines, however, formerly a major part of the winery picture, are expected to make a comeback in the coming months.

Walter S. Richert, winery founder, is a notable figure in the history of California wines. Richert took his degree in chemistry and fruit processing from the University of California in 1932, just before Repeal. For twenty years he served a broadly based apprenticeship. He drew his love of dessert wines from experience in Fresno and Lodi; he learned about table wines in Napa and Sonoma valleys; he served as roving editor for *Wine Review* and *Wines & Vines*; he was a founder of the American Society of Enologists. He did everything from winemaking to sales.

In 1953 he founded a small winery in Morgan Hill and six years later took over the old Paradise Valley Winery at Oak Glen (on Edmundson Avenue, south and west of Morgan Hill). An optimist at heart, he named the winery Richert & Sons. His three sons were then but school children. Even his label, with four oak ovals of descending size, symbolized the proud father and his three male offspring.

The winery's line was trimmed to dessert wines alone in the early seventies. Table wines had been made in the fifties, the winery producing up to forty different private labels at one time. Fruit wines were discontinued in 1972 when the price of sugar tripled and strawberry and apricot crops were disastrous.

Today only six wines are bottled at the winery: Pale Dry Sherry, Full Dry Sherry, Club Sherry, Triple Cream Sherry, Ruby Port, and Tawny Port.

Richert explains the necessity of having two dry sherries: "The 'Full Dry Sherry' is our own innovation. Most dry sherries have the color removed, but some of the native sherry taste is removed in the process. With this sherry we let it age without any such treatment. Thus, we have a full-bodied sherry, quite heavy in the 'nutty' character of a naturally aged dry sherry. It received the highest award at the Los Angeles County Fair for six years running." Pause. "There weren't any competitors in the class until 1975!"

Walt Richert sold the winery to Wines Unlimited of Los Angeles in 1974, but reacquired it, with his brother Hubert, two years later in an out-of-court settlement. (Hubert owns Desert Packing Company, a large date ranch in Indio.) Walter had stayed on as winemaker during that period, but ill health forced him to curtail his activities in 1976. Scott Richert, Walt's son, formerly with Paul Masson, now operates the winery.

San Martin Vineyards Co.

The San Martin Company has undergone as much change in the last four years as any winery in the industry. In that period the winery has experienced two ownership changes, acquired an exciting new winemaker, and radically altered its vinous horizons.

The winery was founded circa 1892 as a cooperative. A group of local vineyardists wanted simply to produce sacramental wines and make wine for their personal use. They operated the winery until Prohibition.

In 1932 the winery was purchased by the Bruno Filice family. The Filices came originally from Cosenza (in the province of Calabria, Italy) and were said to have been able to trace their winemaking ancestors to the early eighteenth century. Under the Filices the winery expanded its vineyard holdings. It became well known for its fruit and berry wines, Aprivette and Strawberry Fraisette among the favorites.

San Martin is given credit for originating sequenced tasting and greatly popularizing the tasting room concept, something they have managed to continue in fine style. The winery now operates no less than six tasting rooms, most of which are open daily. The main tasting room is at the winery, on the Monterey Highway (old U.S. 101), just south of San Martin Avenue. The newest tasting room is at the corner of San Pedro Avenue and Condit Road, Morgan Hill (Formerly a Filice Winery tasting room). Subtitled "Vintage 1892," this location features weekend balloon ascensions and instruction. Others are located in Gilroy (corner of Highways 101 and 25), Camarillo (Santa Rosa Road), Monterey (Wharf #2), and Solvang (Alisal Road). Signs like "Taste the Naked Grape" point the way.

In the spring of 1973 San Martin (pronounced "Marr-teen") was purchased by Southdown, Inc., a Houston based New York Stock Exchange company with interests in sugar, oil, gas, land, beer, soft drinks, candy, and cement. New resources became available to the winery, which was then able to go heavily into Monterey County for premium grapes. A bright new management team moved in, including viticulturist/winemaker Ed Friedrich, whose German and American training had prepared him to approach winemaking with imagination and artistic sense.

The winter of 1976-77 saw another ownership change. By cash sale, San Martin became the property of Somerset Wine Company, a subsidiary of Norton Simon, Inc., which had long been interested in the domestic wine scene. The move seems to put the winery in a better position to market its varied lineup of wines.

Ed Friedrich was born in Trier, Germany, and studied in that town's famed Institute for Viticulture and Enology. In 1959 he came to California, sponsored by Otto Meyer of Paul Masson. Friedrich had originally planned to stay for a couple of years, but he began to realize that there were few new horizons in the German

The Tasting Room at Morgan Hill

wine industry. While he was with Paul Masson (fourteen years), Friedrich was involved in their first crush of grapes from Monterey County in 1963. Three years later he moved to Soledad to supervise Masson's new winery there.

In February of 1973 Ed left Paul Masson for Arkansas. There he worked with the Wiederkehr family, making Concord and hybrid wines in their two million gallon winery and supervising an experimental vinifera program. "We planted over two hundred acres of vinifera while I was there," recalls Ed, "but I soon realized that the wine industry was still in California."

By December he was back in California and signed as the new winemaker at San Martin. Southdown was then in the process of putting $1.5 million into badly needed new crushing, pressing, and fermentation facilities. Even today, when walking through the old and decrepit aging cellars, one begins to realize some of the handicaps that are overcome to make the fine wines that issue from San Martin.

Since the Southdown takeover, the emphasis has been shifted from the fruit and berry wines toward vintage-dated, premium varietal wines. Part of the reason for the success of this program, avers Friedrich, is that the grapes are coming from new and distinctive regions. He points out the earthiness that comes from the well-established, dry farmed vineyards of Amador County, the fruit and body that prevail in wines whose birthplace is Shandon (San Luis Obispo County), and the tremendous varietal characteristics that are showing up in young wines from the young vineyards of Monterey County. It helps that Ed has complete control over San Martin's winemaking, from vineyards to bottle.

Two recent releases have highlighted the change in direction of San Martin. The first is their 1974 Amador County Zinfandel. The grapes were grown in a 35 year old, dry farmed vineyard, and the wine is cherry red in color and has a like aroma and flavor. It is a fruity, distinctively flavored Zinfandel.

The second involves a style of winemaking more than a particular wine. That style is German. Friedrich started with a Chenin Blanc, then added a Johannisberg Riesling. The premise is simple: by controlling the fermentation with low temperatures, the wine is made to have lower alcohol (in the ten percent range), which in turn yields fresh, fruity wines with greatly pronounced varietal flavors.

The first San Martin wines made in this style have been tagged "Soft," an understated, yet elegant descriptive term. San Martin's Soft Chenin Blanc and Soft Johannisberg Riesling will be new tasting experiences for most Californians, one they'll probably appreciate. As Ed says: "We consume wine for flavor components, not for alcohol. The original reason for alcohol in wine was as a preservative for the fruit juice. Alcohol covers all of the niceties that wine has to offer. The higher alcohol content tends to reduce the taste buds' ability to detect and acknowledge the complex nuances of the varietal characteristics of wine."

Sycamore Creek Vineyards

West of Morgan Hill, in the heart of Uvas Valley, exists another example of an abandoned winery being rebuilt with concern. At the corner of Watsonville and Uvas roads is the new Sycamore Creek Vineyards winery, revitalized by Terry and Mary Kaye Parks.

The Parkses are both teachers: Terry teaches fifth grade and Mary Kaye works with gifted students at first to sixth grade levels. They originally moved to the country several years ago because they wanted to participate in the production of their own foodstuffs.

They bought a couple of acres and an old house not far from their present residence. The house had been uninhabited for some fifteen years and required much of their time and efforts in repairs. They spent nearly three years refurbishing the house and "getting into ranching," as Terry puts it. Between goats, chickens, and an extensive vegetable patch, they were able to account for ninety percent of their needs.

When the couple came into a small inheritance they opted to try a larger ranch rather than put the sum into a bank. After much looking and thinking, especially since Mary Kaye was then pregnant and not working, they settled on a rundown sixteen acre ranch.

Two modest houses stood on the property and nearby was what had formerly been a winery. It had been built around 1913 by the Marchetti family, who had acquired the land in 1906. The best guess is that the winery only operated until the onset of Prohibition in 1919, though it is possible that it was used then as well.

Initially Terry and Mary Kaye thought they would sell the grapes from the seven acres of existing Zinfandel and Carignane to home winemakers. But then they got to talking with their neighbors. Ted Knopf, who sold them the ranch, was a home winemaker. He encouraged the Parkses to do the same. John Roffinella, a grape broker down the road, and Tom Kruse, whose winery lies at the end of Watsonville Road, agreed.

So Terry tore out some walnut trees and planted another seven acres to rootstock, to which will be grafted scions of Cabernet Sauvignon and Zinfandel. The winery was cleaned up and a concrete floor covered the dirt one. Sixteen tons of grapes were crushed in 1976 and rose´ wines were produced from Zinfandel, Carignane, Cabernet Sauvignon, and Grenache. A White Riesling was also made.

The Parkses are looking to make wines with a wide range of appeal. The winery will be open to the public. Its location, at a convenient intersection and adjacent to Uvas Meadows (a large private park), make it a natural. Visitors will be welcomed on weekends initially, but daily when school is out.

Kirigin Cellars

Kirigin is the original family name of the Chargin family, who purchased the former Bonesio Winery in August of 1976. The Chargins are from Croatia, on the Adriatic coast (now a part of Yugoslavia). The family name was changed in the 1880's by cousins who were coming to the United States. Their French lawyer had suggested that Kirigin sounded a bit too Irish to be of any business value, so the French-sounding "Chargin" was adopted.

When Nikola Kirigin brought his family to California in 1959 he had no intention of changing his family name. But one of his cousins enrolled his children in school as Chargins. Nikola finally agreed to a compromise: the old family name was to be retained as a middle name.

Nikola Kirigin Chargin (he always uses his full name) earned his degree in enology and chemistry at the University of Zagreb before bringing his family west. From 1960 to 1968 he made wines for San Martin and did some consulting. He then spent three years at Almaden, leaving shortly after National Distillers took over.

He then decided to head east to see what winemaking was like in New York. For four years he was head enologist for the Canandaigua Wine Company. By mid-1975 he had decided to retire. But before he had reached home there were two job offers, one of which he couldn't refuse. So he left for Delano to talk with the late Antonio Perelli-Minetti. When he arrived, Antonio lined up glasses of thirty different wines for Nikola to taste, so as to evaluate their compatibility with one another.

A year later Nikola attempted retirement once again. He even went so far as to purchase a forty acre orange and almond ranch in Madera. It was then that he learned that the sale of Bonesio Winery to Varietal Vintners had soured and that the winery was again on the block. The lure was too great.

The winery had been founded, north of Gilroy, by Pietro "Peter" Bonesio in 1915 and moved to its present location in 1921. Peter's sons, Victor and Louis, took over operations in 1932, but Peter kept his hand in things until his death in 1966. The Bonesios' best wines were bottled under the *Uvas* (Spanish for "grapes") label. Wine vinegar and a bing cherry wine were also featured.

The winery residence was built in 1827, when the 600 acre property was known as the Solis Rancho. Finished in 1853, it is listed as a Santa Clara County Historical Building. Picnic tables in the garden in front of the house benefit winery visitors.

Nikola's son, Nick, handles marketing for the new/old winery. A former college basketballer, Nick is an energetic promoter of his father and his wines. He has already opened the winery's second tasting room at 12549 Harbor Boulevard in Garden Grove, a mile and a half south of Disneyland.

Live Oaks Winery

Eduardo Scagliotti (the "g" is silent), the second son of a large farming family, was born in 1881 in the Italian province of Lisandria, near the town of Casale Monferrato, (Lisandria is in the region of Piedmont.) At the age of nineteen, Eduardo left home to find his own way in the world.

He arrived in Gilroy in 1900 and found work with the firm of Miller & Lux, a vast outfit which handled cattle and fruit. Eduardo's beginning salary was $15 a month. In his second year he was made field foreman and was later promoted to superintendent of the dried fruit department, which included supervision of the cultivation of orchards and vineyards.

But it was not the same as having his own orchards and vineyards. In partnership with three of his brothers, he leased a 200 acre ranch on Watsonville Road, in the UvasValley area. They operated the ranch, producing prunes, apricots, apples, and grapes. By 1912 Eduardo had secured a bonded winery license and begun making wine commercially.

Soon thereafter the four brothers purchased a tract of land, 120 acres, known as the E.H. Farmer Ranch. The toughest job they had to do was to clear land that was heavily wooded with live oak trees, wild cherry, greasewood, poison oak, and other California chaparral growths. They had another problem: an infestation of ground squirrels which devoured new plants. Shooting, trapping, poisoning, and even surrounding each new vine with a wire mesh were tried, with limited success. The furry creatures were finally decimated by an epidemic of Bubonic Plague (between 1915 and 1918).

In 1915 Eduardo resigned from Miller & Lux and the brothers moved their operations wholly to the new ranch. In 1920 Eduardo bought out his brothers. During Prohibition he shipped hundreds of tons of fresh grapes to New York markets. He also sold grapes and grape juice to local families and made sacramental wine.

Eduardo and his wife Amelia had three children: Lillian, William, and Peter (named for his grandfather). In 1937 Eduardo died of a heart attack and, a year later, William was fatally injured in an automobile accident. Peter, who was studying at Heald's Business College in Oakland, returned home to assume control of the ranch and winery.

"We had a fruit dehydrator then," says Peter, "and did about a thousand tons of prunes a year. During the war we finished five hundred pigs a year for the government and raised barley to feed the pigs."

The winery took its name from the grove of trees that once covered the ranch. The few that remain are estimated to be over 350 years old, but are being destroyed by moth's larvae that devour the leaves.

In 1960 Peter, a bachelor, hired Mitsuo Takemoto, a former strawberry grower who had become interested in the art of winemaking. Takemoto is now the winemaker and four members of his family take part in the winery's operations.

Bertero Winery

Alfonso Bertero, born and raised on the outskirts of Turino, Italy, came to this country late in the first decade of this century. No one is quite sure of the exact date, but it is certain that he worked for Standard Oil Company for several years before he was able to start a winery on property that was part of the Las Animas land grant.

Alfonso founded his winery in 1917 and built the present winery and family home in 1924. Even before the winery was in operation Alfonso was raising grapes for home winemakers and wineries making sacramental wines. During Prohibition he continued selling grapes to home winemakers (it was not illegal to make wine at home) and made sacramental wines.

Like most Italian winemakers, Alfonso made a red and a white and sold them directly to his customers, who would bring their own containers to the winery to be filled. They might bring a gallon jug, a five gallon demi-john, or a fifty gallon barrel. It was all very simple and straightforward, a delightful way to do business.

Alfonso's son, Angelo C. Bertero, with his wife Josephine, took over the winery in 1955. Today, Angelo's sons--Angelo Jr. and Carl--assist their father. Angelo Jr. is the winemaker and Carl the viticulturist.

Angelo Sr. has seen many changes in the industry he grew up in: "Things were simpler in the old days. Our customers were our friends. We used to have a route. Once, maybe twice a week, we'd take the wine around to our regulars. We also had a distributor. Just one. Jordano Brothers in Santa Barbara. From the thirties to the early sixties, they kept us alive in this business."

Angelo recognizes that, while many things have changed over the years, some things have remained unaltered: "We're more mechanized today. We have an automatic bottling line that does everything but talk back. But some things never change. Losing money in this business isn't unusual. We've been talking about large surpluses the last couple of years, but we faced a similar situation in 1946. We misjudged it this time and got stuck with a lot of wine. Heck, we still have some of our wine stored elsewhere. You know, we could actually use another short harvest like last year (1976). But the future really looks good, especially in the retail end."

It should. The Berteros have built a nifty new pavilion tasting room, complete with sales and gift shop, that looks out onto seventy-one year old Cabernet Sauvignon vines and, just beyond, the winery and what may be the state's largest live oak tree.

"We've been making a special bottling of the Cabernet (100%) from that 1906 vineyard since 1974," says Angelo. "It's our featured wine, but there's not much of it."

Picnic tables are available under the massive live oak, which experts have estimated to be over 400 years old. Tours of the winery can be arranged by calling ahead.

Thomas Kruse Winery

Thomas Kruse grew up in Chicago. His father was a union organizer and Tom remembers spending summers on a farm in Wisconsin where they made cider. He later majored in English at Northwestern University.

"I worked at an odd succession of jobs before coming to California and entering the wine business," Tom recalls. "I was a truck driver, did steel fabrication, was an escrow officer, and worked as a real estate broker and salesman."

In 1963 he purchased an old cider press at a furniture auction. In California, he reasoned, people make wine, not cider. So he bought some grapes from John Roffinella (whose family has sold grapes to home winemakers since 1920) and fermented a rose′ out of a half ton of Grenache and Zinfandel.

"If that wine hadn't turned out well, I might have quit winemaking then and there. The next year's batch wasn't so hot, though, but I kept trying. I made about four barrels a year and finally came to the conclusion that maybe I could make a living at it."

He purchased an old house and the former winery building (read barn) behind it in 1971. He recalls moving in on the ninth of September and crushing his first vintage twelve days later.

A lanky, angular-jawed young man, Tom Kruse has shown no reluctance at attempting the unusual. He was the first to make and market a Nouveau wine (a Zinfandel) made by carbonic maceration (see label). He'll make a rose′ at the drop of a hat ("A complete dimension of winemaking that is so often overlooked.") and thinks nothing of starting a secondary fermentation with any of his wines. Result: a bone dry, sparkling Zinfandel Rose′ or a Golden Chasselas Champagne. Tom even makes a sparkling Grignolino Rose′ that is alive with flavor.

Tom also made the first *varietal* Thompson Seedless. But that's Alexia's story:

"When I worked with Tom," says Alexia Gadler, "he told me that I had to make a wine all the way through, on my own. So I thought a lot about what I would try. I wanted it to be something different. I was going to make some Rkatsiteli (a Russian variety obtained by the Concannons from the Vivilov Institute), but they didn't have any to spare that year (1974). So, I thought, most of the state's bulk wines have Thompson Seedless in them, but who knows what it really tastes like? So we bought some Thompsons from Mr. Roffinella."

The result was labeled "Alexia Gadler, California, Thompson Seedless." Pale, but not without color, it was a modest and unassuming wine with a hint of grapefruit. And, according to Tom, his retailers had to take two cases of his Cabernet Sauvignon to get one case of the Thompson!

Tom also produces a superb Santa Clara Valley Zinfandel that is light and exceptionally berry-like, with a delightful hint of pepperishness in its aftertaste.

The winery is located at the juncture of Watsonville Road and Hecker Pass Highway, in the shadow of the D'Arrigo Brothers Cactus Pear Farm.

Fortino Winery

Like many Italians who have settled in the Santa Clara Valley, Ernest Fortino's family had made wine in the old country. His grandfather had a small winery in the province of Calabria, but Ernie's father had been born in the United States and yearned to return. In 1959 Michele (pronounced ''Mih-kay-luh'') Fortino brought his family to work the vineyards of California.

After spending ten years in other people's wineries, Ernest and his wife Marie purchased the old Cassa Brothers vineyards and winery in 1970. The winery had been out of production since 1963, due to the death of one brother and the illness (and subsequent death) of the other. Ernie's brother was originally part of the new operation, but soon split the vineyards with Ernie to start his own winery next door.

Ernie and Marie personally welcome visitors to their retail room seven days a week, in addition to running both vineyards and winery. ''I enjoy meeting people,'' he says, ''and it gives me an opportunity to help educate our customers about wine. The biggest problem with the industry today is that the price structure is so unstable. Some wines are too expensive, some are too cheap. The wine business has a wonderful future, but we have to concentrate on making good wines that can sell for reasonable prices.''

Most of Ernie's seventeen wines (including a Charbono and a Grand Noir) are in the $1.99 to $3.25 price range. A robust Barbera, however, brings $3.75, displaying the immense respect Italians have for the variety.

The Fortinos produce around 10,000 cases of wine per year now, but hope to expand the operation to reach an eventual plateau of 30-40,000 cases. ''Whatever we do, though,'' adds Ernie, ''I've got to be able to maintain total control over the quality. If we can reach that size and keep hold of the quality, we'll do it. If we can't, we won't.''

A skilled accordionist in his spare time (''I don't have much!''), Ernie sees the wine industry as a challenge: ''You know, a lot of people get into the business strictly as an investment or as a tax shelter. Some of them make wine by books and machines. We're doing it for a living and we make the wine from our own, personal experience. When I was a kid, we didn't have a choice in our vocation. Your father stomped grapes for a living, *you* stomped grapes for a living. I've done it all my life and I love it. I hope one of my kids will feel the same way, but I won't force them.''

The winery is located on Hecker Pass Road (Highway 152) about five miles west of Gilroy, just past the junction of Watsonville Road. The tasting room, retail store, and gift shop are open daily and Ernie and Marie are happy to show folks around the vineyard and winery. They will even host parties or dinners, with advance notice. They live with wine, they like wine. As Ernest is fond of saying, ''May our wine brighten your mind and strengthen your resolution.''

Hecker Pass Winery

It is a rare treat when winery visitors are able to meet with and talk with the person who grows the grapes and makes and sells the wine. It is rarer still when that person is as warm and as comfortable to be with as Mario Fortino.

Mario does all of those things, and does them well. His speech is direct and sincere. Because of his heavy accent, one is forced to listen intently, but that's not bad.

Mario's grandfather, Joseph, emigrated to the United States, where Mario's father, Michele (known as "Mike") was born in 1905. Joseph worked as a miner in Pittsburg, Kansas. In a cave-in, he was trapped between two rocks and vowed to return his family to Italy if he made it out alive.

In 1911 Joseph started a little winery in the south of Italy, in the town of Cosenza. Many years later, when Mike was required to join the Italian Army (World War II), he lost the American citizenship he had gained at birth. It took eleven years of persistent effort to get through the red tape to regain it. In 1959 Mike moved his own family to Stockton, California. Mario was then twenty-one.

The next year the family moved permanently to Gilroy, to work for the Filices, whose family had also come from Cosenza. After two years in the Filice vineyards, Mario spent thirteen years at San Martin Winery, working at nearly every job the winery had to offer. During that period he also worked two crushes at Paicines for Almaden, all the while gathering the wealth of experience necessary to run a winery from the ground up.

In 1970 Mario and his wife Frances purchased fourteen acres of vineyards and began preparing, part-time, for their own little winery. The building began to go up in 1972 and the winery was bonded for its first crush the following year. It might have been an uneventful first crush but for the fact that Mario had to supervise it with a broken leg. In February of 1975 he left San Martin to devote his energies to his own creation.

In the few years that the winery has been in operation Mario and Frances have garnered a covey of awards from the Los Angeles County Fair. Even a brief examination of his vineyards and winery explain why: both are meticulously cared for and immaculately kept.

Mario ages his wines in small oak barrels. Each is topped every twenty days (most wineries top once a month, many every other month) and sealed with beeswax. He also engages in another practice that well defines his consideration: he fills and corks all his bottles, then allows them to bottle age (several months to a year) *before* labeling and placing the capsules. Why? So he can weed out the case or so in every hundred with bad corks. I know of no other winery using this practice as a matter of course.

The winery is open daily. It is located directly across from what is reputed to be the world's largest cactus pear farm, so it's not hard to find.

Rapazzini Winery

Angelo Rapazzini, born in Milano in 1910, came to California in 1931 after serving three years in the Italian Army. A few years later, he and his bride Vita started an Italian bakery in San Jose, which they operated until 1962. In that year, with their sons Jon and Vic, they took a long term lease on the inactive Perelli-Minetti Winery, three miles south of Gilroy.

In October they opened shop with a limited selection of table wines, featuring a sweet Chenin Blanc. Within a few years, after gauging the interests of his customers, Angelo added a line of fruit and berry wines, which became widely known under the Los Altos Winery label. Dessert wines soon followed.

Operating his own winery was the height of Angelo's dreams, so he chose the Spanish words meaning "the heights": Los Altos. He had no way of knowing that it would be confused with a town of the same name an hour's drive to the north.

His daughter-in-law, Sandra (Jon's wife), remembers his influence: "Angelo didn't speak English well, but people loved to visit him in the tasting room. They always commented on his huge, crystal blue, friendly eyes. He died over five years ago, but people still come in asking for the man with the blue eyes. On the other hand, if someone rubbed him the wrong way he was hell on wheels!"

Jon Rapazzini took over the winery at his father's death in 1972. That year he opened a second tasting room, Rapazzini's Stage Coach Cellars, in an antique complex on the Monterey Highway at Aromas, fifteen miles north of Salinas. This year that tasting room will be closed so that three others can be opened in California. San Diego, Long Beach, and Carmel are the prospective sites.

Vic, who worked with Jon off and on at the winery (he had been a salesman with Paul Masson and United Vintners), sold Jon and Sandra his share of the business a few years ago when he opted for the insurance business.

The Rapazzini's are in the process of phasing out the Los Altos label and the fruit and berry wines as well. They also plan to expand their wholesale and import operations. As importers, they sell Barfede Lambrusco (a sweet, spritzy red), Castle Stra (a rosc'), and Jacob Horz Berncastler Kurfuerstenlay, a soft, sweet white wine.

Rapazzini Winery offers about as complete a wine list as any in the state. There are varietal and generic white, red, and rose' table wines. There are sparkling and dessert wines, brandy and cordials. There are fruit, berry, and special natural wines, including Mead (honey) and Ambrosia (a sweet wine flavored with citrus fruits).

The winery is located on the east side of the Monterey Highway (U.S. 101), south of Gilroy. Nearly all of the Rapazzini wines are available for tasting from nine to six daily (until seven in the summer). The tasting room has an extensive gift shop and is closed on major holidays.

Other Wineries

The Conrotto Winery is one of a dying breed, those smaller wineries whose owners are content to produce a red and a white, for their friends and a few long time restaurant and retail store accounts, and nothing else. No boutique status, no spectacular varietals, no charismatic winemaker. Just buy the best grapes you can get and make the best wines you can make, because that's what you do best.

The winery was founded by Anselmo Conrotto at the termination of Prohibition. The winery was built on two levels, to take advantage of the earth's pull, and Anselmo's son, Chinto, still finds it perfectly adequate. A former collegiate footballer, Chinto and his son-in-law, Jim Burr, continue to make a burgundy and a chablis in half gallons and gallons for the restaurant trade, retail stores, and family friends.

PETER AND HARRY GIRETTI WINERY

Harry Giretti is a gnarled and crusty old fellow who speaks of past and present in salty, forthright terms. He blames Prohibition on women's suffrage, asserts that there were more alcoholics then than now, and blithely states that everybody bootlegged during those difficult fourteen years.

"We had property taxes to pay and children to feed. The 'revenooers' knew it and we knew it and everybody got along as best they could," he says.

Harry is winemaker and his brother, Peter, handles the books. Their Burchell Road winery, built in 1912 (the year of Harry's birth), is a ramshackle barn with a dirt floor and, asserts Harry proudly, remains unchanged in its sixty-plus years. The only wine made--a red made of Zinfandel, Carignane, Mission, and Grenache--is sold directly to family trade in five gallon carboys and 25 or 50 gallon barrels.

"Nothing fancy," says Harry. "No yeast, no SO2, no fining, no filtration. Drinking wine!"

La Purisima Winery
from the monterey county vineyards of
Arroyo Seco Farming Company
Los Coches Road, Greenfield, California
1976 Nouveau
California
Gamay Beaujolais
Lot Number 19
Table wine produced and bottled by
La Purisima Winery, Sunnyvale, California

You might think it strange to walk into a winery through pneumatic, supermarket doors. It is strange. But that's how you must enter La Purisima Winery, because that's exactly what the building used to house: a supermarket! It took an imaginative eye to visualize cooperage and a lunch area where produce and cereals used to reside, wine and cheese storage in the cold rooms, a tasting area where the liquor department used to be, and crushers and fermenters in the back storeroom.

"It's a hard concept to get across to people," explains Doug Watson, winemaster and general partner. "People just don't expect to see a winery in a downtown area, close to people, without acres of vineyards surrounding the building.

Doug Watson (actually Doug Watson IV, but he dislikes the designation) and his father, Doug Watson, Sr., are the owners of La Purisima, so named in tribute to California's Spanish heritage. They opened the doors to the public on July 10, 1976 and crushed their first grapes there that fall. The Watsons own ten acres of vineyards in the Napa Valley, near St. Helena. They also buy some grapes and purchase bulk wine to age and blend for their label.

''A big problem with larger wineries, I would even go so far as to call it a constraint, is the necessity of owning vineyards, so as to balance out the ups and downs of the market,'' says Doug. ''For us it's much simpler to be able to buy grapes under contract, and get specifically what we're looking for, or purchase bulk wines already made.''

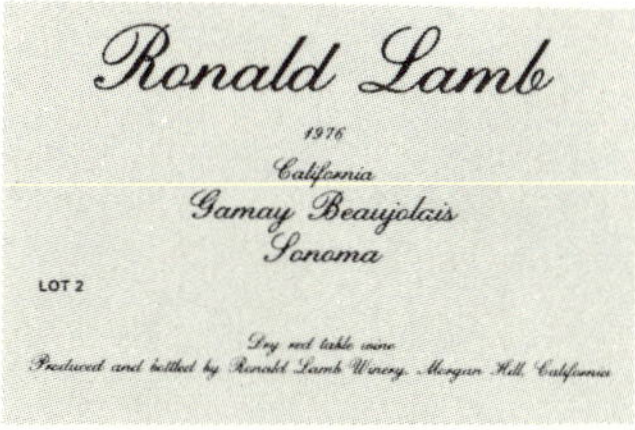

Ron and Aldrene Lamb claim that theirs is the smallest winery in the state. Snugly situated in a 400 square foot garage behind their Morgan Hill home, storage capacity is only 2000 gallons, so the claim seems a valid one.

Ron has several years of experience in wine sales and has been making wine at home for four years. ''They were pretty good,'' he says matter-of-factly. ''Better than many I could buy.''

The first crush for the fledgling winery was 1976, when Gamay Beaujolais, Pinot Noir, Zinfandel, and Cabernet Sauvignon were made. Lamb's next projects are a white Zinfandel and a Beaujolais Blanc (from the Gamay Beaujolais grape). ''It helps to have something different. You can establish an identity quicker.''

The Lambs released their first wine, the Gamay Beaujolais (only 22 cases were made), in June, 1977. Ron stresses that the winery will not have a tasting room, a gift shop, or any pong video games.

SOMMELIER WINERY

After twenty years of home winemaking, Richard ''Dick'' Keezer decided that he'd like to try it on a larger scale. A chemical engineer who does research in materials science, Dick and a fellow scientist, Robert Burnham, joined forces to start Sommelier Winery.

They rented space in a concrete block industrial complex between El Camino and Highway 101 in Mountain View. The building required little insulation to bring it up to snuff for its new use. With fermentation tanks of their own design (featuring ''316'' stainless steel and square, bolted-on portholes), they crushed forty-six tons during their maiden harvest of 1976.

Several varieties were made, including Cabernet Sauvignon, Ruby Cabernet, Zinfandel, and a red Grenache. Keezer and Burnham intend to make only red wines that are ''big, tough wines.'' All will be aged in recycled, well-cared-for, American oak barrels.

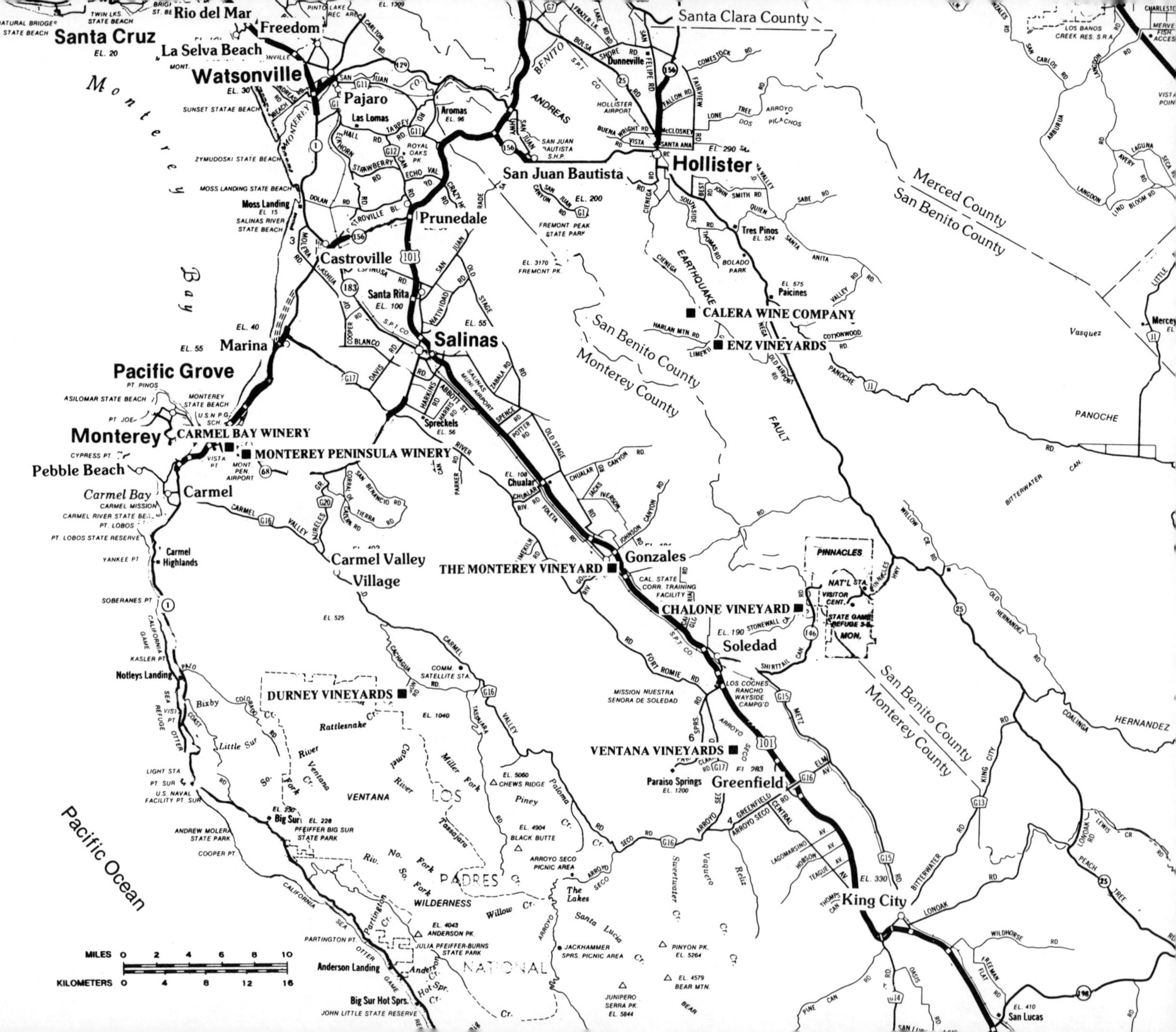

Santa Cruz
Rio del Mar
Freedom
La Selva Beach
Watsonville
Pajaro
Las Lomas
Aromas
Santa Clara County
Dunneville
Hollister
San Juan Bautista
Monterey Bay
Moss Landing
Castroville
Prunedale
Santa Rita
Salinas
Marina
Pacific Grove
Monterey
CARMEL BAY WINERY
MONTEREY PENINSULA WINERY
Pebble Beach
Carmel Bay
Carmel
Carmel Highlands
Carmel Valley Village
Spreckels
Chualar
Gonzales
THE MONTEREY VINEYARD
CHALONE VINEYARD
Soledad
Tres Pinos
Paicines
CALERA WINE COMPANY
ENZ VINEYARDS
Merced County
San Benito County
Monterey County
EARTHQUAKE
FAULT
Vasquez
PANOCHE
PINNACLES
NAT'L STA.
VISITOR CENT.
MON.
DURNEY VINEYARDS
VENTANA VINEYARDS
Paraiso Springs
Greenfield
King City
San Lucas
Notleys Landing
Big Sur
Anderson Landing
Big Sur Hot Sprs.
Pacific Ocean
VENTANA
WILDERNESS
LOS
PADRES
NATIONAL
MILES 0 2 4 6 8 10
KILOMETERS 0 4 8 12 16

Monterey -
San Benito Counties

Enz Vineyards

Susan Enz was born in Tennessee, but didn't stay long. Her father was in the construction business. Bob Enz, Sue's husband, was a civil engineer, having graduated from Colorado State University. After working jobs in the San Francisco Bay Area--including the San Luis Dam project near the Pacheco Pass--Bob decided that moving all the time wasn't the best thing for their four children, now aged from seven to fifteen.

So, in 1967, Susan started looking for a small, five acre ranch in the Hollister area. Just something nice for the children. She ended up buying a 278 acre ranch, with vineyards, at the end of Limekiln Road, in the Cienega district south of Hollister! Since then they have added an adjoining ranch for a total of 750 acres.

Bob's occupation took him to work on the Bay Area Rapid Transit, then into his own firm with a friend. The Enzes continued the practice of selling the ranch's grapes. In 1972 Bob sold his interest in the firm to his partner and began building a small winery. He urethaned the interior of an old redwood barn and built a laboratory and office in its hay loft. Later a Soule' Building was added and a small bottling line built.

The property was once a huge limestone quarry, and some of the original lime kilns are still standing. Several stone foundations also remain, a silent reminder of the days when the quarry was a thriving operation, the railroads came up the valley to the kilns, and over a hundred homes housed the workers.

Vines had been planted as early as 1887 next door to the Enz vineyards. In 1895 Nels Peterson put vines into the coarse, granitic soil on the Enz property. A half acre of Pinot St. George, planted at that time, is still in production.

The first wines were made by Bob and Sue Enz in 1973 and sold to nearby Almaden. The next year they made wines for their own label, a distinctive one with an up-jutting crown displaying the Enz coat of arms. Made under that label are Zinfandel, Zinfandel Rose', Pinot St. George, Golden Chasselas, Burgundy, Chablis, and Rose'. They also do a good deal of private labeling--house wines for such Monterey restaurants as The Sardine Factory, the Old Bath House, and Neil DeVaughn's. Most of the wines sold retail also go to the Monterey Peninsular area.

In the Bicentennial year, Enz scored a coup when his wines were selected by the Imperial Hotel in Tokyo to be served there at the hotel's 4th of July celebration.

When we talk of the Enzes we mean the whole family, because everybody pitches in to do the vineyard and winery work, including tasting and evaluation. The Enzes plan to expand their vineyard plantings slowly, hoping to eventually reach between 100 and 150 acres. Also included in future plans is a tasting room, possibly to be erected upon one of the stone foundations left by Chinese limekiln workers.

Monterey Peninsula Winery

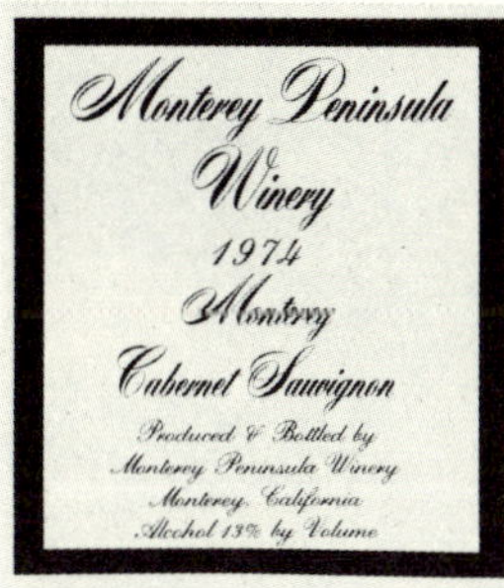

Where other areas have their Vintage and Harvest festivals, the Monterey Peninsula Winery holds an annual "Wine Stomp." The Stomp is what the name implies. Each year, in late September or early October, depending upon how the vintage is progressing, some 300 people will gather at the winery to crush ten tons of grapes by pedestrian means.

The Stomp is a party, with food, wine, and music, but it also serves as a fund raiser for several local charities, which rotate each year. Incidentally, the wine made at the event is kept as a separate lot and released under a "Stomp" label.

The Monterey Peninsula Winery is located immediately west of the junction of Canyon Del Rey and Monterey-Salinas Highway (State Routes 218 and 68 respectively). It is housed in a sprawling, multi-leveled stone complex which is directly in line with the approach pattern at the Monterey Peninsula Airport.

The stone walls are over five feet thick in places and a sixty foot cave tunnels just off the tasting room. The building, part of the former Rancho Saucito, was built stone by stone over a period of 35 years and completed in the 1920's. Seven springs lie on the property, pouring forth water even in the midst of California's worst drought. The pocket valley surrounding the winery has weather that is warmer and more clear than the Monterey Bay area in general, thus being a natural site for the nearby airport.

Roy Thomas and Dick Nuckton (both dentists), along with another friend, Robert Zampatti, had all made wine as amateurs. They decided, in June of 1974, to make the move to professional status. They leased the building and had their first crush and Stomp that fall.

Monterey Peninsula's wines are made as naturally as possible, without fining or filtration, in an attempt to stay as close to the grape as possible. Naturally, many of the reds are huge, muscular wines. They are made in small lots, with vineyards often kept separate. Much experimenting is done. In 1974, three lots of Riesling were made from Pleasanton grapes: one aged without oak, one with American oak, and one with French oak.

If one must characterize the winery, the word would be Zinfandel, for Monterey Peninsula has many different shades of the variety. At least six were offered at the beginning of 1977, including an Amador "Essence" and another Amador subtitled "Big Jim," for vineyardist Jim D'Agostini.

The winery also makes wine under its second label, Monterey Cellars. Included in this line are some outstanding fruit and berry wines, all three of which won medals at the 1976 Los Angeles County Fair. The Plum wine is of particular note.

Monterey Peninsula offers tasting at the winery as well as at a second location, in Carmel. Called "Gifts of Bacchus," it is located on 6th Avenue, between Dolores and Lincoln.

The Monterey Vineyard

It is the general mode for a new winery to start small, establish itself in the marketplace, and then gradually increase its production toward an optimum size. Not so The Monterey Vineyard, which came forth full-formed at its 1974 birth as a two million gallon winery with contracts for nine thousand acres of vineyards.

Though the winery had no *growing* pains, it experienced marketing and internal difficulties, attributable perhaps to the number and diversity of its vineyard partnerships (fourteen at one point). After the dissolution of its marketing arm, the severing of its vineyard contracts, and the presence of many rumors, The Monterey Vineyard was sold, in March 1977, to Richard G. "Dick" Peterson and Dan Lucas. That November it was purchased by Coca Cola of Atlanta, the firm that had acquired Sterling Vineyards of Napa Valley only three months earlier.

It has been Peterson, as winemaker and president, who has maintained the winery's direction through the difficulties. For, despite the side issues, The Monterey Vineyard is a dominant figure in the present and future of winemaking in Monterey County. It is, today, one of only a handful of bonded wineries in a county which boasts the largest wine grape acreage of any of the coastal counties.

A graduate of Iowa State University, Peterson later received a master's in food technology and a doctorate in agricultural chemistry from the University of California at Berkeley. It was while working with Maynard A. Joslyn at Berkeley that Dick began to consider the wine industry as a vocation.

After ten years with Gallo and six seasons at Beaulieu (Napa Valley), Dick accepted the challenge of a whole new region and winery. He was instrumental in both design and construction phases of the large but elegant winery building, which is graced by 25 foot high stained glass windows, created by his professionally artistic wife, Diane.

A large part of The Monterey Vineyard's operations is contract crushing. Though this involves crushing lots of grapes for more than a dozen other wineries (including some of the most prestigious names in the business), The Monterey Vineyard cannot be characterized as a "bulk" operation. With the lone exception of of their own label's "Del Mar Ranch" (a blend of Pinot Blanc and Chenin Blanc, with a touch of Sylvaner), the winery deals exclusively in vintage-dated varietals.

Dr. Peterson says that he is thrilled by making unique wines, "making something that nobody else has made!" With The Monterey Vineyard he has already created two highly distinctive wines. His first was the 1974 "December" Zinfandel. He had to wait out a plot of grapes that were not ripening in predictable fashion, the acid remaining abnormally high until December 6th. The wine turned out lusty, yet fruity. The second is a luscious, botrytised Sauvignon Blanc.

Chalone Vineyard

Vineyards were first planted in the limestone soils at the western base of the basalt Pinnacles formations in 1919 by Will Silvear. A brilliant man, whose love of genetics led him to the development of a new strain of capons, he had hoped to make great sparkling wines. Among the early varieties planted were Pinot Noir, Chardonnay, Chenin Blanc, and Pinot Blanc. Indeed, in the 1940's, sparkling wines were made at Almaden from Silvear's fruit.

Chalone Vineyard as a winery, however, dates only from 1960. Yet in so short a time it has had a tumultuous history. Two San Franciscans, Dr. Edward Liska, a psychiatrist, and Jack Sigman, a stockbroker, purchased the property in the late fifties. In 1960 they hired Philip Togni (now with Cuvaison) to supervise their initial crush. He made Chardonnay, Pinot Noir, Pinot Blanc, and Chenin Blanc and suggested the mountain's Indian name, Chalone, for the winery. The name took, but few wines were made again until 1966.

Dr. Liska sold his interest to Sigman, starting a whole string of events, resulting in strange sales and, eventually, in the tangle of a court battle. In the meantime the grapes went to Windsor Vineyards (Rod Strong) for a while, and later to Mirassou.

In 1966 Richard "Dick" Graff, with money borrowed from his mother, got the winery going again. The court battle was still to come and the 1968 vintage would be lost, but by 1969 Gavilan Vineyards, Inc. had been formed to put the winery on a sound footing. Within two years Dick's younger brothers--John and Peter--joined the operation. John, with a doctorate in chemistry from the University of Chicago, became the winemaker; Peter, a Davis graduate in plant science was a natural to handle the vineyards. The new team was rounded out by the addition of president and managing partner Phil Woodward, a refugee from Detroit and a CPA's desk.

Shortly thereafter a new winery went up, designed and built by Dick Graff and Roland Masse. Completed in 1974, it replaced the former brooding shed used by Philip Togni.

The corporation owns 125 acres of vineyards, planted to Chardonnay, Pinot Noir, Chenin Blanc, and Pinot Blanc. Some of the vines are from the original planting.

The winery's cooperage is French oak and its style is decidedly Burgundian. Dick recalls that it was exceedingly difficult to get information on the care of French oak when he first obtained the barrels. He finally decided it would be most expedient just to go to France. So he did.

Dick Graff is a thin, animated, Harvard grad whose blue eyes sparkle when he's talking wine. It is his ambition to preside over the definitive California Burgundy wines. Anything that does not meet winery standards is bottled under the Gavilan Vineyards label. Limestone soil, low rainfall, and low cropping levels (two tons per acre at maximum) insure that there will not be a lot of wine for the secondary label.

Other Wineries

CALERA WINE COMPANY

Josh Jensen lived in Europe, working a couple of harvests in Burgundy, after taking a degree in history at Yale and another in anthropology at Oxford. He returned home with the thought of finding a plot of limestone soil capable of producing Pinot Noir grapes in the Burgundian manner.

''With Pinot Noir,'' he asserts, ''soil--limestone soil--is everything! But there's not a lot of limestone in California. I looked at one belt in the Sierra foothills that reminded me of the Cote d'Or.'' Josh finally settled on a spot 12 miles south of Hollister and 18 miles north of the Pinnacles. At a 2200 foot elevation he planted one acre in 1974 and another twenty-three acres the following year. (Calera is Spanish for limekiln. Jensen's land is the site of an abandoned limestone quarry and kiln.)

CARMEL BAY WINERY

Thus far, stockbroker Fred Crummey has resisted all attempts to coerce him into calling his new business the ''Crummey Winery.'' At any rate, Carmel Bay Winery is the name Fred and his partner, school teacher Bob Eyerman, have chosen to go with in crushing their first grapes in 1977.

The pair have been amateur winemakers for five years and see the winery as an opportunity to ''get our hobby out of the garage.'' Out of the garage and into a hanger is the whole phrase, for the new winery is located in a 1000 square foot abandoned Navy hanger at the Monterey Peninsula Airport.

With vineyards established nearly a decade ago, William W. Durney has finally decided to make an entrance into the field of winemaking. The president and owner of Carnation Sea Food, he has ranched his Carmel Valley acreage since the early fifties. He ran Belted Galloways (a rare breed of cattle in North America) on the ranch before turning to grapes in 1968, when sixty acres were planted to Cabernet Sauvignon, Gamay Beaujolais, Chenin Blanc, and White Riesling.

VENTANA VINEYARDS

Doug Meador feels that Monterey won't really come into its own as a part of wine country until it has boutique wineries ''scattered around the county.'' He intends for Ventana to be one of those wineries, complete with tasting room.

An ex-Navy pilot, Meador has been farming grapes for five years. He owns 300 acres south of Soledad and is a partner in an adjoining 300 acres. Primary varieties are Pinot Noir, Cabernet Sauvignon, and Chardonnay. He says that the Chardonnay makes a flinty, greenish wine, much like those of French Chablis. As the vines are in rocky, gravelly soils, that is hardly surprising.

Doug expected to be bonded in 1977 and to crush a bit less than a thousand gallons,

San Luis Obispo-
Santa Barbara
Counties

ESTRELLA RIVER VINEYARDS
CONTINENTAL VINTNERS
HOFFMAN MOUNTAIN RANCH VINEYARDS
ROTTA WINERY
PESENTI WINERY
YORK MOUNTAIN WINERY
San Miguel
EL. 620
Estrella
EL. 760
Cholame
EL. 1150
EL. 2000
COTTONWOOD SUMMIT
POLONIO PASS
EL. 1765
NACIMIENTO RES. REC. AREA
EL. 800
Shandon
EL. 1035
Paso Robles
Klau
San Simeon
SAN SIMEON PT
WILLIAM RANDOLPH HEARST MEM. ST. BEACH
HEARST-SAN SIMEON S.H.M. (ADMISSION OFFICE)
(CASTLE)
PIEDRAS BLANCAS PT
SAN SIMEON STATE BEACH
EL. 60
Cambria
Cambria Pines
CAMBRIA AIR FORCE STA.
Harmony
Atascadero
ATASCADERO LK. CO. PARK
DEVIL'S GAP
CURBARIL AV.
STATE HOSP.
Creston
EL. 1110
San Luis Obispo County
PT. ESTERO
Cayucos
MORRO STRAND STATE BEACH
Estero
Morro Beach
ATASCADERO STATE BEACH
MORO ROCK
Morro Bay
MORRO BAY STATE PARK
Baywood Park
Los Osos
Cuesta by the Sea
LOS OSOS OAKS STATE RESERVE
MONTANA DE ORO STATE PARK
PT. BUCHON
Pacific Ocean
Santa Margarita
EL. 1000
LA CUESTA SUMMIT
EL. 1522
SANTA MARGARITA LAKE REC. AREA
Pozo
EL. 1450
San Luis Obispo
EL. 230
MISSION SAN LUIS OBISPO
CAMP SAN LUIS OBISPO
HI MTN. LOOKOUT
EL. 3198
LOPEZ LAKE RECREATION AREA
SAN LUIS OBISPO AIRPORT
Edna
EL. 300
Avila Beach
EL. 80
Port San Luis
AVILA STATE BEACH
LIGHT STATION
PT. SAN LUIS
San Luis Obispo Bay
Shell Beach
EL. 95
Pismo Beach
EL. 70
Grover City
Fair Oaks
Halcyon
Oceano
Aroyo Grande
EL. 114
Los Berros
EL. 215
PISMO DUNES PRESERVE
STATE VEHICULAR REC. AREA
Nipomo
EL. 320
NIPOMO REG. CO. PARK
LEROY CO. PARK
Santa Maria
Guadalupe
TWITCHELL DAM
COLSON PICNIC AREA
SIERRA MADRE PICNIC AREA
Cuyama
101
1
41
46
58
166
227
135
MILES 0 2 4 6 8
KILOMETERS 0 4 8 12

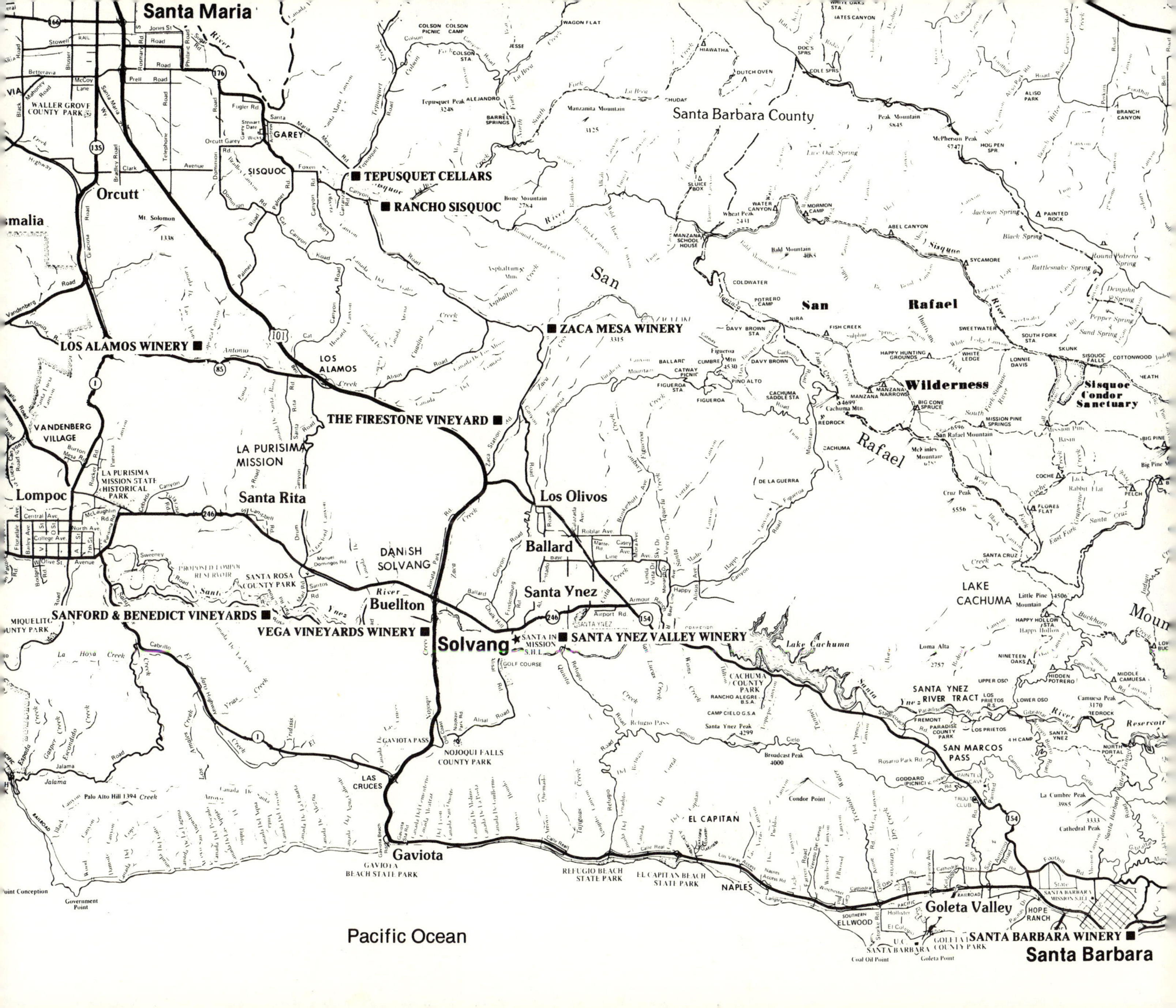

Santa Maria
Santa Barbara County
TEPUSQUET CELLARS
RANCHO SISQUOC
Orcutt
SISQUOC
GAREY
WALLER GROVE COUNTY PARK
ZACA MESA WINERY
LOS ALAMOS WINERY
LOS ALAMOS
THE FIRESTONE VINEYARD
VANDENBERG VILLAGE
LA PURISIMA MISSION
LA PURISIMA MISSION STATE HISTORICAL PARK
Lompoc
Santa Rita
Los Olivos
Ballard
DANISH SOLVANG
Buellton
Santa Ynez
SANFORD & BENEDICT VINEYARDS
VEGA VINEYARDS WINERY
Solvang
SANTA YNEZ VALLEY WINERY
SANTA INES MISSION S.H.L.
SANTA ROSA COUNTY PARK
PROPOSED LOMPOC RESERVOIR
San Rafael
San Rafael Wilderness
Sisquoc Condor Sanctuary
LAKE CACHUMA
Lake Cachuma
CACHUMA COUNTY PARK
SANTA YNEZ RIVER TRACT
SAN MARCOS PASS
NOJOQUI FALLS COUNTY PARK
GAVIOTA PASS
LAS CRUCES
Gaviota
GAVIOTA BEACH STATE PARK
REFUGIO BEACH STATE PARK
EL CAPITAN
EL CAPITAN BEACH STATE PARK
NAPLES
ELLWOOD
Goleta Valley
HOPE RANCH
SANTA BARBARA MISSION S.H.L.
SANTA BARBARA WINERY
Santa Barbara
U.C. SANTA BARBARA
GOLETA COUNTY PARK
Goleta Point
Coal Oil Point
Point Conception
Government Point
Pacific Ocean

Hoffman Mountain Ranch Vineyards

His color photograph hangs in the main residence and in the lab. His imprint extends throughout the winery, in its design, in its style. "We consider ourselves students of his," says David Hoffman. "Everything we do is done under his guidance."

Though "he" is not spelled with a capital "h," it is no matter, for the reference is to Andre Tchelistcheff, unquestionably the dean of California winemakers. And it is he, again unquestionably, who is responsible for bringing Hoffman Mountain Ranch wines into almost immediate credibility in an ever-increasingly competitive business.

Cardiologist Stanley Hoffman purchased the 1200 acre almond and walnut ranch in 1961. (Two hundred acres have since been sold off.) He intended to retire to the life of a country doctor, tend some grapes, and make a little wine each fall. It didn't work out that way. Paso Robles, like any country town, was in woefully short supply of cardiologists. So Dr. Hoffman found himself as busy as ever.

Fortunately, two able-bodied sons were waiting in the wings. In 1965 and 1967, 62 acres of Chardonnay, Pinot Noir, Cabernet Sauvignon, and Franken (Sylvaner) Riesling were planted. In 1974 a drip irrigation system was installed to supplement an annual rainfall of between 25 and 30 inches. An additional fifty acres of Pinot Noir, Chardonnay, and Cabernet will be planted in 1978 or 1979, depending upon the availability of water.

The elevation varies at different locations on the Hoffman ranch, located in the eastern foothills of the Santa Lucia Mountain Range. From 1500 to 1800 feet is David's best guess on an area with several microclimates, averaging about 3000 heat degree days per season (from high Region II to low Region III). The soils are the key, however. They are shallow, gravelly, with a good deal of lime shell. Tchelistcheff refers to the area as a "jewel of ecological elements."

The proof of any such claim lies, of course, in the wines. Thus far, the statement is sound. The first wines were made in 1972 in a small building adjacent to Dr. Hoffman's garage. The following year brought Tchelistcheff into the picture, resulting in a Chardonnay (1973 vintage) which was a gold medal winner at the 1975 International Wine Competition in London.

By 1975, Michael Hoffman was making the wines in a spacious, airy, partially open-to-the-elements redwood facility. The bottling line is glass enclosed and looks out over an almond grove on the opposite hillside. On the same, open level are two rows of stainless steel, jacketed Mueller tanks. The lower level, which follows the natural slant of the hillside, encloses over 30,000 gallons of oak cooperage.

Chardonnays are fermented in French oak and possess an exquisite grapefruit-like quality. Cabernet Sauvignons, aged in American and French oak, are flavorful and long in finish. Pinot Noirs are fermented with stems to add body to their already rich character.

Pesenti Winery

Pesenti Winery, though it produces 100,000 cases of wine annually, can still be classified as a ''district winery,'' one whose distribution is confined to a limited area near the winery itself. Most of its wines, in fact, are sold within San Luis Obispo County, though Bakersfield, a hundred miles to the east, and northern Santa Barbara County are also major markets.

Victor Pesenti's 65 acres of Zinfandel supply but a fraction of the winery's needs, so grapes and wines must be purchased. As Pesenti offers the widest possible range of wines, he draws on the resources of wineries like Weibel, San Martin, and Gibson to flesh out his popular line.

Victor's father, Frank Pesenti, first planted vines near Templeton in 1923. Though Prohibition was in its early years, grapes were in great demand. At the termination of the ''Noble Experiment '' Frank built and licensed a winery. Additions were made in 1941 and 1947 to keep pace with consumer demand. After serving in the Army during World War II and participating in the Invasion of Sicily, Victor returned home to the family business. His father continued working at the winery until the late sixties.

The winery's marketing comes under the supervision of Aldo Nerelli, vice president and general manager. Nerelli, who worked for a San Luis Obispo wholesale liquor distributor before leaving with his two brothers for World War II, returned to marry Frank Pesenti's daughter and join the winery family. Nerelli's own family had operated the Templeton Winery, at the foot of York Mountain, from Repeal until the war. Aldo's son, Frank, and Victor's sons, Steven and Michael--all active at the winery--are expected to carry on the family winegrowing traditions.

Zinfandel is the prime stock in trade of the winery. Though his vineyards are immediately adjacent to the winery, Victor nevertheless uses a Mortl System field crusher-stemmer to insure that his Zinfandel is as fresh as possible in preparation for its many uses. Under both his ''Pesenti'' and ''FP'' labels, Victor bottles dry, sweet, and rose' Zinfandels. Victor believes he might have been the first to commercially produce a Zinfandel Rose' in California, having started in the early sixties.

A friendly, outgoing person, Victor Pesenti spends a good deal of time waiting upon customers in his brightly decorated tasting room. He attests to the validity of the tasting phenomenon whereby people talk dry and drink sweet, offering as evidence the fact that his Sweet Zinfandel and Chateau d'Oro (a sweet white) are big sellers. In addition to his wines, Victor also offers nuts, books, wine glasses, T-shirts, and baseball caps (the last three with the winery's name imprinted) in the tasting room.

Pesenti welcomes visitors. The tasting and sales room is open daily from eight until six, Sunday from ten to six. Take the Vineyard Drive exit west from Highway 101, about seven miles south of Paso Robles. Tours will be given upon prior request.

York Mountain Winery

York Mountain Winery was founded in 1882. It has had a new owner since late 1970, a man not new to the business of winemaking. At that time, Max Goldman purchased the property from Wilfrid York, grandson of founder Andrew York.

After graduating from Whittier College in 1933 with a degree in chemistry and physics, Max Goldman started a distinguished career in winemaking and management that has spanned over forty years to date. He has worked at Roma, Petri, Sanger Cellars, United Vintners, Waterford Winery, and Great Western. He has also spent seven years with Bohemian Distributing Company, been president of the American Society of Enologists, and currently serves on the board of directors of the Wine Institute.

Goldman says that he jumped at the opportunity to have his own winery. He has much work to do to restore both vineyards and winery, which are seven miles from the Pacific and 1500 feet above sea level. Old vines are being uprooted and a conservation program instituted to reclaim soil lost to severe erosion. Annual rainfall ranges from 45 to 60 inches and culverts were up to eight feet deep.

A five acre test plot has been planted while the land is farmed to grains and grasses to restore the hillsides. Chardonnay, Pinot Noir, Cabernet, Gamay Beaujolais, and Zinfandel are being observed before the seventy acres available for vines will be planted. When planting does get under way, it will be done in small segments and will likely be completed by the middle of the next decade.

Max's son Steve is making the wines. Previously a student of graphic design, Steve is learning by doing, under his father's supervision. In what has always been a strong Zinfandel region, that variety will pace a wine list that will eventually be composed of four reds, four whites, and, perhaps, a couple of sparkling wines. The reds will be Zinfandel, Pinot Noir, Cabernet Sauvignon, and a generic. The whites will be Chardonnay, Chenin Blanc, either White Riesling or Pinot Blanc, and a generic.

The winery itself has grown around the original building of stone, which measures about 25 by 40. Some of the original redwood tanks are still in use, but Steve contends that they were second hand when installed at what was then called Ascension Winery. In 1892 the winery was enlarged, using bricks made from clay found on the property. The thick redwood columns supporting the second floor of the addition came from the pier at Cambria, after steamship lines were put out of business by the arrival of Southern Pacific Railroad in the latter half of the last century.

York Mountain wines are in limited distribution, mostly to local restaurants and wine shops. The Goldmans are intent upon building up an inventory of aged wines before seeking distribution in Los Angeles and the San Francisco Bay Area. Most of the wines are sold in the tasting room at the winery, where a log is always flaming on the hearth to ward off the lingering chill of the mountain nights.

Los Alamos Winery

Mary Vigoroso was born in Boston. When she was three, her father moved the family to Italy where Mary's grandfather had a vineyard and sold winc. Thcy would remain there nine years, through the First World War. Mary remembers learning about wine even then: ''When the harvest came, as long as you could walk, you learned to make wine, from beginning to end. We crushed the grapes with our feet, and that's the God's honest truth!''

In 1923 the family returned to Massachusetts. Mary's father worked as a laborer and farm hand: ''Anything to get bread in the house,'' as she recalls. And she helped make wines for the family's use during Prohibition.

Now, over half a century later, Mary Vigoroso is the winemaker, tour guide, and salesperson of a small winery owned by her son-in-law, Los Angeles attorney Samuel D. Hale, Jr.

Hale and a partner had purchased a vineyard near Paso Robles in 1968, but Hale later sold his share to purchase a 680 acre ranch in the Los Alamos Valley, four miles west of Los Alamos, in 1971. The following year, under the supervision of viticulturist Dale Hampton, 350 acres were planted to Cabernet Sauvignon, Pinot Noir, Gamay Beaujolais, Merlot, Chardonnay, and White Riesling.

A working oil well sits conspicuously in the midst of vine rows, which are adjacent to the tin roofed, concrete block winery. The building is the former Jensen Dairy. Oval stainless steel dairy tanks are set along one wall, a basket press rests in a corner, and a row of French oak casks faces the dairy tanks.

Mary Vigoroso and Sam Hale made their first wines in 1974--2500 gallons of Cabernet, Pinot Noir, Zinfandel, Chardonnay, and White Riesling. The grapes that they were unable to use were sold to other wineries. Since then, because of the winery's limited capacity, several of the wines have been made for Los Alamos by The Monterey Vineyard.

Mrs. Vigoroso's Zinfandels are most characteristic of the winery's style. They are big, heavy wines, yet retain their native fruitiness. The 1975 vintage, which sells for five dollars a fifth, was harvested late (26 Brix, 0.9 acid). A huge wine, it is smooth and has lost no flavor to alcohol.

Mary Vigoroso makes no apologies for her style. She admits that it's old fashioned winemaking: ''A light wine seems like water to me. I like heavy, full-bodied wines. That's the way I was taught. They use good terminology these days, but it's all the same as it was in Italy. I have a personal feeling about every one of the wines I make.''

A genuinely friendly lady, she welcomes visitors to the winery, but requests that they call ahead to make sure that she is going to be there. Los Alamos is one of the last areas in the state to have toll stations, so that one must dial ''Operator'' and ask for Area Code 805, Los Alamos 2391. It's a novel experience for those who never knew the early days of the telephone.

The Firestone Vineyard

It won't be long before the phrase "Ask a friend about Firestone" will have become a piece of American folklore and humor. Originally intended for the oft-advertised tire and rubber company, it may easily find a wider, more popular use in reference to the wines of A. Brooks Firestone, scion of former United States Ambassador to Belgium, Leonard K. Firestone.

To be sure, Brooks Firestone paid his dues to the family business; twelve years worth. But it wasn't quite right. In 1972 his father made a commitment to wine grapes. He chose the Santa Ynez Valley, an unsullied Eden between Santa Barbara and San Luis Obispo. "I had always liked California," says Brooks. "The research looked good on the area, the budget looked good, but the big question was, 'Where do we sell the grapes?'"

The winery was thus born of a tripartite partnership between Brooks, his father, and Leonard's close friend Keizo Saji, chairman of the board of Japan's largest producer of wines and spirits, Suntory, Ltd.

"I was my own contractor on the winery," notes Brooks. "We decided what we wanted *in* the winery, then clothed it in an architectural building. It wasn't cheap, but we didn't make any mistakes." We're looking at a long period of investment and our financial situation is such that we can last and won't be pressured into rapid, uncontrolled growth."

Firestone--lank, angular-jawed, suntanned--feels that the winery will be defined, in size and quality, by the vineyards. Nearly three hundred acres encircle the winery. Over a third of the acreage is planted to Cabernet Suavignon; equal sections are planted to Merlot, Johannisberg Riesling, and Pinot Noir; there are lesser plots of Chardonnay and Gewurztrasminer.

Tony Austin, a quiet, ingenuous young man, is Firestone's choice for winemaker. Formerly with Simi, Austin joined Brooks in the fall of 1974. "I was fortunate to be able to work with designer Dick Keith through the design phase," Austin recalls. "I was able to set up the 'process flow'--where things move and how--so that I could best control it all as winemaker. I can see everything in the winery from the lab ."

The wines are showing the care, attention, and artistry of the two men. Austin has an infectious enthusiasm for his Pinot Noir. Grown in an outwash of gravel bar and lime and aged in Burgundian oak, it reaches a ripe, rich maturity in the glass. Brooks is proud of his 1976, botrytised Johannisberg. With lower than normal alcohol and 2.4 percent residual sugar, the wine tastes of apricots and peaches.

The Firestone Winery has an innovative label program. The labels will change with each varietal, each year. Brooks has commissioned artist Sebastian Titus to create these labels. Sebastian will record the development of the winery, and try to capture the different moods of the winemaking procedures and surrounding landscape.

Sanford & Benedict Vineyards

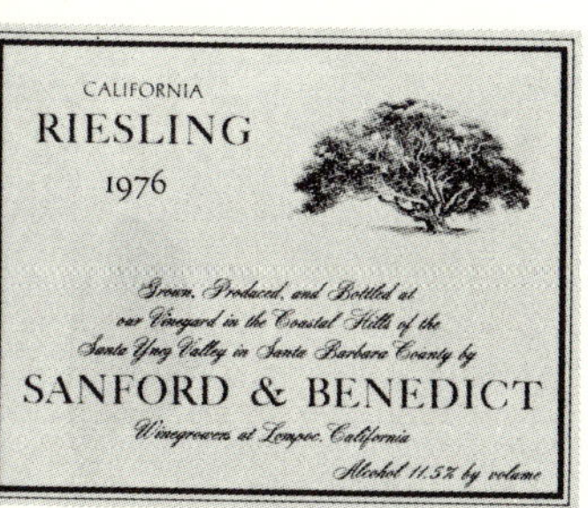

Sanford & Benedict Vineyards was founded in the winter of 1970 by Richard Sanford and Michael Benedict, primarily as an outgrowth of a a series of discussions they had about wines in general and more specifically about how the physical situation of various European vineyards affected the quality of the wines they produced.

The partners had been pursuing other careers: Sanford as the head of a small television production company and Benedict as a member of the faculty at the University of California, Santa Barbara, where the two had originally met as students.

The partners' discussions about wine produced a series of concepts which had irresistible appeal for them as the fundamentals of a great adventure. The concepts were basically that great wines were very much the product of specific physical environments; that the traditional winegrowing areas in California were quite measurably different from the best winegrowing areas of France; that there existed in coastal California specific regions that were quite comparable to some of the best in the Burgundy regions of France and that these regions had been mostly overlooked by California winegrowers; and that the varieties that had previously and conspicuously been the least successful in California and which offered the greatest promise of improvement were the great Burgundian varieties--Pinot Noir and Chardonnay.

With these concepts in mind, the partners decided to investigate the potential winegrowing regions in coastal California with regard to a certain set of physical parameters, primarily Burgundian, and to let these parameters be the sole determining factor in deciding where to plant their vineyards.

A year and one half and thousands of road miles later their search ended with the purchase of land in a small valley which was once part of the Old Rancho Santa Rosa, a Spanish land grant which occupied the extreme western portion of the Santa Ynez Valley.

The ranch and vineyard are located on an elevated, north facing bench within a wooded upland valley which overlooks the Santa Ynez River about 9 miles west of the town of Buellton.

In 1972 the first forty-eight acres were planted followed by an additional sixty-two acres in 1973. The varieties planted are Pinot Noir, Chardonnay, Riesling, Cabernet Sauvignon and Merlot. In 1975 the vines produced their first commercial harvest. Most of the grapes were sold with the exception of a small quantity which the partners reserved for the producetion of experimental wines.

Because of the promising quality and pronounced regional characteristics of these early wines, the partners decided to go ahead with the construction of a small commercial winery within an old barn on the ranch. The rustic exterior of the building was preserved, but the interior was completely rebuilt to accommodate the production of wine in a pleasing and traditional environment.

Santa Ynez Valley Winery

A 1976 start in the wine business. The winery is a converted dairy barn. There are a few wineries that fit such a general description, but only one that lies just east of the quaint Danish community of Solvang: Santa Ynez Valley Winery.

The ranch itself has quite a distinctive history. Called Old College Ranch, its owner Boyd Bettencourt asserts that the adobe ruins near the winery building are the remains of Our Lady of Guadalupe, the first college in California, which was founded in 1843 and later moved to Moraga (1863) under the name of St. Mary's. The family home, since expanded, was originally the college chapel and it is plain to see that what is now the pantry was once a confessional.

Mrs. Bettencourt's family purchased the land in 1923 and started a dairy two years later. It remained so for over fifty years, having finally been closed in 1976. In the meantime, Bettencourt saw that grapes, and perhaps wine, might be a more profitable business than milk. So, in 1969, he began planting small blocs to grape vines. He believes he has the first commercial plantings in the Santa Ynez Valley.

Today he has ninety acres. The largest planting is to Cabernet Sauvignon (55 acres). Fifteen acres each are in White Riesling and Chardonnay. Additionally, a five acre bloc was planted experimentally to Gewurztraminer, Sauvignon Blanc, Pinot Noir, Chenin Blanc, and Gamay Beaujolais. The first two have done well and will be represented in future plantings.

Grapes from the early harvests were sold to Paul Masson, but a lot of home wines were tried out before the Bettencourts and their next door neighbors, the Davidges, pooled their resources to start a winery. C. Frederic Brander, a Davis graduate with experience at Dry Creek, was recruited as winemaker. A bond was obtained just before the 1976 crush and three thousand gallons were made.

Seven wines were made from the first crush, including two Cabernets (a red and a light rose'), a Pinot Noir Blanc, and what Boyd's son, Lee (winery president), jokingly calls their "swamp white," an unusual blend of White Riesling and Chardonnay. Winemaker Brander plans to keep the wines dry and medium bodied. "A winemaker shouldn't make wines that only satisfy himself," he says.

The two families intend to keep the winery small, expanding to a maximum size of perhaps 20,000 cases within a ten year period. Boyd notes that there is a natural tourist market for their wines in nearby Solvang, which received over five million visitors in 1976. He expects southern California will be his main market, but will distribute as far north as San Francisco.

The winery is located three miles east of Solvang, just off of Highway 246 on Refugio Road. Visitors are requested to make an appointment prior to their arrival.

Santa Barbara Winery

Until a few years ago, Santa Barbara Winery was the only producing winery in the county. Though owner/winemaker Pierre Lafond plans a continued slow expansion, the winery will remain a regional winery. For Lafond sees his operation as serving a "community market": He has no intention of pursuing a statewide market and is content to distribute his wines within a hundred mile radius, from Los Angeles to San Luis Obispo.

Thus, his marketing boundaries are virtually coincidental with the area from which he draws his raw materials: grapes and other fruits. With the exception of cranberries (Washington) and pomegranates (Bakersfield), everything comes from an area bounded by San Luis Obispo to the north and Oxnard to the south.

Lafond started the winery in 1962. It was mostly a garage operation until 1965, when it was moved to its present location in Santa Barbara, just blocks from the beach. The facility has been expanded several times since and Lafond sees additional expansion ahead. The winery currently bottles 35-40,000 cases a year and Lafond looks upon 100,000 cases as a reasonable goal. In 1971 he purchased a vineyard site on the north bank of the Santa Ynez River, about five miles west of Buellton. He hopes eventually to move crushing and production facilities there, but will retain the Anacapa Street facility. It's a good location for distribution and retail sales.

Lafond, with viticulturist Bill Collins, has planted forty-two acres between 1972 and 1976 and has another thirty acres which can be used. Varieties are: Cabernet Sauvignon, Zinfandel, White Riesling, Chardonnay, and Chenin Blanc. Also planted among the vines are ollalieberries, the main ingredient in another of Lafond's wines.

His premium wines are made from the fruit of his own vines and bear a unique label, which depicts an historical view of the Santa Barbara coastline in color. None are more than three dollars a fifth. Lafond also "produces" a line of fruit wines himself, bottling them under the Solvang Fruit Wines label. Two inexpensive bulk lines, made from wines purchased in bulk, are bottled under labels with the Santa Barbara Mission enclosed by an oval border.

Mr. Lafond has strong feelings about ecological matters. He already uses recycled soft drink canisters for his restaurant trade. He anticipates, with the acquisition of a nearby building, a recycling center complete with bottle washing capability. He feels that the limited distribution area he works in will make it easier to accomplish a successful recycling program.

Lafond originally got into the wine business when he obtained a bonded winery license so as to be able to hold tastings at his El Paseo Cellars retail store. Eventually, he transferred that license to what is now his Solvang tasting room, located at 1656 Mission Drive in the famed Danish community. Open daily from ten to five, tasting is offered daily during the summer and on weekends in winter.

Other Wineries

The 38,000 acre Rancho Sisquoc is owned by San Francisco businessman James Flood. With 60,000 acres of leased grazing land in the nearby Los Padres National Forest, some 1000 steers, 800 cows, and 600 calves are run on the ranch. In addition wheat, barley, oats, alfalfa, and garbanzo beans are raised on the ranch. And wine grapes.

Vineyard planting began in 1970. Today 120 acres of Cabernet Sauvignon overlook the Sisquoc River, along with smaller plantings of White Riesling, Merlot, and Sylvaner. The total is just under two hundred acres.

Ranch foreman Harold Pfeiffer began making small lots of wine experimentally in 1972. Most of the grapes have been sold to Geyser Peak, who has them contracted for through 1978. Geyser Peak's winemaker Al Huntsinger was so impressed with the ranch's 1974 vintage of Cabernet that he kept the lot separate. The wine was released last year as "Santa Maria Limited Bottling."

Flood now has a small winery bonded at the ranch, but is in no hurry to make a lot of wine. A label has been designed. It shows the 1875 Foxen Chapel, which stands on a rise at the entrance to the ranch.

TEPUSQUET CELLARS

Wines are currently being marketed under the Tepusquet (Tep-uhss-kay) Cellars label, but there is, as yet, no Tepusquet Winery. There won't be, either, until at least 1978. For the partners involved in Tepusquet Vineyards and Santa Maria Vineyards--with a total of 2585 acres of prime varieties planted in Santa Maria, Shandon, and San Luis Obispo--are attempting to begin with a 25,000 case market before going ahead with a winery.

The partners in Tepusquet Vineyards (1832 acres) are brothers Louis (managing partner) and George Lucas Jr., and Alfred J. Gagnon. Santa Maria Vineyards, also managed by Louis Lucas, is owned by Jack Niven, former head of Purity Stores. The vineyards have been planted since 1971 and Cabernet Sauvignon (937 acres) is the prime variety, with healthy plantings of White Riesling, Chardonnay, and Pinot Noir.

In addition to selling grapes to Napa and Sonoma wineries, Tepusquet Cellars has had wines made from their grapes by The Monterey Vineyard and Beringer. If the group's test marketing goes well, a Mission-styled winery, designed by Richard B. Taylor, may be under construction by 1978. It will be located in Edna Valley, southeast of San Luis Obispo.

President of Tepusquet Cellars is Lee Stewart, founder of Souverain Winery.

Like a handful of prospective winery owners, Louis Marshall Ream, Jr. is being quite deliberate in planning his venture. Instead of slapping up a winery right off, the former Atlantic Richfield vice president has already had wines made from his grapes so as to satisfy himself of their quality.

Marshall and Connie Ream purchased the 1500 acre Zaca Mesa Ranch in the Santa Ynez Valley in 1972. Cattle, forage, and row crops are raised on the ranch. Winegrape planting began the following year. Today, 160 acres are clothed in vines. Cabernet Sauvignon, Pinot Noir, and White Riesling head the list.

In 1975 Ream had the first wines made for his label by The Monterey Vineyard: Cabernet and Pinot Noir. A Chardonnay was added the following year. Grapes were again crushed at The Monterey Vineyard in 1977 and finished at Zaca Mesa, where winery construction will soon begin.

The wines will bear the label "The Vineyards at Zaca Mesa." As implied, there are separate vineyards on the ranch. Ream owns Chapel Vineyard (named for the cinder block chapel he has built on the ranch); Mariposa Vineyard is owned by real estate developer John Cushman; other partners own Toyon Vineyard and Zaca Mesa Vineyard. The specific vineyard will be identified for each wine by a neck label, which will also designate the vintage.

VEGA VINEYARDS WINERY

Dentist William Mosby and his sons, Gary and Michael, expected to be bonded for the 1977 crush. They plan an 8000 case winery, which will be housed in an elegant, almost frilly red barn located at the corner of Santa Rosa Road and Highway 101, just south of Buellton. The Mosbys also plan a tasting room in the adjacent Rancho La Vega adobe, built by Dr. Roman de la Cuesta in 1853.

A native of Klamath Falls, Oregon, Dr. Mosby has been in practice in Lompoc since 1958. He liked the area so much that he was able to convince his two brothers to set up their dental practices in the same building. In 1973 he planted ten acres of White Riesling across the Santa Ynez River from the winery site. He planned to put in another ten acres of Gewurztraminer in the spring of 1977.

Son Gary, a Davis grad, will be winemaker; Michael, from Cal Poly, will handle the vineyards. In addition to the two whites, the Mosbys expect to crush Cabernet Sauvignon and Pinot Noir.

CONTINENTAL VINTNERS

In 1969 a limited partnership, headed by actor Wayne Rogers and real estate investment man Herman Schwartz, purchased the 2500 acre Rancho Tierra Rejada, thirteen miles east of Paso Robles. The name means "furrowed earth" in Spanish and the primary crops were wheat, barley, and alfalfa. The ranch also boards and breeds thoroughbred horses.

Two years of study convinced the partners (which also include actors Jack Webb, Peter Falk, and James Caan) that the ranch had a climate similar to areas of Napa Valley. In 1973, 500 acres of Merlot, Cabernet Sauvignon, and Zinfandel were planted. Their 210 acres of Merlot is one of the largest single plantings of the variety in the state.

The group holds a wholesale license under the name Star Crest Vineyards, which will probably be the winery label when the first wine is released, probably in early 1978.

ESTRELLA RIVER VINEYARDS

Estrella River Vineyards (pronounced "Ess-tray'-yuh") is an aggressive vineyard operation which promises soon to be an aggressive winery operation. Under the leadership of Gary Eberle, who once studied to be a medical school instructor, Estrella has 570 acres of established vineyards (started in 1972) and planted another 140 acres in 1977.

Winery construction was begun this spring. The building is set in a sparse grove of oaks on a low rise and the first phase was ready for a 1977 crush of about 60,000 gallons.

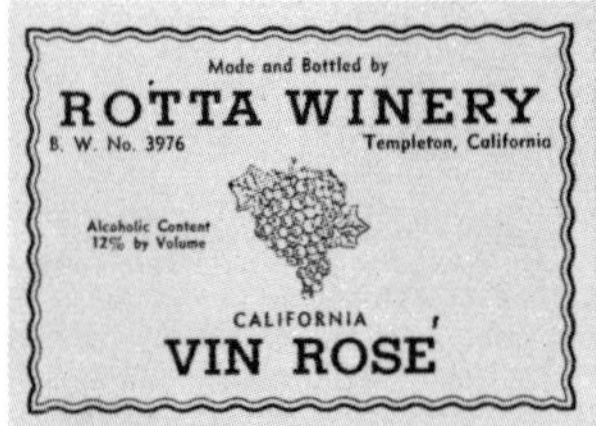

The small wooden building that is Rotta Winery stands not much more than a hundred yards up the road from Pesenti Winery. In Zinfandel country it is, fittingly, a Zinfandel winery.

Frenchman Adolph Siot is said to have first planted vines along what later came to be known as Winery Road in 1856. A winery was probably built there circa 1890. In 1905 Joe Rotta, an Italian raised in Switzerland, purchased vineyards and winery, beginning his family's control of the winery that would last over seventy years.

Joe's brother, Clemente, farmed the vineyards from 1925 until Joe's son, Mervin, took over in the forties. Mervin, assisted by his mother Romilda, operated the winery until December of 1976, when he sold the winery to John and Della Mertens.

Conclusion

I have several times in this volume voiced my optimism for the future of California winegrowing. It is relatively easy to see that future now for an industry which has overcome natural disasters (earthquakes and vineyard pests, like phylloxera) and man-made disorders (wars, depressions, dry counties and dry states, and even national prohibition), and yet remains a vital, healthy segment of the American economy. It could not have been easy, however, to see that future in the last century, before California's wine industry had faced even a small share of those problems. But someone did see it, from Boston no less. A remarkable feat. So we close this book with the thoughts of that uncited author who penned the following words of prophecy, whose fulfillment was only a century off the mark. They appeared in the May issue of *The Atlantic Monthly* in 1864. The article was entitled "California as a Vineland."

"Our Pacific sister [California], from whose generous hand has flowed an uninterrupted stream of golden gifts, has announced the fact that henceforth we are to be a wine-growing people. From the sparkling juices of her luscious grapes, rich with the breath of an unrivalled climate, is to come in future the drink of our people. By means of her capacity in this respect we are to convert the vast tracts of her yet untilled soil into blooming vineyards, which will give employment to thousands of men and women, -- we are to make wine as common an article of consumption in America as upon the Rhine, and to break one more of the links which bind us [as] unwilling slaves to foreign lands.

* * *

It only remains for the vintners to keep their wines pure, and always up to the highest standard, and to take such measures as shall insure their delivery in a like condition to the consumers, to build up a business which shall eclipse that of any of the great houses of Europe. Thus will the State and nation be benefited, by keeping at home the money which we annually pay for wine to foreign countries, and the people will be led away from the use of strong, fiery drinks, to accept instead the light wines of their native land."

So there you have it--the call to patriotism, quality control, and wine as the drink of moderation. It may sound overblown at first, but beneath an emotional form lies the substance of sound thought.

It should also bring to our attention the fact that we may obtain, from California's Central Coast, a broad spectrum of wines, from those which will stand with the finest in the world to those which may be drunk with pleasure at our daily dinner table without discernable damage to our pocketbooks. It is that range of opportunity and ability that makes the region worthy of our notice.

Appendix

AHLGREN VINEYARD Page 124
Address: 20320 Highway 9, Boulder Creek 95006
Phone: (408) 338-6071
Facilities: Visitors by appointment
Winemaker: Dexter Ahlgren
Wines: varietal, sparkling
Vineyards: 2.5 acres
Volume: 5,000 gallons storage, 2,000 gallons fermenting, 500 cases

ALMADEN VINEYARDS Page 151
Address: 1530 Blossom Hill Road, San Jose 95118
Phone: (408) 269-1312
Hours: Mon.-Fri. 10-3:30
Facilities: Tours only
Winemaker: Klaus Mathes
Wines: varietal, generic, dessert, sparkling, brandy
Vineyards: 6,748.2 acres
Volume: 26,500,000 gallons storage, 3,000,000 gallons fermenting, 6,500,000 cases

BARGETTO'S SANTA CRUZ WINERY Page 123
Address: 3535-A No. Main St., Soquel 95073
Phone: (408) 475-2258
Facilities: tasting & sales daily; tours if asked
Winemaker: Larry Bargetto
Wines: varietal, generic, fruit & berry, dessert
Volume: 130,000 gallons storage, 18,000 gallons fermenting, 35,000 cases

BERTERO WINERY Page 173
Address: 3920 Hecker Pass Hwy., Gilroy 95020
Phone: (408) 842-3032
Hours: daily 8-5
Facilities: tasting, sales, tours by appt.

DAVID BRUCE WINERY Page 113
Address: 21439 Bear Creek Rd., Los Gatos 95030
Phone: (408) 354-4214
Facilities: tour & tasting every other Sat. by appt.
Winemaker: Steve Millier
Wines: varietals
Vineyards: 40 acres
Volume: 35,000 gallons storage, 15,700 gallons fermenting, 5,000 cases

CALERA WINE COMPANY Page 194
Address: P.O. Box 342, Hollister 95023
Phone: (408) 637-2344
Facilities: No tasting, tours, or sales at present
Winemaker: Josh Jensen
Wines: varietal
Vineyards: 24 acres
Volume: 13,000 gallons storage, 6,000 gallons fermenting, 6,000 cases

CARMEL BAY WINERY Page 194
Address: P.O. Box 2496, Carmel 93921
Winemakers: Fred Crummey & Bob Eyerman
Wines: varietals

CHALONE VINEYARD Page 193
Address: Stonewall Canyon Road, The Pinnacles, Soledad 93960
Phone: (415) 441-8975 for tour appts.
Facilities: tasting, tours by appt.
Winemaker: John H. Graff
Wines: varietal
Vineyards: 125 acres
Volume: 48,000 gallons storage, 12,000 gallons fermenting, 12,000 cases

CHANNING CELLARS Page 100
Address: 2157 Clinton Ave., Alameda 94501
Phone: (415) 523-1544
Winemaker: John Channing Rudd
Wines: varietal
Volume: 2,000 gallons storage, 800 gallons fermenting

CHATEAU VINTNERS Page 101
Address: 1688 Timothy Rd., San Leandro 94577
Phone: (415) 352-5425
Hours: Saturday 11-4
Facilities: tasting, tours, sales
Winemaker: Richard Carey
Wines: varietal and generic
Vineyards: 1 acre
Volume: 10,000 gallons storage, 4,000 gallons fermenting, 12,000 cases

CONCANNON VINEYARD Page 89
Address: 4590 Telsa Road, Livermore 94550
Phone: (415) 447-3760
Hours: Mon.-Sat. 9-4, Sun. 12-4:30
Facilities: tasting, sales, tours
Winemaker: James J. Concannon
Wines: varietal, generic, dessert
Vineyards: 250 acres
Volume: 430,000 gallons storage, 150,000 gallons fermenting, 40,000 cases

CONGRESS SPRINGS VINEYARDS Page 149
Address: 23600 Congress Springs Rd., Saratoga 95070
Phone: (408) 867-1409
Hours: 10-5 Fri.-Sun.
Facilities: tasting, tours, sales
Winemaker: Daniel Gehrs
Wines: varietal
Vineyards: 7 acres
Volume: 7,500 gallons storage, 5,000 gallons fermenting, 2,000 cases

A. CONROTTO WINERY Page 183
Address: 1690 Hecker Pass Road, Gilroy 95020
Phone: (408) 842-3053
Facilities: No tasting or tours
Winemaker: Chinto Conrotto
Wines: generic
Vineyards: 2 acres
Volume: 120,000 gallons storage, 20,000 gallons fermenting, 18,000 cases

CONTINENTAL VINTNERS Page 214
Address: Shandon Star Rte., Paso Robles 93446
Phone: (805) 238-2562
Wines: varietal
Vineyards: 500 acres

J. E. DIGARDI WINERY Page 101
Address: 3785 Pacheco Blvd., Martinez 94553
Phone: (415) 228-2638
Facilities: tours wknds. by appt., no tasting, sales at Liquor Store daily
Winemaker: Francis J. Digardi
Wines: generic
Volume: 90,000 gallons storage, 15,000 gallons fermenting, 2,000 cases

DURNEY VINEYARDS Page 194
Address: Star Rte., Box 152, Carmel Valley 93924
Phone: (408) 659-4716
Facilities: No tasting or tours
Winemaker: Ken Roberts
Wines: varietal
Vineyards: 60 acres
Volume: 15,000 cases

ENZ VINEYARDS Page 187
Address: 1781 Limekiln Rd., Hollister 95023
Phone: (408) 637-3956
Facilities: tasting, tours, sales by appt.
Winemaker: Robert W. Enz
Wines: varietal, generic

Vineyards: 30 acres
Volume: 25,000 gallons storage, 9,600 gallons fermenting, 3,500 cases

ESTRELLA RIVER VINEYARDS Page 215
Address: Paso Robles 93446
Phone: (805) 238-0751
Winemaker: Gary Eberle
Wines: varietal
Vineyards: 710 acres
Volume: 300,000 gallons storage, 120,000 gallons fermenting, 25,000 cases

FELTON-EMPIRE VINEYARDS Page 119
Address: 379 Felton-Empire Rd., Felton 95081
Phone: (408) 335-3939
Facilities: tasting, tours by appt.
Winemaker: Leo McCloskey
Wines: varietal
Vineyards: 15 acres
Volume: 5,000 gallons storage, 2,500 gallons fermenting, 2,000 cases

THE FIRESTONE VINEYARD Page 207
Address: Zaca Station Rd., Los Olivos 93441
Phone: (805) 688-3940
Hours: Mon.-Sat. 10-4
Facilities: tasting, tours, sales
Winemaker: Anthony Austin
Wines: varietal
Vineyards: 297 acres
Volume: 110,000 gallons storage, 90,000 gallons fermenting, 20,000 cases

JULIUS FIRPO WINERY Page 102
Address: Sellers Ave., Knightsen 94548
Phone: (415) 625-2915
Winemaker: Edward Firpo
Wines: generic & dessert
Vineyards: 6 acres
Volume: 32,000 gallons storage

FORTINO WINERY Page 177
Address: 4525 Hecker Pass Rd., Gilroy 95020
Phone: (408) 842-3305
Hours: Daily 9-6
Facilities: tasting, tours, sales
Winemaker: Ernest Fortino
Wines: varietal & generic
Vineyards: 20 acres
Volume: 95,000 gallons storage, 40,000 gallons fermenting, 10,500 cases

FRICK WINERY Page 126
Address: 3965 Bonny Doon Rd., Santa Cruz 95060
Phone: (408) 426-8623
Facilities: visits by appt., no tasting
Winemakers: William and Judith Frick
Wines: varietal and generic
Vineyards: 2 acres
Volume: 5,000 gallons storage, 1,150 gallons fermenting, 1,000 cases

GEMELLO WINERY Page 131
Address: 2003 El Camino Real, Mt. View 94040
Phone: (415) 948-7723
Facilities: tours & tasting Saturday, retail store
Winemaker: Mario Gemello
Wines: varietals, dessert
Volume: 66,000 gallons storage, 20,000 gallons fermenting, 10,000 cases

PETER & HARRY GIRETTI WINERY Page 183
Address: 791 5th St., Gilroy 95020
Phone: (408) 842-3857
Facilities: no tasting or tours
Winemaker: Harry Giretti
Wines: generic
Volume: 12,000 gallons storage, 5,600 gallons fermenting, 4,000 gallons per year

EMILIO GUGLIELMO WINERY Page 157
Address: 1480 Main Ave., Morgan Hill 95037

Phone: (408) 779-2145
Hours: 9-5 daily
Facilities: tasting, sales. tours by appt.
Winemaker: George Emilio Guglielmo
Wines: varietal, generic, dessert, sparkling, brandy
Vineyards: 150 acres
Volume: 550,000 gallons storage, 63,000 gallons fermenting, 60,000 cases

HECKER PASS WINERY Page 179
Address: 4605 Hecker Pass Hwy., Gilroy 95020
Phone: (408) 842-8755
Hours: daily 9-6 (9-5 winter)
Facilities: tasting & sales daily, tours by appt.
Winemaker: Mario Fortino
Wines: varietal, generic, some dessert
Vineyards: 14 acres
Volume: 16,000 gallons storage, 4,000 gallons fermenting, 2,700 cases

HOFFMAN MOUNTAIN RANCH Page 199
Address: Adelaida Rd., Star Route, Paso Robles 93446
Phone: (805) 238-4945
Hours: 10-5 dly at Black Oak, cnr. Hwys 46 & 101
Facilities: tasting, sales, tours by appt.
Winemaker: Michael Hoffman
Wines: varietal
Vineyards: 62 acres
Volume: 80,000 gallons storage, 50,000 gallons fermenting, 25,000 cases

KIRIGIN CELLARS Page 169
Address: 11550 Watsonville Rd., Gilroy 95020
Phone: (408) 847-8827
Hours: daily 9-6
Facilities: tasting & sales
Winemaker: Nikola Kirigin Chargin
Wines: varietal, generic, fruit
Vineyards: 35 acres
Volume: 100,000 gallons storage, 26,000 gallons fermenting, 10,000 cases

THOMAS KRUSE WINERY Page 175
Address: 4390 Hecker Pass Rd., Gilroy 95020
Phone: (408) 842-7016
Hours: daily 12-6
Facilities: tasting 50¢ (unless purchase), sales
Winemaker: Thomas Kruse
Wines: varietal and sparkling
Vineyards: contract and farm 50 acres
Volume: 9,000 gallons storage, 4,000 gallons fermenting, 2,500 cases

LA PURISIMA WINERY Page 183
Address: 725 A Sunnyvale-Saratoga Rd., Sunnyvale 94087
Phone: (408) 738-1011
Hours: Wed.-Sun. 11-7:30
Facilities: tasting, sales
Winemaker: Rudy Madrigal
Wines: table wines (generic/varietal)
Vineyards: 10 acres
Volume: 15,000 gallons storage, 3,000 gallons fermenting, 1,250 cases

RONALD LAMB WINERY Page 183
Address: 17785 Casa Lane, Morgan Hill 95037
Phone: (408) 779-4268
Facilities: no tasting room, sales, or tours
Winemaker: Ron Lamb
Wines: varietal
Volume: 2,000 gallons storage, 1,200 gallons fermenting, 600 cases

LIVE OAKS WINERY Page 171
Address: 3875 Hecker Pass Hwy., Gilroy 95020
Phone: (408) 842-2401
Hours: 8-5 daily
Facilities: tasting and sales
Winemaker: Mitsuo Takemoto

Wines: mostly generic
Vineyards: 55 acres
Volume: 150,000 gallons storage, 20,000 gallons fermenting, 25,000 cases

LLORDS & ELWOOD WINERY Page 97
Address: 315 S. Beverly Drive, Ste. 306 (office), Beverly Hills 90212
Phone: (213) 553-2368
Facilities: no tours, tasting, or sales at winery
Winemaker: Richard H. Elwood
Wines: varietal & dessert
Volume: 150,000 gallons storage, 10,000 gallons fermenting

LOS ALAMOS WINERY Page 205
Address: 2635 Highway 135, Los Alamos 93440
Phone: (805) Los Alamos 2391
Hours: Tues.-Sun. 11-5, but call first
Facilities: tasting, sales, tours
Winemaker: Mary Vigoroso
Wines: varietal
Vineyards: 350 acres
Volume: 5,000 gallons storage, 2,500 gallons fermenting, 10,000 cases

PAUL MASSON VINEYARDS Page 139
Address: 13150 Saratoga Ave., Saratoga 95070
Phone: (408) 257-7800
Hours: 10-4 daily
Facilities: tasting, tours, sales
Winemaker: Joseph Stillman
Wines: varietal, generic, dessert, sparkling
Vineyards: 4,725 acres
Volume: 28,202,371 gallons storage, 7,316,143 gallons fermenting, 4,000,000 cases

MIRASSOU VINEYARDS Page 135
Address: Route 3, Box 344, 3000 Aborn Road, San Jose 95121
Phone: (408) 274-3000
Hours: Mon.-Sat. 10-5, Sun. 12-4
Facilities: tasting, tours, sales
Winemaker: Don Alexander
Wines: varietal, generic, sparkling
Vineyards: 1,100 acres
Volume: 2,250,000 gallons storage, 200,000 gallons fermenting, 300,000 cases

MONTCLAIR WINERY Page 102
Address: 910 81st Ave., Oakland 94621
Phone: (415) 962-9492
Facilities: tasting, tours by appt. sales through R.K. Dove (at residence)
Winemaker: Richard K. Dove
Wines: varietal
Volume: 3,000 gallons storage, 2,000 gallons fermenting, 500-700 cases

MONTEREY PENINSULA WINERY Page 189
Address: 2999 Monterey-Salinas Hwy., Monterey 93940
Phone: (408) 372-4949
Hours: 10 a.m. until dark
Facilities: tasting, sales, informal tours
Winemaker: Roy Thomas
Wines: varietal, generic, fruit, dessert
Vineyards: 6 acres (leased)
Volume: 60,000 gallons storage, 15,000 gallons fermenting, 10,000 cases

THE MONTEREY VINEYARD Page 191
Address: 800 S. alta St., Gonzales 93926
Phone: (408) 675-2326
Hours: daily 10-5
Facilities: tasting, tours, sales
Winemaker: Richard G. Peterson, Ph.D.
Wines: varietal
Vineyards: 900 acres (contracted)
Volume: 2,000,000 gallons storage, 1,600,000 gallons fermenting, 40,000 cases

J. W. MORRIS PORT WORKS Page 83
Address: 1215 Park Ave., Emeryville 94608

Phone: (415) 655-3009
Facilities: winery open by special appt. only
Winemaker: Jim Olsen
Wines: Port & Angelica only
Volume: 15,000 gallons storage, 3,000 gallons fermenting, 3,000 cases

MOUNT EDEN VINEYARDS Page 147
Address: 22000 Mt. Eden Rd., Saratoga 95070
Phone: (408) 867-5783
Facilities: tours by appt., sales daily, no tasting
Winemaker: Bill Anderson
Wines: varietals
Vineyards: 22 acres
Volume: 9,000 gallons storage, 2,000 gallons fermenting, 2,000 cases

NEPENTHE CELLARS Page 126
Address: Scotts Valley
Winemaker: George L. Burtness
Wines: varietal
Vineyards: 10 acres
Volume: 7,000 gallons storage, 7,000 gallons fermenting, 2,000 cases

NICASIO VINEYARDS Page 126
Address: 14300 Nicasio Way, Soquel 95037
Phone: (408) 423-1073/423-1578
Facilities: tasting, tours Sat. p.m. by appt.
Winemaker: Dan E. Wheeler
Wines: varietal, sparkling
Volume: 5,000 gallons storage, 1,000 gallons fermenting, 200 cases

NOVITIATE WINES Page 155
Address: College & Prospect Aves., Los Gatos 95030
Phone: (408) 354-6471
Hours: Mon.-Sat. 9-4
Facilities: tasting, sales, tours
Winemaker: Bro. Lee Williams, S.J.
Wines: varietal, generic, dessert, altar
Vineyards: 650 acres
Volume: 650,000 gallons storage, 60,000 gallons fermenting, 40,000 cases

OAK BARREL WINECRAFT-WINERY Page 103
Address: 1201 University Ave., Berkeley 94702
Phone: (415) 849-0400
Hours: Mon.-Sat. 10-6:30, Sun. 11-6:30
Facilities: tasting & retail sales (wine & equip.)
Winemaker: John Bank
Wines: generic & varietal
Volume: 6,280 gallons storage, 1,200 gallons fermenting, 10,000 cases

OX MOUNTAIN Page 127
Address: Route 1, Box 2Q, Half Moon Bay 94019
Phone: (415) 726-6465
Winemakers: Paul & Sandy Obester
Wines: varietal
Volume: 4,000 gallons storage, 2,500 gallons fermenting, 1,000 cases

PAGE MILL WINERY Page 111
Address: 13686 Page Mill Rd., Los Altos Hills 94022
Phone: (415) 948-0958
Facilities: by appt. only
Winemakers: Dick & Ome Stark
Wines: varietal
Vineyards: 1 acre
Volume: 4,000 gallons storage, 3,000 gallons fermenting, 1,000 cases

MICHAEL T. PARSONS WINERY Page 127
Address: 170 Hidden Valley Rd., Soquel 95073
Phone: (408) 475-6096
Facilities: visits by appt. only
Winemaker: Mike Parsons
Wines: varietal
Vineyards: 1 acre
Volume: 5,000 gallons storage, 1,500 gallons fermenting, 500 cases

PEDRIZZETTI WINERY Page 159
Address: 1645 San Pedro Ave., Morgan Hill 95037
Phone: (408) 779-7380
Hours: daily 10-6
Facilities: tasting, sales at 19500 Monterey Hwy., tours by appt.
Winemaker: Ed Pedrizzetti
Wines: varietal, generic, fruit, dessert, sparkling
Vineyards: 55 acres
Volume: 325,000 gallons storage, 85,000 gallons fermenting, 62,500 cases

PESENTI WINERY Page 201
Address: Rte. 1, Box 169 (Vineyard Drive), Templeton 93465
Hours: daily 8-6, Sun. 10-6
Facilities: tasting, sales, tours by appt.
Winemaker: Victor Pesenti
Wines: varietal, generic, fruit, dessert, sparkling
Vineyards: 65 acres
Volume: 128,000 gallons storage, 30,000 gallons fermenting, 100,000 cases

RANCHO SISQUOC Page 214
Address: Rte. 1, Box 147 (Foxen Canyon Rd.), Santa Maria 93454
Phone: (805) 937-3616
Facilities: visitors by appt. only
Winemaker: Harold Pfeiffer
Wines: varietal
Vineyards: 194 acres
Volume: 5,000 gallons storage, 3,000 gallons fermenting, 1,200 cases

RAPAZZINI WINERY Page 181
Address: 4350 Monterey Hwy., Gilroy 95020
Phone: (408) 842-5649
Hours: 9-6 daily (2 locations)
Facilities: tasting, sales
Winemakers: Jon P. Rapazzini & John Gordon
Wines: varietal, generic, fruit & berry, dessert
Vineyards: 50 acres
Volume: 98,000 gallons storage, 76,000 gallons fermenting, 20,000 cases

MARTIN RAY VINEYARDS Page 145
Address: 22000 Mt. Eden Rd., Saratoga 95070
Phone: (415) 494-8922
Facilities: visitors by appt. only
Winemaker: Peter Martin Ray
Wines: varietal
Vineyards: 5 acres
Volume: 6,500 gallons storage, 1,500 gallons fermenting, 1,500 cases

RICHERT & SONS WINERY Page 161
Address: 1840 W. Edmundson, Morgan Hill 95037
Phone: (408) 779-5100
Facilities: tasting, tours, sales by appt. only
Winemakers: Scott Richert & Walter S. Richert
Wines: dessert (to start varietal & fruit)
Volume: 20,000 gallons storage, 3,000 gallons fermenting

RIDGE VINEYARDS, INC.___Page 143
Address: 17100 Montebello Road, Cupertino 95014
Phone: (408) 867-3233
Hours: Sat. 11-3 by appt. only
Winemaker: Paul Draper
Wines: varietal
Vineyards: 50 acres
Volume: 100,000 gallons storage, 32,000 gallons fermenting, 18,000 cases

ROTTA WINERY Page 216
Address: Rte. 1, Box 168 (Winery Road), Templeton 93465
Phone: (805) 434-1389
Hours: daily 8-6
Facilities: tasting, tours, sales
Winemakers: John & Della Mertens
Wines: varietal & generic
Vineyards: 40 acres

P AND M STAIGER Page 115
Address: 1300 Hopkins Gulch Rd., Boulder Creek 95006
Phone: (408) 338-4346
Facilities: no tasting, tours or sales at winery
Winemakers: Paul and Em Staiger
Wines: varietal
Vineyards: 4 acres
Volume: 4,500 gallons storage, 1,500 gallons fermenting, 400 cases

STONY RIDGE WINERY Page 87
Address: 840 Vineyard Ave., Pleasanton 94566
Phone: (415) 846-2133
Hours: 11-5 Thurs.-Sun.
Facilities: tasting, tours, sales
Winemaker: Lanny Replogle
Wines: varietal, generic
Vineyards: 200 acres
Volume: 220,000 gallons storage, 40,000 gallons fermenting, 10,000 cases

SUNRISE WINERY Page 117
Address: 16001 Empire Grade Rd., Santa Cruz 95060
Phone: (408) 423-8226
Facilities: visitors weekends by appt. only
Winemaker: Keith Hohlfeldt
Wines: varietal
Vineyards: 35 acres
Volume: 10,000 gallons storage, 5,000 gallons fermenting, 1,500 cases

SYCAMORE CREEK VINEYARDS Page 167
Address: 12775 Uvas Road, Morgan Hill 95020
Phone: (408) 779-4738
Facilities: tasting, tours, sales weekends (daily in summer)
Winemaker: Terry Parks
Wines: varietal
Vineyards: 14 acres
Volume: 5,000 gallons storage, 3,000 gallons fermenting, 1,000 cases

TEPUSQUET CELLARS Page 214
Address: Route 1, Box 142, Santa Maria 93454
Phone: (805) 937-2043
Wines: varietal
Vineyards: 2,585 acres

TURGEON & LOHR WINERY Page 133
Address: 1000 Lenzen Ave., San Jose 95126
Phone: (408) 292-1564
Hours: daily 12-4
Facilities: tours, sales, & tasting
Winemaker: Peter Stern
Wines: varietal & generic
Vineyards: 280 acres
Volume: 118,000 gallons storage, 58,000 gallons fermenting, 20,000 cases

VEGA VINEYARDS WINERY Page 215
Address: 526 So. L. St., Lompoc 93463
Phone: (805) 736-2600
Winemaker: Gary Mosby
Wines: varietal
Vineyards: 20 acres
Volume: 20,000 gallons storage, 10,000 gallons fermenting

VENTANA VINEYARDS Page 194
Address: P.O. Box G, Soledad 93960
Phone: (408) 678-2306
Winemaker: Doug Meador
Wines: varietal
Vineyards: 600 acres

CONRAD VIANO WINERY Page 81
Address: 150 Morello Ave., Martinez 94553
Phone: (415) 228-6465
Hours: daily 9-12 & 1-5
Facilities: tasting, sales daily; tours if asked
Winemaker: Clement Viano
Wines: generic & varietal
Vineyards: 60 acres

Volume: 75,000 gallons storage, 35,000 gallons fermenting, 15,000 cases

ROUDON-SMITH VINEYARDS Page 121
Address: 513 Mountain View Rd., Santa Cruz 95060
Phone (408) 427-3492
Facilities: visitors by appt. only
Winemaker: Robert Roudon
Wines: varietal
Vineyards: 4 acres
Volume: 5,000 gallons storage, 2,000 gallons fermenting, 2,000 cases

SAN MARTIN VINEYARDS CO. Page 163
Address: 13000 Depot St., San Martin 95046
Phone: (408) 683-2672
Hours: 9-5:30 daily
Facilities: tours, tasting, sales
Winemaker: Ed Friedrich
Wines: varietal, generic, fruit, dessert
Vineyards: 10 acres
Volume: 2,200,000 gallons storage, 800,000 gallons fermenting, 325,000 cases

SANFORD & BENEDICT VINEYARDS Page 209
Address: Santa Rosa Road, Lompoc 93436
Phone: (805) 688-8314
Facilities: tasting, tours, & sales by appt. only
Winemakers: Richard Sanford & Mike Benedict
Wines: varietal
Vineyards: 110 acres
Volume: 12,000 gallons storage, 7,000 gallons fermenting, 2,000 cases

SANTA BARBARA WINERY Page 213
Address: 202 Anacapa St., Santa Barbara 93101
Phone: (805) 962-3812
Hours: 10-5 daily
Facilities: tasting & sales, no tours
Winemaker: Pierre Lafond
Wines: varietal, generic, fruit, dessert, sparkling
Vineyards: 42 acres
Volume: 55,000 gallons storage, 18,000 gallons fermenting, 35,000 cases

SANTA CRUZ MOUNTAIN VINEYARD Page 126
Address: 2300 Jarvis Road, Santa Cruz 95065
Winemaker: Ken D. Burnap
Wines: varietal
Vineyards: 12 acres
Volume: 6,000 gallons storage, 3,500 gallons fermenting, 750 cases

SANTA YNEZ VALLEY WINERY Page 211
Address: 365 N. Refugio Rd., Santa Ynez 93460
Phone: (805) 688-8381
Facilities: visitors by appt. only
Winemaker: Frederic Brander
Wines: varietal and generic
Vineyards: 90 acres
Volume: 7,000 gallons storage, 3,200 gallons fermenting, 4,000 cases

SHERRILL CELLARS Page 109
Address: 2975 A Woodside Rd., Woodside 94062
Phone: (415) 851-1932
Facilities: open by appt. only
Winemaker: Nathaniel D. Sherrill
Wines: varietals
Vineyards: 2 acres
Volume: 4,000 gallons storage, 2,000 gallons fermenting, 600-800 cases

SOMMELIER WINERY Page 183
Address: 2560 Wyandotte St., Section C, Mtn. View 94043
Phone: (415) 969-2442
Winemakers: Dick Keezer & Bob Burnham
Wines: varietal
Volume: 10,000 gallons storage, 6,000 gallons fermenting, 3,000 cases

VILLA ARMANDO Page 85
Address: 553 St. John St., Pleasanton 94556
Phone: (415) 846-5488
Hours: daily 10-5:30, Sun. 12-5:30
Facilities: tasting, sales
Winemaker: Anthony D. Scotto
Wines: varietal, generic, dessert
Vineyards: 170 acres
Volume: 1,500,000 gallons storage, 250,000 gallons fermenting, 150,000 cases

VINE HILL VINEYARD Page 127
Address: 2317 Vine Hill Rd., Santa Cruz 95065
Phone: (408) 438-1260
Facilities: no tours, tasting or sales
Winemaker: Leo McCloskey
Wines: varietal
Vineyards: 13 acres
Volume: 3,500 gallons storage, 3,500 gallons fermenting, 2,600 cases

WEIBEL CHAMPAGNE VINEYARDS Page 99
Address: 1250 Stanford Ave., Mission San Jose 94538
Phone: (415) 656-2340
Hours: daily 10-5
Facilities: sales daily, tours Mon.-Fri. 10-3
Winemaker: Oscar Habluetzel
Wines: varietal, generic, dessert, sparkling
Vineyards: 380 acres
Volume: 1,300,000 gallons storage, 66,000 gallons fermenting, 500,000 cases

WENTE BROTHERS Page 93
Address: 5565 Telsa Road, Livermore 94550
Phone: (415) 447-3603
Hours: Mon.-Sat. 9-5, Sun. 11-4:30
Facilities: tasting, sales, tours (Mon.-Fri.)
Winemaker: Eric P. Wente
Wines: varietal, generic
Vineyards: 1300 acres
Volume: 2,360,000 gallons storage, 412,000 gallons fermenting, 400,000 cases

WINE & THE PEOPLE Page 102
Address: 907 University Ave., Berkeley 94710
Phone: (415) 549-1266
Hours: Mon.-Sat. 10-6, Sun 11-5
Facilities: tasting, sales, tours
Winemaker: Peter Brehm
Wines: varietal
Volume: 8,000 gallons storage, 3,000 gallons fermenting, 1,250 cases

WOODSIDE VINEYARDS Page 107
Address: 340 Kings Mountain Road, Woodside 94062
Phone: (415) 851-7475
Facilities: tours, tasting & sales by appt. only
Winemaker: Robert Lee Mullen
Vineyards: 5 acres
Volume: 3,800 gallons storage, 700 gallons fermenting, 600 cases

YORK MOUNTAIN WINERY Page 203
Address: Rte. 1, Box 191 (York Mtn. Rd.), Templeton 93465
Phone: (805) 238-3925
Hours: 10-5 daily
Facilities: tasting & sales, tours by appt.
Winemaker: Steve Goldman
Wines: varietal & generic
Vineyards: 5 acres
Volume: 70,000 gallons storage, 18,000 gallons fermenting, 8,000 cases

ZACA MESA WINERY Page 215
Address: Foxen Canyon Road, Los Olivos 93441
Phone: (805) 688-3763
Wines: varietal
Vineyards: 160 acres
Volume: 20,000 cases per year

END.